COLDITZ RECAPTURED

Also by Reinhold Eggers

COLDITZ: THE GERMAN STORY

COLDITZ RECAPTURED

COMPILED BY

REINHOLD EGGERS

EDITED BY

JOHN WATTON

ROBERT HALE & COMPANY · LONDON

Robert Hale & Company
63 Old Brompton Road
London S.W. 7

PHOTOSET AND PRINTED
BY REDWOOD PRESS LIMITED
TROWBRIDGE, WILTSHIRE

Contents

Illustrations

Dedicated

To my beloved wife Margaret who hid, smuggled and treasured my diaries, photographs and notes through both wars with their aftermaths of fear and confusion. In those days it would have been far safer for her to have burnt all my papers, but she saved them, as she has saved me through nearly sixty years of marriage.

Colditz Castle

The first historical reference to Colditz Castle was in 1014. Surviving the Thirty Years War it was used as a hunting lodge and residence for the Dukes of Saxony up to 1753. The castle became a prison in 1800; a lunatic asylum in 1828; a concentration camp in 1933; an Arbeitsdienst camp for Hitler Youth in 1934; a Sonderlager or special camp for dangerous prisoners of war from 1939 to 1945. Since the war it has been part hospital, part home for the aged.

Preface

BY REINHOLD EGGERS

It is well known that men are children of their historical period; that the conditions and events of their time shape the main features of men's attitudes, behaviour and general views. No phenomenon of life has a single root; the causes of all things are complex.

In Colditz all the German officers were born in the last fifteen years of the nineteenth century; they had been moulded by the achievements of that time; the foundation of the German Kaiserreich under Prussian leadership; victory over their old sworn enemy France; the industrialisation of the new Reich; the introduction of the first measures for preventing serious distress by disease, age and invalidity through the social laws of the eighties; the revival of Rousseau's old "back to nature" cry with the Wandervögel movement; the suppression of the Marxist organisation by the Sozialisten-Gesetze, and the prohibition of the social-democratic party up to Bismarck's dismissal under William II. All this was something to be proud of. Our remarkable achievements nourished a belief in the invincibility of the Reich. This exaggeration was personified by The Kaiser with his naval politics and colonial activity. The "gleaming weapon", the army, too long trained in the tradition of 1870–1, fostered an ideal of invincibility.

World War I may have proved us wrong, but it also proved that the old caricatures symbolising the typical dandy German officer with his eyeglass and arrogant bearing were wrong too. Those types were the exception, not the rule. The battlefields showed the true quality of the masses of our officers and soldiers. The politicians had confronted them with an impossible task: to defeat the whole world single-handed, except for an ally of doubtful qualities –Austria.

The consequence of this shaped a new model of a soldier–the front line fighter, called in the jargon of the trenches *Frontschwein*. No one subscribed now to the old ideal: the officer or soldier attacking the enemy to a drum roll under the waving regimental colours, with bayonets fixed and swords drawn. In 1914 very few of these main subjects of our training were carried out, still less the formidable cavalry charges of peace-time manoeuvres. The *Frontschwein* soon laughed at these. Hand-to-hand fighting became a rare event. The killing of the enemy became mechanised, part of an enormous, anonymous machine. There was no use for a bayonet or sword in the destroyed trenches. Hand-grenades, revolvers and machine guns decided the outcome. The stress on human nerves, souls and physical endurance reached limits unknown until then. The *Frontschwein* had to stand them and he only, indefinitely. Exposed to bombardment from innumerable mortars and guns for hours and even days, seeking shelter in shell holes, in the midst of crying wounded and the silent corpses of the victims who decayed, unburied, for days . . . the *Frontschwein* had to stand all this, cut off from any communication with the back lines.

I remember an oil picture called *Return from the Front*. It showed a lonely road about six kilometres behind the front lines, with some ruins at the side, some bare tree trunks without branches, on a rainy day in December. The road was covered ankle-deep with liquid mud, churned up by the numerous horse-drawn carriages and guns that had ploughed through it during the night. On one side of the road the *Frontschweine* returned after four days in the front line and four days in the support line into this dreary landscape to some dirty and windy barracks for rest. They marched in single file. You could not distinguish officer from man for their uniforms were covered with clay and mud. Soon they would reach some uncomfortable shelter. It would be hoped that the straw there was dry and that the roof was waterproof, and that the stoves would give some warmth to dry boots and clothing. It was expected that these men after a rest of four days – if there was no alarm – would return for a second or third period of twelve days to their shell-shattered line; again to be exposed to the merciless *Trommelfeuer* and to defend this 'line', imaginary though it was, against attacks. Those who survived could hope to leave this hell, for a longer rest in some region far from this zone of death.

All of them dimly felt their situation to be hopeless, that all this was a kind of madness. Yet nobody saw a way out and so duty alone stood the stress as long as fate demanded it.

This was the ordeal through which almost all men of the Colditz staff and most of the guard company had gone, twenty-five years before. It had left traces in their souls, characters, attitudes; somehow it shaped them into different people from those who had not experienced it. They had become front-line fighters – *Frontschweine*.

Some people had managed to get around these hardships or had only read or heard about them. They made the best of their own situation – They were the *Etappen-schweine* who worked as in peace time, reliably enough, but clinging onto the good things in life as much as possible.

When the reader judges the men of the German staff described in this book, he may bear the above in mind. In short, the characteristics of the *Frontschwein* are these. He puts his duty first; he sticks to his word; he never leaves his comrades in the lurch; he forms a unit with his crew; he despises the little human vanities like titles, decorations, stilted behaviour, dandylike clothing; he hates self-glorification, boasting, exaggeration of any kind; he esteems and honours the achievements of the simple soldier. According to this scale I weighed the actors at Colditz. I hope I have done justice to everybody; at least I have tried to do so.

I have also tried to present the unusual situation of how I, the old German jailer at Colditz, can co-operate with my former prisoners in preparing this book. I now acknowledge with gratitude to all concerned the help freely given to me when I asked them for their recollections of Colditz.

Naturally, some politely refused; others have not yet replied. But those Polish, French, Dutch and British ex-Colditz prisoners who did respond to my invitation gave me more than words: they gave me their good will, for which I am doubly grateful.

Their good will has shown itself in other ways, too, for I have found among my former enemies men whom I now esteem as my greatest friends. I am proud to publish the contribution of Jedrzej Giertych who expresses the fine Polish sense of honour, discipline and common sense I admire so much. The Dutchman Oscar Drijber wrote to me to say that although the time he spent in Colditz was none too pleasant he did not consider it lost time, but as an experience he would not have missed for anything in his life. The French had more to complain about than most, after the wars of 1870, 1914–18 and 1939–45, when much of the fighting had been on their soil and three or four generations had suffered in succession. But I had word from the French Colditzer, Jean Bréjoux, who said, "I have to admit we were rather a wild lot who loved to organise a riot. We sang, shouted insults and sometimes behaved like men in a mad house. In spite of this, you, our jailers, understood us and behaved correctly."

Most of all, I found new friends among my former enemies, the British, who have that glorious gift of weeping with one eye while laughing with the other; which reminds me of how my old prisoners, Dick Howe and Sir Rupert Barry, whom I recently met again in London returned to me, with their compliments, my German Army Pass Book that had somehow been 'liberated' from me nearly thirty years ago.

Bodman/Bodensee
1973

Prologue

BY REINHOLD EGGERS

All authors of memoirs are tempted to justify or glorify themselves. I am not without such human vanity but I shall present no self-drawn character study of myself. Instead I shall let other people's comments on me stand, and leave the reader to judge the evidence. Here I shall simply outline the background against which I grew up to find myself eventually a guard at Colditz.

I was born in 1890 at Roklum, a village near Brunswick where my father was a blacksmith. It was a peaceful agricultural district. My mother died giving birth to her second son a year after I was born, and we were later looked after by a housekeeper. Soon my father started to buy me picture books and read me the captions which I quickly learned off by heart – I could even impress my father by reading them although it didn't matter to me if the pages were upside down.

My father also taught me to play cards – the 'devil's prayer-book'. I learned the game of Skat in my youth but had little time to enjoy it – until my post-war captivity in Russian hands. And then although we had plenty of time to play we had no cards! Twice we were able to get hold of some cardboard and marked some out with a stump of pencil. Punishment for this crime was twenty-one days' arrest in a dark cellar on bread and water. When our home-made cards became so dirty that they stuck together and we could no longer see the pictures, we had at last to give up this pastime before we were caught.

I attended the village school at Roklum from 1896 to 1904. The older pupils (aged from ten to fourteen) were in the charge of a *Cantor*, a teacher in his thirties who besides having his school work was organist, sexton and cantor of the village church. When the number of pupils at the school rose to over 150 a third teacher was engaged; except for the cantor all our teachers were beginners, aged about twenty, and they constantly changed – I enjoyed the methods and temperaments of six different ones during my time at this school.

As I did well in my lessons the school suggested that I attend a gymnasium, but my father said that he would not be able to afford the cost of this followed by several years at university. He agreed instead to my going to training college and qualifying at the age of twenty as a teacher with a monthly salary of 62,50 marks and free lodging. This was cheaper and took less time.

My father was satisfied with my successes at school but, an energetic man himself, he was often impatient with his day-dreaming son. I would forget where I had put a tool, or I would forget an order, not through disobedience, but absent-mindedness. All this made him really angry and he would shout, *Droemeker!* (Dreamer), and he would bang his fist on the table to bring me back to reality. If the case was more serious, he became furious and called me "*Maankop!*" (moon-head). Why a head similar to the good old moon was the best symbol for imbecility, I do not know. He then continued: "If someone dropped it on you from a great height you wouldn't notice it." For a more definite awakening he ordered me into the *gute Stube* (best room) where he kept a cane hidden in a cupboard, and he would use it on my backside on the advice of the Bible: "He who loves his child punishes him by the rod." This did not happen too often, perhaps because my stepmother tried to stop my father in the fulfilling of his biblical duties. I was well aware that my father loved me and that he was quite right to wake me up, yet I could not change my nature and my inborn inclination to ponder on problems, childish though they might have been. My strange dreaming moods even increased with adolescence. My parents were not able to tell their son the facts of life and he had to find them out for himself . . .

This absent-mindedness remained a lifelong fault although really it is nothing other than the highest concentration of mind absorbed completely with a problem. Happily my wife has abstained from shouting at me, but she has grown used to repeating her wishes or demands two or three times before I pay attention to her. "I know," she says, "you are away in another world. Your ears still hear well, but they do not always convey the sounds they hear to your brain." True enough. I can work in noise or during a concert, and probably it will remain so – as long as I have problems to think about, like Colditz.

In 1904 I was one of the happy candidates admitted to the new and modern college at Werferlingen near Helmstedt. Our director was perhaps thirty years old, and the other teachers were younger. Except for the ten prayers per day I found it wonderful – a library full of hitherto unknown treasures, sports, a beautiful landscape. The Wandervögel started and I joined at once. I continued my studies with enthusiasm and success, finally becoming top of my class.

My father (who had married for the third time in 1897 and had another son) died in 1905 at the age of 62, and the Prussian state gave me an allowance until my training was complete. I qualified in 1910 as cantor, sexton and organist as well as gaining my teacher's certificate. My results were so good that the Magdeburg education committee decided to trust me with one of their more difficult schools. The lonely village of Siestedt near Werferlingen had driven the previous teacher to leave in despair. I replaced him and taught the 96 pupils there for three years, later aided by a second teacher when the number had risen to a hundred. My task of training the local choir for both church and public performances was complicated by the poor state of the organ and my own low standard of musicianship – but by trusting in Providence I managed to keep it going and even got the choir to win a prize in a competition of village choirs. But my happiest Sundays were those when the congregation numbered less than three, and the parson would call up to me in the organ loft, "Herr Cantor, it's no use today!" – and we could go home.

With my boy pupils I dug the first village swimming pool and taught them to swim. I introduced Wandervögel walks and conducted big walking tours with the boys in the summer holidays. Each evening I had a short cross-country run to a nearby wood. As I was also a teetotaller and a non-smoker, my peasant neighbours shook their heads and concluded, "Our cantor is mad." Well, their children did not share their opinion. As a schoolmaster I enjoyed some of the best years of my life there, as a lord in my own kingdom, though my inspectors, parson and superintendent did not much care for my methods.

I took my final examination in 1912, but not with the same good written work as before! That June I asked my former teacher's daughter if she would marry me. She consented – neither realising how much I had fallen in love with her nor what she could expect in the future. Now she knows: nearly sixty years later!

This happy period ended in March 1913 when I had to report for my military service.

By nature and through my father's influence and my education I was a German patriot, devoted to my country. As a sportsman, now twenty-three years old, I had no fear of becoming a soldier nor of going through the required training. Not seeing the consequences I was proud of my country, particularly of her new navy. I wanted to serve there so I asked the 2nd Battalion of Marine-Infantry at Wilhelmshaven if I could serve my year with them and I was accepted. I would have to spend one month in barracks, because men like me had first to learn to march and to salute, I was told.

The Battalion Commander was Major von Lettow-Vorbeck, later famous as a bush-general in East Africa. He had already lost one eye in our colonial wars. My Company Commander, Captain von Hanstein, trusted his administration wholly to his sergeant-major, a man known as 'The Horror of the North Sea'. The young corporal who trained me was nick-named *Kleiner Schleifstein* (little grindstone). Well, the reader can imagine my life with this old Prussian-style training. After six months Major von Lettow-Vorbeck personally made me a *Gefreiter* (a lance-corporal) as we say, the first step to becoming a fieldmarshal! Then he was made a lieut.-colonel and sent to East Africa, so I asked to be transferred to the machine-gun company, where I had the happy chance of finding a fine chief, Lieut. von Gerlach. I finished my training on 31st March 1914 and was promoted to the rank of *Unteroffizier* – a full corporal.

I planned to take all the examinations required to become a teacher at a training college, so I had to find an appointment in a university town. I applied at Halle/Saale during my time as a soldier and I was accepted after a personal interview and a trial lesson. I started my new job on 1st April 1914, and began studying for my first exams.

In June the Crown-Prince of Austria was murdered at Sarajevo. The Kaiser and his government decided to stick to the Dreibund treaty and to risk a war . . . On 1st August 1914 I was ordered to join the First Regiment of Marine-Infantry at Kiel. World War I had started. With my regiment I went through fifty-one dreadful months.

I fought at Antwerp, the mouth of the Yser in Flanders, Ypres, the Somme, Flanders, the great break-through of 1918 and in our retreat from France in November 1918. I won the Iron Cross second class on 8th May 1915 in Flanders, the Iron Cross first class and the Hesse Medal for bravery on the Somme in December 1916. I was wounded slightly by a French bullet, in June 1915. During my first leave I got married. Our son was born in 1916. Then the end. Complete defeat in November 1918. Back to Halle on 1st January 1919.

At home everything was upside down – hunger at Halle; gangsters in and around the town. Halle was the Red Heart of Germany. Sinowjew personally came there to attempt to found a Soviet Republic. There was civil war. Gone were my plans for becoming a training college teacher for thousands of us teachers streamed back from the lost Eastern Provinces. For years we had a surplus of teachers. The colleges were closed.

During 1919 pupils were fed in the schools by donations from the Quakers. We were all hungry; people in bigger towns died of hunger. Clemenceau's Treaty of Versailles was the Personification of the old French-German enmity's hatred and revenge, causing us to take measures for our survival whatever happened. My wife and I sold all we had of our fortune – mainly war bonds (little more than 10,000 marks). We bought about an acre and a half of land at Reideburg, a village outside Halle. A primitive house had to be built. The cost was all of 28,000 marks, helped with an advance on my pay of 10,000 marks.

On 1st August 1920 we moved to our new home. Our second son had just been born. (He was later killed in World War II in May 1943, as a pilot in North Africa.) All our spare time from now on was devoted to our vegetable garden. We had neither Sundays off nor holidays until conditions improved after the inflation. We had nothing to lose, except some money held by my stepmother. Her son had been killed in March 1918 in France, so I became the sole heir to my father's fortune, which now, in 1923, was nothing. One two-kilogramme loaf of bread cost 1,000,000,000,000 marks. Our old fortune in money rose to about 30,000 marks, for which you could not buy even a slice of bread. My salary at that time was quite a good number of billions monthly – that was why we lived at Reideburg on our own ground, producing everything: milk from two goats; eggs from a dozen hens; meat from one or two pigs and some geese and ducks; potatoes, fruit, vegetables, wheat, barley, rye for home-baked bread, all from our own land. But what did this mean? Work, work, work. In 1927 prices were so low that the peasants could not sell their products for even the very lowest prices. "Germany is starving with full barns" was a saying then.

When conditions had stabilised I decided to switch over from gardening to studying. For seven years I took courses to get my certificate of secondary school teaching and for matriculation to the university. My studies included philosophy, education, modern languages and national economy, and my thesis was on "The theory and practice of school reform in England from Victorian times to the present day". I was awarded the degree of Doctor of Philosophy by Halle University in 1934, *magna cum laude*; with this I planned to achieve higher positions in our school administration such as Inspector of Schools.

However I had failed to anticipate the meanness of my colleagues, for in 1933, just after Hitler's coming to power, six of them denounced me for such crimes as opposition to future wars and being a friend to England*, having a tendency to lean to the left, and being an adversary of the NSDAP.

In the summer of 1933 I was summoned to appear before the commissioner of the NSDAP with our regional government at Merseburg who had full powers to clear out officials hostile to Hitler's politics. The result of his investigations was the following decree:

> I have been ordered by the minister to acquaint you with the law for restoration of professional officials from 7–4–1933, but I have to exhort you seriously to fulfil your duties with inner devotion and all eagerness in the spirit of our new state leadership. Your activity in office will be supervised by special measures. The inspector of schools will report on you after a year and I reserve the right to transfer you elsewhere.

On 1st April 1933 I was transferred to a primary school and in 1934 to another one, the headmaster of which was an "SA-Standartenführer". My career was finished, yet in 1939 with the help of a friend I regained a post in secondary education at the half-private Francke Stifungen school at Halle. Some months later World War II was started by Hitler.

I was fifty in 1940 and again I was a soldier, a lieutenant with Erzatz-Battalion 11 Leipzig, for training. Soon officers who knew foreign languages were asked for so I reported, was examined at Dresden as an interpreter and transferred to the PoW service. After an apprenticeship at Oflag IVB I arrived at Colditz on 26th November 1940. I served there under all three commandants except for the months of June and July 1942 when I was transferred to IVA, the generals' camp at Königstein after the escape of General Giraud. Together with Captains Priem and Püpcke I went through the trouble, provocations and attacks of the Colditz prison. As a schoolmaster I drew on my experience and some well-tried principles:

(1) Never show any emotion.
(2) Keep smiling whatever happens.
(3) Punish disobedience with energy, but only up to the limit allowed.
(4) Use arms only in cases of self-defence.

I openly declared to the senior officers: "I shall treat you as I would wish to be treated if I had become a PoW." I had the opportunity of seeing the other side of the coin from 16th April 1945 to

* In 1932 I organised a holiday exchange between the schools of Halle and Cheltenham grammar schools. I had already stayed in England for some months in 1929 and in Paris in 1930.

8th August 1945 as an American PoW, and from September 1946 to 28th December 1955 in Russian and German captivity. I am sorry to report that my jailors did not follow my last principle. Certainly some of them did not treat me as they would choose to be treated had they been in my position.

Lieut. Jedrzej Giertych

Jedrzej Giertych

Born 1903 in Poland. Master of Law at Warsaw University. Writer and politician. Author of more than twenty books including *Wrzesniowcy* (*The Soldiers of the September Campaign*, dealing with the campaign of 1939, PoW camps and escapes). Wounded in the war of 1920. Later sub-lieutenant in the Polish Naval Reserve. Before 1939 in the Polish Ministry of Foreign Affairs; member of the City Council of Warsaw 1938–9. Captured October 1939 on the Peninsula of Hel. Six escapes from PoW camps. Spent the winter of 1940–1 in solitary confinement in Colditz Castle. Subsequently imprisoned in Spitzberg, Sandbostel, Lübeck, Dössel. Liberated by US forces in April 1945. Rejoined the Polish Navy in Great Britain. Made secret trip to Poland with false documents to rescue his wife. Became a teacher in St Ignatius College, Enfield. Father of nine children.

First in Colditz

BY JEDRZEJ GIERTYCH

I was the first Allied officer in the Second World War to be imprisoned in Colditz Castle after an escape, and for this reason I like to
consider myself the father or founder member of the Colditz community.

As a lieutenant of the Polish Naval Reserve I took part in war
operations in the Polish sector of the Baltic Sea and in their final
stages I was a member of the garrison of the besieged Peninsula of
Hel which surrendered on the night of 1st and 2nd October 1939. I
tried, with five friends, to escape in a rowing boat across the Baltic
to Sweden, but we were unsuccessful. The boat capsized on the
sandbanks not very far from shore and by morning I found myself
in German captivity.

In early November I escaped to Western Germany from a train
when in transit from one camp to another. After two days and three
nights of freedom and a journey of 500 kilometres in German trains
I landed in the central Gestapo prison at Alexanderplatz, Berlin.
After two rather unpleasant weeks and apparently because of police
doubts about my status, I was handed over to the German military
authorities who imprisoned me in Colditz Castle.

Colditz Castle was at that time an ordinary prison camp for
Polish officers, but I was placed in solitary confinement with no
contact with the inmates of the camp; so my cell became the starting
point of a special camp for escaped prisoners.

I spent two weeks in this cell before being moved to the Murnau
camp in southern Bavaria, also an Oflag for Polish officers, where
again I was placed in solitary confinement. There were now four of
us in four separate cells there: apart from me, another lieutenant
punished for an unsuccessful escape, and a naval captain and divi-
sional commander (with the rank of a colonel) for some political, or
disciplinary reasons.

From Christmas Eve 1939 we could communicate with each
other and soon afterwards we were joined by a general (an army
commander) and a major (who before the war was deputy military

attaché at the Polish Embassy in Berlin), both there for political reasons. I must add to this that I too was among this selected group of people not only because I escaped, but also partly on political grounds as I had in the past served in the Polish Ministry of Foreign Affairs, and immediately before the war I had been a politician and a political author and publisher. In my writings I had expressed the view that Germany was our main enemy and a danger to Poland, and that Poland must count in the near future on the possibility of a German war of aggression. I had also written about the problems of the persecuted Polish minority in Germany's Eastern provinces and stated that in my opinion the Versailles territorial settlement had been unfair to Poland. (I learned after the war that some of my books had in pre-war times been translated into German, printed in editions 'For private circulation only' and put secretly at the disposal of German authorities and personalities interested in Polish problems.)

In January 1940 all six of us were moved – after a quite pleasant journey in an ordinary train through Munich, Salzburg and Vienna and across occupied Czechoslovakia – to a Silesian place called Silberberg in German, and Srebrna Góra in Polish. Near this place, high up in the mountains, was Fort Spitzberg, built by Frederic the Great during his frequent wars against Austria to block the passage through the Sudeten Mountains from Austrian Moravia and Bohemia to Silesia which had been conquered a short time earlier by Prussia.

This was a picturesque ruin, partly hidden underground, and the life there was not without hardships. Our sleeping quarters were dark, wet underground casemates with inch-long stalactites already forming on their vaulted ceilings.

We had been treated harshly and had been reminded persistently that we were members of a beaten nation and could neither expect a satisfactory future, nor tolerance or pity. I do not have bad memories of that place, however, but it stands out vividly as a place of magnificent views through two or three narrow windows, of towering mountains; of snow in brilliant sunshine in winter and of ravishingly green forests in spring; of the vigorous and pleasant smell of the larch and fir trees which covered the slopes of the mountain on which our fortress stood; of scores of colourful, quite exotic looking butterflies and of wild flowers blossoming in the cracks of the walls. But above all, I remember the joy of being in good company, among real friends, strong, loyal, noble, manly companions, worthy of attachment and respect.

Together with us arrived seven other Polish officers from other camps, so our special prison camp now had a strength of thirteen.

Soon however our numbers substantially increased, especially with the coming of spring when more escape attempts were made in all prison camps. Soon we numbered ninety, most of us young and having escaped. There was no room in the fort for more.

Our attempts to escape were not successful as this was really a very well chosen place for the purpose of guarding turbulent prisoners. It had already been used as a prison in the nineteenth century, and in about 1835 a quite prominent German poet and revolutionary, Fritz Reuter, had managed to escape. We knew about this and envied him – but in spite of diligent endeavours we were not able to follow his example.

In April, however, in view of the need for more room, a branch of our camp was opened in Fort Hohenstein, on another mountain, a mile or two away. This was considered to be an even worse place; a real eagle's nest high up over a precipice. Twenty of us – allegedly the worst among us – were sent over there.

We discovered a weak spot in the surveillance system, and got into a room which was out of bounds to us, made a hole in the wall and climbed down the outside wall on a rope made of bed sheets. Ten of us had to stay in the fort to cover the absence of the other ten. Thus 50 per cent of the inmates of the fort got away in the night, and it was some eight hours before our absence was discovered.

We split into three groups, but we all had the same aim: to reach neutral Hungary and then the new Polish Army in France or Polish Navy or Air Force in Britain. Only one group succeeded; we got a message from them from Istanbul later and we learned after the war that they had been lucky enough to be able to take part, with a Polish Brigade, in the defence of Tobruk and later, with the Second Polish Army Corps, in the Italian Campaign.

I walked for nearly eleven nights with my friends (we slept during the days in the forests), but were arrested near Olomouo in Moravia when trying to cross the border between the Sudetenland, incorporated into Germany, and the Bohemian–Moravian Protectorate. I was brought back to Fort Hohenstein and later transferred to Fort Spitzberg again.

The limits of the capacity of the forts near Silberberg had been reached. Then a new problem arose for the German prison camp authorities, with many more prisoners attempting to escape, French, British, Dutch, Belgian, Norwegian this time, and among them more Poles.

In autumn 1940 the special camp was moved from the Silberberg forts to Colditz Castle in Saxony where there was much more room. We had already one French airman among us, but the camp remained essentially Polish for some days. Suddenly, lorryloads of French and British prisoners started to arrive, almost fresh from battle, some still in steel helmets, evoking vividly for us the great turmoil of the Western front, of the French battlefields, of Dunkirk, and of Norway – things we knew of only from German newspapers and in which we longed so poignantly during the 1939–40 winter to take part. I watched their arrival from the window of a punishment cell, as I had to complete a fourteen-days prison sentence immediately after my arrival from Silberberg to Colditz.

The international community of the Colditz inmates crystallised at once into a group of good friends tied together not only by the comradeship of arms, but by the much closer bond of having passed through the same experience of escape and its consequences.

We all agreed not to try to escape from Colditz Castle before a given date in the spring. In the winter, the chances of successful escape were very slight; it was better not to spoil the existing possibilities. Only by such an undertaking could the more impatient ones among us be restrained. We also undertook not to compete with each other in exploiting existing possibilities. A sort of an international patent office was established. The first to invent a way of escape had to register his priority and nobody else had the right to pursue the same idea.

We discussed the possibilities of escape – it is amazing how much one can learn in this matter from the experience of other men – and in the remaining free time we lived an animated, interesting and exhilarating social life with discussions, lectures, the teaching and learning of languages, theatrical performances, or simply conversations, telling each other's life stories, etc. As this was, on the whole, a community of strong characters and colourful individuals, it was certainly an interesting change and entertainment for us Poles, who were already bored with one year of captivity.

I belonged to this community for only about six months because early in the spring of 1941 twenty-seven of us were called out and sent – as Captain Priem expressed it – "home" – which was back to Fort Spitzberg near Silberberg again. I do not know to this day what was the cause of this transfer, but we did not stay there for long, for by the summer we had been moved to a large Oflag for Polish officers at Sandbostel near Bremen, and in the autumn the whole camp including ourselves had been moved to Lübeck. (I escaped on the way by jumping from the train at night, but was rearrested the next day, after arriving in Hamburg.) I spent three years at Lübeck – an international but predominantly Polish and French camp into which later most of the other Polish, French, Belgian and Yugoslav inmates of Colditz Castle found their way, and where I made a close acquaintance with the Soviet lieutenant Dju-gashvili, the son of Stalin. I escaped from this camp three times, but the nearest I got to Britain was to reach the border between Germany and occupied Denmark west of Flensburg where I was arrested by the frontier guards.

In 1944 the Polish part of the camp was moved to another camp at Dössel in Westfalen – and it was there that we were liberated by the Americans on 1st April 1945 and from where I was able to rejoin the Polish Navy in London before the Second World War ended. I have written, in Polish, and published in London, a book about my life during these years – not only just a story of my six escapes and my more than thirty unsuccessful attempts, even if all this occupied a large part in it, but about the miseries and joys and disappointments of a soldier who during a war cannot take part in war operations which he eagerly wishes to be won; of a sailor who reads about sea battles and convoys, while sitting enclosed in a room; of a father in perfect health who cannot support his family; of a Christian who does not want to hate but has so many reasons for hate; of a believer who fervently prays to God for salvation for his country and nation in situations when everything seems to be irretrievably lost; and of a participant in a war which became a victory for his side, but a defeat for his country and himself. Also, about my trip from London to Poland in August 1945, when I travelled one way pretending to be a Polish agricultural slave-worker and Displaced Person seeking repatriation to Poland, and came back with my family pretending to be a former French prisoner of war who escaped from a camp, hid for two years in Poland among the Polish population and married there a Polish widow with four children. This book became, on the modest market of Polish émigré literature, quite a best seller.

As can be seen, in spite of my role as the founder member of the Colditz special camp for escaped prisoners, my Colditz experiences form only a fairly limited part of the long story of my captivity in Germany. This gives me, however, perhaps the chance of forming a somewhat wider view upon the problem of prison camps in Germany during those years.

On the whole, I can sum up my experiences by saying that we prisoners of war cannot complain about our fate. On the contrary, we were the lucky ones. In a Germany which destroyed in concentration camps millions of human beings (among them probably some two or three million Polish Jews and some two million Poles) and in a world in which 12,000 Polish officers, captured in 1939 by the Soviet Army, disappeared without trace, or rather leaving a very conspicuous trace in the form of the mass graves of more than 4,000 bodies with bullets in their necks in the Katyn wood – the Oflags and Stalags in Germany were really something like an oasis of traditional chivalrous methods of conducting war and treating captured enemies.

Germany was not altogether blameless in the way she treated her prisoners of war. One can say that the principles of the Geneva Convention were not fully applied to Polish prisoners of war until the summer of 1940 and ceased to be really applied to anybody after early in 1944. But between 1940 and 1944 the prison camps were run, on the whole, quite strictly, and sometimes even very strictly according to the established rules of international law. With one great exception – the Russians.

The treatment of Polish prisoners of war in 1939–40 I can illustrate by a conversation which I had with a German officer in December 1939 or January 1940 at the time of my solitary confinement at the Murnau camp.

This officer was called Doctor Falke and was an elderly lieutenant and member of the Abwehr, the German Military Intelligence. I was called from my cell to his office; another German officer whose name I do not know was also present.

Doctor Falke told me that he had something to say to me. He told me that if I tried another escape I would be shot. "*Erschossen.*"

I answered: "You mean that I may be hit by the bullet of a guard? Yes, of course, I realise that this is a risk which has eventually to be taken when trying to escape."

"*Nein, Sie werden füsilliert* [No, you will be executed]."

"I am not in a position to do anything," I retorted, "except accept this as the existing situation. But how can this be reconciled with the text of the Geneva Convention?"

"What convention?"

"The convention about prisoners of war."

"Do you know Latin? If you do, you should realize that the word *convention* comes from the word *convenire*. And for *convenire* two parties are necessary. The Geneva Convention has ceased to be applied to you because Poland has ceased to exist. It has been extinguished by way of *debellatio*, an accepted concept of international law. You are now a subject of the Reich who for security reasons has been placed in internment for the time of the war. It is only an act of benevolence and also a matter of convenience that you have all been put under a regime which is essentially an application of principles similar to those of the Geneva Convention, but with some exceptions. One of these exceptions is that you are not permitted, under the penalty of death, to try to escape. And remember: whatever privileges you enjoy, the privilege of being treated as an officer and so on, are not your right, but only a favour which was given but may be withdrawn."

I replied that a *debellatio* of Poland had not taken place because the invasion and conquest of Poland had started a world war and this war was still in progress which meant that neither had the Polish resistance ceased nor had the collapse of Poland been tacitly recognised by the community of nations. Besides, I was sufficiently well informed to know that the Polish government had settled in Paris; that a new Polish Army was being organised in France and a part of the Polish Navy, of which I was an officer, had reached Great Britain and continued to fight. Poland still legally existed and we were her subjects; not subjects of the Reich. What I was now told was a violation of international law.

"Poland has ceased to exist and will never rise again," answered Doctor Falke.

"*Deus mirabilis, fortuna variabilis,*" I replied. "These are well-known words which were said by a prominent Pole three hundred years ago on the occasion of a similar Polish defeat. They were proved right at that time and at other times. And they will prove to be right again."

The two German gentlemen whispered something among themselves – and then Doctor Falke said: "With your attitude you cannot hope for an improvement in your condition."

The conversation was finished and I was sent back to my cell.

That conversation explained clearly to me that it was not the intention of the German Army to apply the Geneva Convention towards us, Polish prisoners. This is certainly true. And I cannot deny that I left Doctor Falke's office indignant and angry.

But the matter had another side. Considering the matter calmly after thirty years I must admit that my – and our – position had aspects which were rather satisfactory after all.

I must concede some favourable aspects even in that particular conversation. It was, after all, quite courteous. I have since met so many compatriots who suffered not only humiliating insults but severe beatings and tortures from the hands of functionaries of the German Gestapo and other German police bodies, from the Russian KGB, German and Russian concentration camp guards, and also from Polish Communist interrogators after the war. That I could conduct a discussion and defend my political point of view when a prisoner in the hands of my enemy seems to me quite like a miracle.

In fact, having been a notorious political opponent of Germany, having remained in her hands throughout the whole war, and having given so many occasions for reprisals by the simple fact of my many escapes, it is miraculous that I stayed alive. Furthermore, I was never struck by anyone, which seems to me extraordinary luck; but this is not enough. I must admit that in spite of the character of the Nazi regime, Germany treated her prisoners of war (with exception of the Russians) in a way which was essentially humane and broadly in accordance with international law. The Russians, however, were not only treated badly, but were in terrifying numbers literally starved to death. I have seen something of this myself and learned a lot about it more indirectly.

The truth is that the German Armed Forces were, throughout the greatest part of the war, not really subject to Nazi rule. They were a kingdom apart and were governed by principles of their own. I cannot say that I approve of all those principles which were not all in accordance with mine nor those of most other European countries. The German Army was exceptionally ruthless not only in 1939–45, but also in 1914–18, 1870–1 and earlier. For example, the German methods of executing hostages and making collective reprisals seem to us all revolting and barbarous. But the German Army had strict rules of conduct and rigid principles of what was admissible and in accordance with honour and what was not – and was pedantic and legalistic in adhering to these rules, one of which was that prisoners of war should be treated as prisoners of war and not as criminals, nor as people condemned to extermination. (Again, I must still repeat that in the treatment of the Russians this rule was not applied.)

I have reasons to believe that in November 1939, when I was in the hands of the Berlin Gestapo, I was saved by a demand from the German military authorities to be handed over to them.

And besides, the threats of Doctor Falke were not fulfilled in my case after all. When I was captured in Moravia after my second escape and brought back to Silberberg, I was conducted at night along a steep, meandering road through forest to the fort on the top of a mountain, during a fog, in a darkness hardly dispersed by one or two swinging barn lanterns, surrounded by more than a dozen German soldiers with sub-machine guns at the ready and by several police dogs on leashes. I was sure that I was being conducted to execution. It was really a pleasant surprise to learn, at the fort, that my punishment was to be ten days' solitary confinement and to hear from the mouth of the very strict and haughty grey-haired Prussian aristocrat, who was the camp commandant, a few polished words of praise about my escape and conduct and a solicitous enquiry about my health.

It is true that this was already towards the end of May 1940, when the German offensive in the West was already in full swing;

when the German Army met new Polish brigades and divisions in Norway and France, not counting the Polish Naval units in the North Sea; when many Germans were already in Allied captivity and when obviously the German High Command decided to retreat from its previous stand that the Poles were subjects of the Reich and to consider them to be PoWs on the same footing as the French or British.

It is also true that the whole German policy towards prisoners of war changed in 1944. In that year a number of my French colleagues in Lübeck and about thirty of my Polish colleagues in Dössel – some of them my close friends – were executed after great escapes through tunnels. In 1944 I had to make a journey which lasted several days and nights and in handcuffs, from Lübeck to Dössel, but in the years 1940–4 we were, as I said, in an oasis of respect for international law and of conditions of life which were rather like those in the war of 1914–18, or in the nineteenth century.

Colditz was in particular a place where the principles of the Geneva Convention were applied in a conscientious way. Perhaps it was the intention of the German High Command to be careful not to infringe these principles in this special camp in which many notorious and influential people were concentrated. (It is enough to say that a nephew of Sir Winston Churchill; a son of the former French Prime Minister M. Léon Blum; a member of the French Rothschild family; a famous Catholic theologian Père Yves Congar O.P., were all in this camp.) But it seems to me there was also another reason. There were still different traditions in the different parts of Germany and they could be felt also in the army. Colditz was in the old kingdom of Saxony, certainly one of the most civilised, most humane and most liberal corners of the Reich – and one could feel this in many respects. For instance, one noticed this in the attitude of the Saxon military courts. (I must add that we Polish prisoners noticed a similarly humane and just attitude in a military court at Hamburg.) For example after one of the unsuccessful attempts at escape from Fort Spitzberg one of my friends was caught with a rucksack which he made himself from a piece of old linen taken out from his mattress and with a water-filled lemonade bottle for which he had paid a deposit. He was placed before a Prussian Military Court and condemned to a heavy prison penalty for theft. He appealed. After we were transferred to Colditz, his legal case was transferred with him to a Saxon Court, where his sentence was cancelled completely on the ground that his taking of an old rag and not returning an empty bottle, for which he had paid, were only minor accessory facts connected with the plans of an escape which he was perfectly entitled to undertake. During the session – which was very brief – the members of the Military Court did not conceal their indignation and contempt for the attitude of the Prussian Court which tried the matter in the first instance.

Or another example. On our arrival in 1940 at Colditz, when we were still in a large hall awaiting screening and search, German soldiers brought for us a kettle with soup and spilled part of this soup on the floor. A German sergeant ordered one of the Polish officers to take a rag and a broom and to clean the floor. He refused. A great row developed. The camp commander arrived and gave the same order to a dozen or so Polish officers one after another, myself included. We all refused and were immediately sentenced to fourteen days' solitary confinement.

Our attitude was that we did not object to cleaning the floor and we would have done this anyway on our own initiative in our own interest if not told to do so, but we couldn't obey such an order from a sergeant. After having served our fourteen days we wrote, each of us, a complaint to the Saxon Corps Commander against an unjust punishment. We received complete satisfaction; each of us received in writing an answer that our punishment was just because we refused to obey an order but the order was incorrect because the camp commandant had no right to give such an order to captured officers.

Our French and British colleagues could not understand our inclination to conduct quarrelsome little wars in such petty matters. After all, we had already served our sentence and could not win through our complaint anything useful except the anger of our German superiors. But for us this was something quite important: a struggle for law and justice, a reflection of our national character. I read somewhere, in a literary discussion concerning Joseph Conrad, a British observer's remark that the Poles (including Conrad) show an odd trait: they easily endure great misfortunes but are extremely sensitive to small injustices. But this is quite natural. The great misfortunes are usually results of *force majeure*, or the consequences of deliberate crimes – and they have to be accepted as blows of unavoidable fate. But small injustices come from petty disrespect for law and fairness and they can be put right. Therefore they should be opposed – on principle and for justice's sake, even at some cost.

On the whole I have good memories from Colditz. Even when in solitary confinement in 1939, when my cell was very unpleasant and cold and I had to sleep on bare boards, I did not feel there was any reason for complaint. I considered that my situation after an escape was perfectly consistent with the Geneva Convention. Spending my time in prayer for my country and my family (not having a Rosary I used my ten fingers), in declaiming aloud whatever poetry I could remember, in composing poetry myself, in singing Polish songs and in systematic thinking, I simply waited patiently for the moment when I would no longer be alone.

And I must say that my loneliness was alleviated by visits from Second Lieutenant (later Captain) Priem, who regularly came and had long conversations with me, sitting on the edge of my bed of boards. The same man later escorted me on a long railway journey from Colditz to Murnau in the Bavarian Alps, and who, later still, welcomed me on my second arrival at Colditz, half mockingly and half friendly, as an old acquaintance, and continued to embark regularly into conversations with me.

If anyone should have been a conscious and embittered enemy of my country and in consequence, in a way, of myself, it was certainly he. By profession he was a teacher, and if I remember well, also the son of a teacher. He was born in Poland, in the province of Poznan which was under Prussian rule. He was a member of this German minority which was settled by the occupying power among the population of occupied Poland and it was his job to take part in the ruthless and systematic effort of the Prussian government to eradicate the Polishness of the conquered territory by trying to make Polish children into Prussians and Germans. When in the winter of 1918–19, a Polish rising drove out the German troops and authorities from Poznan, he fought against the Polish insurrection as a second lieutenant in the so-called Free Corps – a troop foreshadowing in some way the later Nazi military formations. Now he was an elderly veteran, still lamenting the German defeat of the First World War.

But all this had no bearing upon our relationship. I remember him rather as one remembers good comrades in arms. He was a good companion, laughing and gay, fond of good stories, friendly and helpful – of course within the limits of his power – and taking the attitude of a colleague not a jailer. We spoke about politics rarely – but if we spoke, we did this in discussions which were conducted without bitterness. I cannot blame him for the fact that he was a German patriot and that he was elated by the German victories. On the other hand, he had some understanding of Poland and certainly held her in respect. When I think now about him I cannot help feeling a sort of pity for him for the fact that before he died, his patriotic expectations were frustrated in a great war for the second time.

I remember particularly vividly my railway journey from Colditz to Murnau with him and two sergeants. He was now free to give me newspapers to read – and I eagerly devoured the *Völkischer Beobachter* and other papers from which I could learn what was going on in the world. (During my solitary confinement I was originally not allowed to read anything at all. However, during the last few days, Priem brought me a few German books; but still no papers.) I learned now, to my astonishment, that a war was going on between Finland and Germany's ally, Soviet Russia. Having read the papers I started interrogating Priem about this war and he told me a lot of interesting things. He told me also – in tones of condolence – about the loss of the Polish transatlantic liner *Pilsudski* which was sunk in the North Sea by the German Navy. It was sad news for me indeed, not only because she was one of the most beautiful ships of the Polish Merchant Navy, but because I personally knew her master, Captain Stankiewicz, who perished in this disaster.

I also remember from this journey a lot of Priem's Prussian joking about Saxony and his imitating the Saxon accent. It was quite funny.

Between Leipzig and Munich, Priem, two guards and I had a compartment to ourselves – and we travelled during the night. I said jokingly that as they did not know my plans they should not sleep but they should watch me and not let me escape. But I could sleep because I knew my plans and I could act accordingly. Priem thought my remark was sensible and told me to lie down on one seat and sleep – and they sat, all three, on the opposite seat watching me.

Priem has been dead a long time. But if he were alive he would be one of my wartime acquaintances whom I should be really glad to meet again. I would slap his shoulder, greet him jovially and invite him for a glass of beer and for a long, friendly and humorous chat. I thought that it would not be bad to end my modest contribution to a collective German and Allied book about our common experiences in Colditz with these memories of a German officer from that camp – at the same time an enemy and quite a pleasant companion – just to show that friendly and tolerant feelings can also exist between enemies and that for us prisoners of war at least, not everything was as bad in Germany as for other people.

Polish–German enmity and political opposition are probably irreparable, not only for our generation but also for some generations to come. But this does not mean that there should always be enmity between individuals. I must say that I consider Germany to be a country which is often pleasant to be in. I find the Rhine Valley quite beautiful; many German cities interesting; the German landscape and many German villages most charming. I also find some members of the German nation delightful, interesting and most worthy of respect and friendship.

In the same way I must say that what I remember from my Colditz days is not only the exhilarating international community and of the friendship with so many Poles, Frenchmen, Britons and Belgians, but also the interesting architectural surroundings of the old Saxon castle; the ravishing view from the top windows over the Saxon hills, over the snow-covered plains and the charming valley of the river Mulde, and also the atmosphere of our sojourn in a stronghold of Saxon military traditions which were on the whole civilised and good.

Major Sir Rupert R. F. T. Barry, Bt., MBE

Captain Rupert Barry, Colditz, 1941

Educated at King's School, Canterbury
A Professional soldier, Royal Green jackets

II

Cooking up a Code

BY RUPERT BARRY

For some time Dr Reinhold Eggers has been asking me if I would write an article on the activities carried on in the prisoners' kitchen at Colditz, of which I was in charge. I think he suspects my prime interest there was not cooking as one would expect. If he did not suspect at the time, he certainly knows now as I told him the awful truth earlier this year when he came to stay with me in England. The kitchen was in fact the spy-centre of Colditz. Cooking was a minor consideration and as the prisoners' staple diet consisted of bread and assorted jam material, potatoes boiled in large steam vats complete with skins, earth and whiskers, one did not have to be a genius at cooking to get by. Dividing the finished product into precise proportions to nationalities, ladle by ladle, was a much more delicate operation as any mistake here could – and indeed did – cause international difficulties of the first order.

I will return to the reasons why the kitchen became the centre for collecting information later, but first it is necessary to go right back to early PoW life. Readers will know by now that Colditz was the Top Security Prison for Allied officer prisoners-of-war. As far as the English were concerned, it started life with eight of us in November 1940, to be joined later by others in ones and twos over the period of the war. Nearly all were officers who had been recaptured after escaping from other prison camps. All of us had much the same story to tell – fairly easy to get out of a camp but much more difficult to travel across Germany; all had been caught doing this. The general drill at this time (winter 1940–1) was as practised successfully during the 1914–18 war, viz. walking across Germany by night, being seen by no one, and eventually turning up at some neutral frontier. It very soon became obvious to us that this drill just did not work any more – either that, or we were just not good enough. Our fathers before us could do it, yet we apparently could not. Why?

I have very vivid memories of sitting up, very often all night, for many nights with the other members of the British party who were not on night shift in the canteen tunnel. We would sit around a bar-rack-room table with a small fat lamp spluttering between us, dis-cussing this problem, which was of course of immense importance to us, especially as the canteen tunnel was showing very real possi-bilities of being able to launch us into the outside world.

There seemed to be no very definite answer to our problem but it appeared to us that walking some 400 miles across Germany at night was not a very good thing. Firstly, Germans in general did not go about at night. They went to bed when it got dark and got up at some unearthly hour in the morning when it got light. Therefore anyone seen moving about during the hours of darkness by police or other officials, or indeed any other German who happened to be about, was automatically under suspicion and would be reported. Secondly, Germans if nothing else are a very thorough people. Any prisoner escaping, when the fact became known to them, would immediately have his details circulated to all police stations within the Reich and this would quickly be backed up with photographs and finger prints. The main difference from 1914–18 was the speed with which this could be done. Our main enemy seemed to us to be the improvement in communications techniques which had taken place between the wars. Although this discovery might have been a softening of the blow to our pride it remained a very serious prob-lem which had to be faced and overcome.

It seemed to us that a high priority had to be given to speed – we could no longer afford the time to walk 400 miles with any hope of getting away with it. How could we shorten the time? The obvious came to mind and we discussed hitching lifts in cars, pinching cars, pinching bicycles, travelling by rail, even pinching aircraft. Each posed further problems. Travelling by rail as a fare-paying pas-senger seemed to offer the best opportunity.

At this time of the war we had no aids whatsoever to help us, our German was, to say the least, indifferent and we had no German money to buy tickets. Also we did not have access to train time-tables and we could not really expect the Germans to supply them. It will be seen that although train travel seemed the most feasible, nevertheless quite considerable problems still had to be solved. The time question could be reduced from weeks to some forty-eight hours and if we could fix the parades so that the Germans would miscount we could hide the fact that a prisoner had escaped. If this fact was not known to the Germans then of course they would not be looking for anyone. Later we were able to carry this out on many occasions to our intense amusement and satisfaction.

As always in planning, one thing leads to another. We would need information; we would need money, compass needles, tools, hacksaw blades, maps, details of frontiers and how they were guarded, and clothes. Although we were developing our own industries some things were unobtainble and unmakeable – but all could be obtained from England if only communications could be established. Could they?

Lock-picking, forgery, stealing, deception with false forms; indeed skulduggery of all kinds did not form any part of the curriculum for officer training when I was at Sandhurst, yet as a PoW one had to become a master of all these arts. In fact, it was interesting to see how fast officers and gentlemen developed those skills and the degree of proficiency they attained.

None of us in Colditz had ever considered that he could, or would, become a prisoner of war. In fact this is a phenomenon common to all the men I have met who have shared the same fate. Many considered death; some their winning the Victoria Cross, but none ever imagined being taken prisoner. All who suffered this fate were totally unprepared for it. No-one in Colditz had taken the precaution of arranging a code with wives, parents or friends in England – and this was what we wanted at this time more than anything else.

I remember one night in early December 1940 sitting over our inevitable fat lamp, planning with Pat Reid that if we could make contact we could have forged Swedish passports sent out showing six of us to be Swedish diplomatic passengers travelling in Germany and, amid much laughter, we visualised ourselves travelling first class direct to Switzerland and freedom. Pat Reid, in spite of what I said before, informed me that he had arranged with his girl friend in Ireland a simple code and that, although he was sure she had forgotten it, he would nevertheless try. Not to be outdone I told him my wife was really highly intelligent especially where crossword puzzles were concerned; she always finished *The Times* puzzle before she had drunk her early morning tea. I was sure if I put a clue in one of my letters she would be able to decode it. Both of us wrote our separate letters; checked, rechecked and checked again and then each rechecked the other's letter. We were certain that they were correct. Although the contents of each letter was in perfectly good English the substance was obviously going to be absolute nonsense to our relations as we had talked about quite fictitious persons. Pat Reid drew a complete blank. I was not to know what kind of reception mine received until after the war. The message was:

Go to the War Office, ask them to send forged Swedish diplomatic papers in shovehalfpenny boards for Reid, Howe, Allen, Lockwood,

Elliott, Wardle, Milne and self.

My wife's immediate reaction on receipt of this letter was that I had gone mad – "Poor old Rupert, they have got him down already!" At the time she was working as secretary to the head of a firm making aircraft valves in Maidenhead, Berkshire; she showed this letter to him and he was not able to offer any immediate advice. Then that night while lying in bed thinking, she suddenly hit upon the clue. She got up and started working on my letter and was able to get as far as, "Go to the War Office . . ." but could not make out anything further. By then it was past midnight but she rang up her boss and told him of her partial success. He asked her to come round immediately with the letter so that they could work on it together. By dawn, well supplied with coffee by the boss's wife, they had got it out although my wife always maintained that I had made a mistake when encoding! At nine o'clock next morning she presented herself at the War Office main door and asked the commissionaire if she could see an officer in the Military Intelligence Department. She was presented with a form to fill in in which she was asked, among other things, for details of the subject she wished to discuss. This she refused to state, saying that the matter was secret. A violent argument ensued and as it became clear that she was not going to be allowed in she explained her difficulty to an officer in uniform who came by, and told him that she had come to discuss a secret matter with an officer in Military Intelligence and not with the commissionaire, and could he help her. It so happened that he could, he would, and in fact did help her. My wife was instructed to write back to me in clear saying that she had met an old aunt of mine called Christine Silverman who had not seen me since I was a child and was distressed to hear where I was and that she would write to me. I, of course, had no aunt of that name and, as things turned out, I in fact received 'Christine's' letter before my wife told me of her chance but happy meeting. However, it only took me a few seconds to rumble what had happened. We set about the letter with great expectations only to have our hopes destroyed by the message, "The War Office considered the use of Swedish Diplomatic papers to be too dangerous". Our reply to this was, "We will consider the danger and not the War Office. Would you please expedite". Suffice it to say that after this somewhat unnecessary delay and because shovehalfpenny boards were no longer acceptable to the Germans as they had already found naughty things hidden in them, we never received our Swedish papers! However, communications had been established and these grew and grew.

Obviously this simple code could not go on with any degree of safety. Something much more sophisticated was needed and this was forthcoming. Still using our simple code we were informed that parcels of clothing sent by various 'good works' institutions (although the British Red Cross and Order of St John were never used for these purposes) had been sent to Peter Allen and Kenneth Lockwood. One contained amongst the clothing a packet of Smarties, and the other six handkerchiefs each with a different coloured border. We were further told what we had to do with these, which was to place the yellow Smartie in a mug of water, then place in this water the handkerchief with the green border, stir for a few minutes, take out, read and destroy. The developed handkerchief contained detailed instructions for the operation of two really quite complicated codes. These were immediately taken into use, discarding the previous simple one.

The immediate consequence was better security and we were able to spell words which were otherwise unmentionable and also to indicate figures without using numbers. We could send longer messages in one letter – up to approximately forty words. Each message sender would have a different frequency and we could use as many senders as required providing the War Office had prior knowledge of their names. It was possible to link parts of a long message, say 500 words, together by means of serial numbers. Different parts would be written by different people. Further, it was easily possible to write anything we wanted to say in good English so that letters could be sent to anyone without that person having any idea that a message was contained in them. In fact, very few did know. Both codes stood the test of time and both were in full operation when the war finished and, as far as I know, the Germans had no idea what was going on. Obviously they were suspicious and they did, from the beginning of the war to its end, test every single letter that ever came in or went out of Colditz for invisible ink. To my knowledge, invisible ink was never used.

As things developed we were able to receive messages in certain BBC programmes and to this end and also for the purposes of news gathering Jim Rogers taught himself shorthand. In Colditz we never at any time had a transmitter – a possibility the Germans were fully alive to.

I have so far talked about how we obtained our vehicles of communication. Having got them, what did we use them for?

In the early stages we were primarily interested in obtaining the necessary hardware for escape – spanners, compasses, maps and tools of all kinds. We could and did make suggestions for the concealment of these in certain articles in prisoner-of-war parcels. Later when Dick Howe had perfected his technique for stealing

whole parcels before the Germans opened them it was only necessary to specify our requirements. With the exception of the Swedish
diplomatic papers all our demands were fully and professionally
met. We had tremendous faith in and admiration for the department of Military Intelligence which dealt with us.

It was not long before we really had everything we needed dupli-
cated and triplicated. Useful information of enemy activity on
frontiers, sentry positions, wire entanglements etc. etc. were coming
in all the time.

When Douglas Bader arrived in Colditz we were not slow to realise that to get him home would be no small propaganda scoop.
Douglas of course, as always, was game for anything. We suggested
to the War Office that the Air Ministry might be willing to consider
the possibility of landing a light aircraft on the autobahn to the
north-east of Colditz at a prearranged time and date. If so, we
would see to it that Douglas Bader was there with others to meet it.
To my utter astonishment the Air Ministry seemed to be interested
and lengthy messages on what was known to us as 'Plane Plan'
started to be exchanged only to come to naught in the end. On
reflection I am convinced that the Air Ministry had no intention of
putting such a plan into operation. Risking a plane and pilot on
such a doubtful mission was really just not on. However, our
morale was boosted no end and this is what was probably intended.

Life was full of surprises – for example, we asked for and received
from London by the magic handkerchief method a plan of Colditz
Castle floor by floor. We required this because at the time we were
interested in possible old drainage systems and possible bricked-up
cavities in the massive castle walls. Each room was shown under the
name of the then occupant, Graf von So-and-So, Gräfin von somebody else. Enquiries after the war revealed that these plans had
been obtained from the archives of the British Museum.

As the traffic in messages concerned with escaping diminished so
the traffic in passing information back to Britain increased. In fact,
as the war progressed more and more information came in. This is
when the kitchen assumed an importance outside its normal role.
No prisoner of any Allied nation, including Russia, passed through
Colditz without having some contact with the prisoners' kitchen.
The prisoner had to be fed and his rations were supplied from this
kitchen and taken to him and we saw to it that Solly Goldman got
the job. Solly hailed from the Whitechapel area of London and had
all the wit that one associated with that area. He was also a Jew and
said so and his strength of character and charm was such that, in
spite of the times, the Germans liked, admired and respected him.
He had the rare gift of being able to communicate with anybody

although speaking no language but his own. He always came back with a fund of useful information, most of which was worth sending on.

Only once did he almost fail and oddly enough with fellow British prisoners. Six Commandos *ex*-Norway had arrived in the Colditz local police lock-up in the village. We knew they were there and rations for six were duly ordered. We knew nothing of them, not even their names, but we did know that because they were Commandos their position in Germany was, to say the least, insecure. Goldman was asked to obtain any details that he could but at the very least he must get their names. As things turned out they were not prepared to talk at all, neither would they divulge their names as they did not know who Goldman was. It was not until the next day that they believed he was who he said he was and not, as they had suspected, some enemy agent. He did then obtain all their names. These were immediately sent back to Britain by code. As events turned out this was important because later on the Germans tried to make out that they had all been killed in the operation they were engaged on in Norway, whereas they were murdered by the Gestapo in Berlin a few days later. Many of our longest messages were reports at the request of the War Office on suspected traitors, and one suspect was later charged with high treason at the Central Criminal Court in London and found guilty.

Codes

Message No. AY
Message to be sent
German aircraft recognition signals Dresden Area Sep 20th – 30th Red over Red Sep 30th – 9th Oct Green over White.

Number of words 20 (4 × 5)

AY	German	Aircraft	Recognition
Signals	Dresden	Area	Sep
20	30	Red	Over
Red	Sep	30	Oct
9	Green	Over	White

Frequency 46E
Spelling on or off – The or and

Figs on or off – A or an
End of message – but

A = W	G = C = 3	M = I = 9	T = P
B = X	H = D = 4	N = J = 0	U = Q
C = Y	I = E = 5	O = K	V = R
D = Z	J = F = 6	P = L	W = S
E = A = 1	K = G = 7	Q = M	X = T
F = B = 2	L = H = 8	R = N	Y = U
		S = O	Z = V

Letter in Code

Oflag IVC
Germany
24th Sep 42

My dear. . . . .

      Your last letter which arrived today gave me very great pleasure. Please dont send white handkerchiefs, khaki has the advantage over white in that the dirt does not show. I keep washing them as you know, even so they are permanently a dirty yellow. The other things you sent including green toothpaste etc. were a great success. Did you ever go to see mother, Norman, and the others? Do when an opportunity arises otherwise etc. etc. . . .

    Having described in some detail how codes were obtained and to what purpose they were put, the time has now come to explain how a message was put into code and how it could be decoded. The method is set out in the diagram overleaf. It needs some explanation. Starting from the top of the diagram you will see Message No. AY. This does not mean that copies of messages sent were kept – they were not, as all workings were burnt immediately. The message number was useful at the receiving end for two reasons: firstly, it enabled the authorities to discover if a message had slipped through the system undetected and, secondly, some messages were in more than one part, in which case after the alphabet letters we would add 1, 2, 3, etc. for continuity.

    The message to be encoded was always in telegraphic form and had to be an even number of words including the message number. The message or part of a message had also to be the right length so that it could be contained in one letter-card or postcard. Each prisoner-of-war could write three letter-cards and four postcards a month. We were issued with these by the German authorities. They were printed forms similar to airletter cards but on glossy paper designed not to take invisible ink. Each letter-card had precisely the same number of lines. Prisoners were only permitted to write on the lines but there was no restriction on the number of words. With a sharp hard pencil and a certain amount of practice it was quite remarkable how many words could be crammed on to a line. Ink was a prohibited commodity. The writer of a message had to decide on the number of words in the message, which had to be divisible by factors, and then decide on the form in which it would be set out. In the example shown there are 20 words, divisible either by 4 × 5 or 5 × 4 and 2 × 10 or 1 × 20. The last word of the first line of the finished letter-card and the first word of the second line indicate to the decoder the size of the box containing the code message so that the 2 × 10 and 1 × 20 could be discarded as impracticable. Having decided that the box will be 4 × 5, the blank box is then drawn out to accommodate four words across and five words down making twenty spaces for the message, which is then written in in the normal way from left to right.

For security reasons or for ease of encoding it was sometimes necessary to spell words and at other times it was necessary to include numbers in messages. These were dealt with by means of the off-set alphabet.

Each sender had his own frequency and the one shown is 46E. These numbers were known to the authorities in England. The 46 indicates the sequence of words in the letter which are of interest and the E indicates where the off-set alphabet starts.

To encode his message the writer's first consideration is to indicate the size of the message being sent. He must, therefore, finish his first line with a word of four letters and start his second line with a word of five letters. (The decoder now knows the sender's frequency and the size of the message he is about to deal with.) After the first full stop the first word of the message to be sent will be the last word of the message, "white". This will appear as the fourth word after the full stop. As this word is not suspicious in itself it can be written in clear. The next word of the message to go into the letter is "over" and as this is also a normal word it can be given in clear as the sixth word after "white". Words will continue to be put into the letter reading on the diagonal from bottom left to top right from the box containing the message. This has the effect of jumbling the words of the message so that they do not appear in sequence in the letter.

The third word to go into the letter is therefore "Oct" and for demonstration purposes this has been spelt out. In fact, it is a word which could have interested suspicious minds so would probably have been spelt anyway. Continuing in the same 46 frequency "Oct" should go in as the fourth word after "over" but as it is going to be spelt out you will see that the fourth word is in fact "the" meaning "spelling starts". Continuing on 46 frequency the first letter of each word involved is taken and read off its off-set alphabet equivalent until the word "the" falls in the frequency again. The decoder now knows that spelling is finished and that the message will continue normally. To encode numerals the system is as for spelling except that the starting and finishing sign for figures is either "a" or "an" falling in the frequency sequence. At the end of the message as a double check that all is finished the word "but" would appear as the next frequency word.

Like most things of this nature it all grew from small beginnings – only two people in the first instance, then four, then six, developing as the war progressed to some twenty or more senders in the net. All realised the gravity of the situation had they been discovered so that no one ever took any chances.

We asked Military Intelligence for much and we received all we asked for and more. Nothing ever seemed to be too much trouble and for this support and encouragement we were grateful then as, indeed, we are still.

Lieut. Frédéric Guigues

*Frédéric Guigues –
a pastel drawing by
John Watton, Colditz,
1942*

19th Battalion, African Light Infantry. Chevalier de la Légion d'Honneur by decree of 20th March 1948. Extract from this decree: "An élite officer, a matchless technician, who used his exceptional skill and audacity to resist the enemy in all PoW camps where he was interned. He succeeded in installing and preserving a prison radio service particularly in the international reprisals camp to which he was transferred. His unique achievements evoked the admiration of all, and particularly of the British PoW officers who were with him."

III

Open Sesame!

BY FRÉDÉRIC GUIGUES

Our French escapists soon realised the importance of the German parcels office where our parcels were kept and opened by the Germans behind a wire grille in the presence of the recipients. The contents were checked and sometimes X-rayed; then, if no contraband was found, the grille was raised and the contents of the tins and parcels handed to the owners.

In spite of the Germans' scrutiny of all parcels, some very small amounts of skilfully-concealed contraband escaped their notice, but if we were to receive parcels containing sufficient forbidden material to use for escaping, we should have to be able to enter the German parcels office whenever we wanted to. All we had to do was to make a key to fit the lock of the parcels office door which opened into the prisoners' courtyard.

Theoretically, it seemed easy to make a key which would fit. The lock was of a very old type, massive and showing more ironwork than mechanical achievement in its construction. The Germans, however, had rendered it burglar-proof by fitting in it a second lock which required a cruciform key to open it.

To start with I had to examine the lock itself. Fortunately, my friends had managed to get one from a door in the British quarters. I was thus able to study the highly complex function of the lock and so arrive at the exact specifications required for a key. In doing this, I had to make an enlarged model of the lock from cardboard boxes, which enabled me to find out how to cut a cruciform key to fit. I knew how the key should be cut, but I needed not only a rough key to work on, but the tools to cut the complex arrangement of notches in it. As I jokingly said, "If we had eggs we could make a rum omelette, if only we had some rum."

It was my friend L'Ouragan (Vidal) who had the idea of making a saw from razor blades bonded with screws between two pieces of tin. He found he could cut teeth into the edge of the blade with a pair of scissors, doing it so skilfully that very small scales of steel were removed leaving angular teeth. Of course, it needed a great deal of skill to use this saw properly, but after a while, even the less gifted of us could cut steel bars 20 millimetres thick. We used this saw to cut metal from the clock in the tower. Martin L'Avocat, whose lack of skill was legendary, was able to cut out so much metal that the clock hands had to be wedged to stop them waving in the wind.

We had few other tools, but Pierre Boutard, my companion in an escape attempt at Munster, had a pair of pincers and we had a few dentist's tools given to us by the camp dentist, René. Pierre worked with me as a kind of surgeon's assistant, handing me tools to my instructions, rather like in certain films where surgeons are operating on a patient.

We were now ready to work on the parcels office lock which would mean dismounting it and cutting the key to fit. A team of ten skilled prisoners were given the job of taking the lock from the parcels office door and distracting the Germans. I had decided not to take part in this particular operation so that my nerves would be in a fit state to make the final fitting of the key. All we needed was a favourable opportunity to distract the Germans. They furnished this themselves when one of their superior officers came for a visit. Bébert and L'Ouragan triumphantly brought their trophy and the work was started at once.

"Scissors, scalpel" – one after the other, the six notches were cut into the partly prepared cruciform key. I tested it in the lock and found, with a little bit of margarine, it worked.

We replaced the lock and the Germans noticed nothing. I waited anxiously for the German parcels officer, 'Le Beau Max', to unlock the door with his own key. He, too, noticed nothing. We were beginning to win.

Now we planned our entry into the German parcels office. This meant close team work with seventeen prisoners involved. Each one had a specialist role to enable one of us to get into the parcels office in safety. It meant a drill which we rehearsed repeatedly. I had to open and to shut the door, working with my hands behind my back, so that I could watch the guards and my stooges who signalled when it was safe for me to go ahead, without arousing suspicion. Once inside the parcels office, I was not hindered by the other locked doors, the locks of which were of a normal type and could easily be opened with a couple of hooks. My training with the African Light Infantry familiarised me with such problems.

Now I was in the position of a child to whom a fairy says, "Tell me what parcel you would like to have; it will be sent to you at once and you can get it without any difficulty." My wish was to get a parcel of saws, files, scissors, engravers' tools, screwdrivers. With such tools we could make anything we required to escape from the castle.

Lieut. Fernand Couve, a gunner I had met in Fort Charny to the north of Verdun at the beginning of June 1940, and with whom I had been taken prisoner, had arranged a code with his fiancée. In a letter twenty-seven lines long, he included a coded message in seven or eight of the lines. Through this channel I ordered two 5-kilogramme parcels of tools to be sent to me by my wife. The tools were to be hidden in rags. The wrapping of the parcel was to be made of black cloth sewn all round. We relied on Lieut. Jung* to let us know in good time when the parcel arrived. Our friend Jung was even able to tell us the number of the mailbag which contained a 'Dynamite Parcel' – the code name we used to refer to parcels containing a mass of unconcealed contraband.

After several interminable weeks, Jung at last announced triumphantly that the first of the Dynamite Parcels had arrived. It was in bag number 3. I watched the unloading of the mail and had seen that my parcel was there. We had prepared an identical parcel full of harmless material, to replace the one we were after.

Our plan to retrieve the Dynamite Parcel went ahead with the utmost care, as we did not wish to be caught by any stupidity or oversight. As the issue of parcels was to take place on the following day, I had to assemble my team of seventeen confederates and get into the parcel office almost at once. In full view of the courtyard I opened the door behind my back, turning the cruciform key in my right hand. I held, concealed as well as I could, the replacement parcel in my left hand. When the door was open I gave the cruciform key to one of my friends, in case I should get caught. The signal was given to me that the guards were not watching, so I entered the holy room, shutting the door behind me.

It took me only a few minutes to open the doors which separated me from the room where the parcel bags were kept. I broke the seal of sack number 3, withdrew my parcel addressed "Lieut. Guigues, Frédéric. . . ." and replaced it with its harmless double. A pair of pincers for resealing the sack again was within reach of the office of

* Lieut. Colonel Le Brigant, then French Senior Officer, asked the Commandant, Colonel Schmidt, to allow a French officer to help the German NCO in the town post office to record and collect the parcels. Often the French addresses were difficult to read. Parcels were sometimes damaged, and a witness was needed to check that the German soldiers on guard had not taken anything from the parcels. After some hesitation Schmidt agreed to this. Lieut. Jung had to give parole (1) not to escape, (2) not to try to contact civilians, (3) to do nothing to the disadvantage of the German Reich.

Captain Lange, the German Security Officer, sometimes supervised Lieut. Jung. He could find no cause for complaint and as far as Lange could see Jung's behaviour was always correct – *Reinhold Eggers.*

the German in charge, 'Le Beau Max'. I could have left the office
then with my parcel, but I wanted to check if the back door could

Sergeant Grünert,
'Le Beau Max'

be opened. It led to another room in the Cellarhouse* and into a
small corridor near the foot of the French staircase, and there was
an entrance to the hospital as well. It was child's play! Besides a
normal lock, the door was fastened by two long iron bars across the
whole door locked by a padlock, the keys of which were hanging on
the wall – so I could open the door quite easily. I signalled to my
friends to come and join me so that we could make an inventory of
the contents of the room. We found there all our contraband possessions which had been confiscated by the Germans after various

* The west side of the prisoners' quarters, above the cellars.

searches in the past. We retrieved only a selected few items. Then I gave the signal for retreat and handed the dynamite parcel to Bébert while I locked all the seven doors as before. The last one was the most important as it led straight into the prisoners' courtyard.

I signalled my friends that I was ready to leave the parcels office, by pushing a piece of paper through the space under the door, so that a corner of the paper appeared outside. As soon as I heard the word "Go!" I opened the door and at once shut it again behind my back and locked it with the cruciform key, which one of my team passed to me. All was well.

This whole enterprise cost our priest, the Abbé Jean-Jean, a bottle of Mass wine to celebrate the event. I shall never forget the three of us, L'Ouragan, Bébert and myself, reporting to General Le Brigant "Operation accomplished". We repeated the whole operation again when the second parcel with 5 kilogrammes of tools arrived and we succeeded in the same way. The French were now the richest contingent of prisoners in the castle.

When we realised how our trick of entering the parcel office presented no problems, our requests for radio sets and other contraband reached their climax. Our orders were sent by code to Madame Guigues* who sent most of the Dynamite Parcels addressed to me, for it was better to limit the risk to a single person.

I could scarcely believe the success of our enterprise. So many dynamite parcels were on their way to Colditz I did not dare to leave my place to one of our team. The opening of the first door was easy because we had the cruciform key, but it was not the same with the inner doors, the locks of which I hand-picked one by one. Let me say, I alone had the fingers necessary for this.

One day we had an urgent warning when several of us were in the parcels office. We received the signal from our German-watchers that the parcels office staff were coming on duty unexpectedly. All

---

* Madame Guigues became an unseen member of the Colditz Castle team. Both Germans and Allies recognised her skilled work in packing the parcels and silently taking the great risk of discovery and punishment if one of her dynamite parcels blew up. Her exemplary courage should be acknowledged by awarding her 'The Colditz Cross', an order still to be founded.

Before the British started to send bulk contraband to Colditz, the same careful considerations were made in London. How would the Germans react? Some feared that at least there would be reprisals. But nothing happened. The Germans did not expect to be confronted with such masses of contraband, so no special measures or reprisals were made. Simply, the objects that were discovered were confiscated. Perhaps in the back of the Germans' mind, it was admitted that a prisoner had a moral right to try these clandestine methods of escaping. Nevertheless, the risk was there and in those days nobody could know what might happen. In the name of the German staff I may state here that we acknowledged the skill, the daring and audacity of the escape attempts of our prisoners. Also the skill and courage needed to create and maintain such efficient secret communications with the outside world. – *Reinhold Eggers*.

but I at once left the office through the back door. I had to stay behind to lock all the doors and to leave the rooms by door number one with the cruciform key. The Germans would soon come in. I felt a funny kind of anxiety, but my mind was calm as I knew my friends outside would do all they could to hinder and to delay the Germans until I had got out. All the same, I knew my limitations.

I was all ready to go when I saw the cat with her newly-born kittens in the first room. She fled from me into the second and then into the third room. I had to get out, as the Germans could be diverted for only a short time, so I did all I could to get the damned cat back to her kittens in the first room, but to no avail. I had to lock the doors and managed to get out in the nick of time, leaving the cat locked in the third room.

The surprise of the Germans was boundless when they later found the kittens locked in one room and their mother locked in another. This looked so suspicious that the Germans ordered a general search throughout the French quarters. We lost civilian clothes, money, false documents and, to crown it all, they took away the keys of the padlocks of the last door. The team of Le Beau Max and his German parcels staff installed a second cruciform lock instead.

Soon I made a second cruciform key in the same way as the first one, but this time by using real tools. From now on I had to leave the parcels office by the main door as the back door had been walled up.

Once, I was almost overwhelmed with fear. I had entered the parcels office in order to look for two dynamite parcels and I was waiting behind the door for the "all clear" signal. In vain. An English officer had been caught in some other forbidden room of the castle and the Germans had ordered a special crash roll-call. The yard was at once flooded with German soldiers who invaded the staircases and living quarters, hustling the prisoners out onto parade. Every effort was made to delay the roll-call so as to give us sufficient time to hide any tools our escape specialists might be working with and to remove any evidence of escape preparations. Many of the prisoners rushed to the toilets to insert their creepers, which were tubes filled with false papers and money. A dozen German guards were posted around the yard.

All this time I was waiting in the parcels office for L'Ouragan to give me the "all clear". I could hear him on the other side of the door saying, "It would be suicide for him to come out now." This was not very reassuring. My nerves tightened as I imagined the coming moment when everyone but I would be on parade.

I had to do something now or be caught and be responsible for our whole scheme being discovered, so I cut the strings binding the two parcels and opened up the packing material, making it look as if the parcels had been checked out by the Germans and had already been issued to me, the legitimate addressee. I went through the Cellarhouse rooms past the French staircase and through the door to our now empty quarters, and temporarily hid the parcels. Then I hurried out of our building, past the guard at the door, as if I had been held up and was a bit late. The guard took no notice. After the roll call I simply went back and locked the door with the cruciform key.*

Caught in my own trap

I don't know the precise circumstances which caused the Germans to install a safety device on the door to the parcels office in the Cellarhouse, but I am sure that the contrivance did not work before the 1st May 1942. Here are my reasons.

More escape experts joined us from other prisoner-of-war camps and reinforced the Colditz French contingent. Among them were two young officers, Yves Desmarchelier, known as Le Petit, who was of the same seniority as I, but from the Lille school; and Robert LaLue, known as Le Conscrit, from the Cluny school. He was two years younger than I. These two were both extraordinarily gifted and if I add that they were particularly experienced, one can understand what a rich team the three of us made; we were inseparable.

L'Ouragan and Bébert were still active and certainly devoted to the common task, but they had not the manual skills of the new comers. At our colleges of engineering, arts and handicrafts, three years were spent in the workshops at twenty-five hours per week. This was how our skills were acquired.

Our German-watching service had reported to me a suspicious noise during the night in the region of the parcels office. We started

---

* In 1942 Captain Lange, the German Security Officer, and Captain Vent, who was in charge of the castle post office with his assistant Sergeant Grünert ('Le Beau Max'), were certainly no match for Guigues and his team. But even so, they were aware that the prisoners made secret visits to the parcel office and the Cellarhouse rooms, and decided to wall up the back door which opened into the corridor at the foot of the French staircase. This back door could only be opened from the inside, as it was secured with big iron bars, but Guigues and later Captain Howe managed to get inside.

Extra guards and cruciform locks made no difference: the parcels office was still being burgled by the prisoners, so Lange laid a trap to catch them. With great secrecy, an electric alarm was installed. The opening of the door rang a bell in the guardroom, except when Le Beau Max and his German team were at work. Guigues found out and mounted a counter plot which rendered the German plan a failure. A most ingenious and scarcely believable achievement involving the use of cruciform keys, understanding of electrical appliances, a quite extraordinary vigilance and a meticulous knowledge of the changing of German guards, all contributed to the success of the French counter measures. – *Reinhold Eggers.*

a twenty-four hour listening post to find out what was going on.

One fine morning, when there was no distribution of parcels, I saw the parcels office door had been left ajar. I glanced in and saw a pair of pliers near the door frame, but my attention was attracted to a small, new copper fragment stuck between the two parts of the lower hinge. I abandoned my first intention to take the pliers and waited until after the next distribution of parcels, so as to see what had been changed in the parcels office. I discovered that the locks had been fitted with an electric alarm system. The conducting wires of thin steel plates covered parts of the door. A ring of moist plaster indicated where the copper wiring led and I noticed that it finished, as far as I could see, in the entrance to a small room where all doubtful parcels were meticulously examined by X-ray.

General Le Brigant has described in detail, in his book *Les Indomptables*, the means by which we became masters of the situation. How, even before the Germans had completed the alarm system, we intercepted their wiring which connected the device in the hinges of the door with the alarm bell in the guard room. Our interception in the X-ray room was completed by 1st May 1942, on the feast of St Philip, the same day that General Le Bleu was moved to another camp. Le Petit and I had done the wiring, taking three hours. Le Conscrit completed the wiring in our quarters in the first floor of the Cellarhouse. Once more we reported to General Le Brigant and to my great friend Commandant Cazabat, "Operation accomplished". Once more the Abbé Jean-Jean opened a good bottle of Mass wine.

We could now not only shut off the alarm to the German guard room, but raise the alarm as well whenever we wanted to. Once we had to do just this.

It happened one day when one of our English comrades, strong as a devil, boxing like a professional, but undergoing some sort of psychological crisis as was not uncommon among prisoners, decided to open the parcels office door by means of an attack upon the cruciform lock with a simple wire hook. I at once appealed to Dick Howe, chief of the English escape committee, and asked him to stop this prisoner damaging the lock. I was not inclined to manufacture another cruciform key as I knew the difficulties only too well. After some attempts to stop our friend from breaking the lock, it was evident that he could not be prevailed upon to abandon his project. Then I said to Dick Howe, "Either you grab him and keep him safe, or I will deal with the situation myself within the next minute or two."

"All right, go ahead," was his answer.

I gave a signal to Le Conscrit who was watching me from a first-floor window in the French quarters. According to our arrangements Le Conscrit switched on the alarm in the German guard house. We did not have to wait for more than a few seconds before a squad of guards rushed into the courtyard and fell upon the English officer who was tampering with their parcels office lock. Our device was proved to function properly. We were masters of the alarm system.

Our easy access to the parcels office allowed us to order, receive and dispose of a thousand forbidden things: radio sets, secret addresses, maps, money, arms, paint, false documents and alcohol. Madame Guigues sent us alcohol in two-litre tins used for motor oil. A single name "Olazur", on the tin indicated the contents. We did not say, "I am taking a glass of alcohol." We said, "I am drinking a cup of 'Olazur'."

By the way, before I go any further, I must give you a recipe for an apéritif which we made:

Lighter fuel bought in the canteen. Methylated spirits from the sick room. Eau de Cologne received from relatives in parcels. Saccharine graciously provided for us by our German guardians. Aspirin from the sick room.

The two latter ingredients served on the one hand to reduce the bitterness and the other to limit the dreadful headache that was caused by drinking the mixture. Needless to say, this beverage, in view of its composition, was not within reach of all of us.

Our organisation worked well, but I always feared failure. I was haunted with the thought of finding myself in the parcels office, suddenly face to face with one of the German guards armed to the teeth. I told my team that we had always to be one jump ahead of the Germans and to be prepared to forestall them without hesitation.

This was how we countered the German security over our parcels sent from home. When a parcel of tinned food had been thoroughly examined by the guards, we had two choices: either to take the contents after they had been emptied into the bowls or plates we provided, or to leave the tinned food in the storeroom from where we could call for it to be opened by the Germans on some future occasion.

In the second case we were allowed to read the labels from behind a high grille of thick wire mesh which ran down the centre of a waist-high solid counter separating us from the guards. But to let us read the handwritten labels on home-made preserves the Germans raised the grille and handed the tins over the counter for us to take in our hands. Now I prepared in advance tins identical in size and appearance to those that I wanted to get. I filled these dummy tins with vegetable rubbish from the kitchen and then had the contents contaminated with urine to make them go so bad they would never be opened but thrown out as soon as the tin had been pierced. Le Petit did the soldering with equipment which we now had available. On the dummy tin we stuck a label which we had kept from a previous similar tin, a label which always read *Marcassin en Sauce*. The tins labelled *Marcassin* in the parcels were filled with contraband, i.e. clandestine correspondence, money, German Marks, and addresses. This was how we got hold of it.

When I took a tin of this kind from the Germans to read the label, I feigned clumsiness and allowed the tin to slip from my hands down to the floor on my side of the counter. At the same instant, Le Conscrit, who was crouched between my legs, caught the falling tin and handed me up the dummy one which I returned to the guard, saying that I did not want it yet and that it should be kept in store. In this way we avoided using our whole organisation to steal a single tin of contraband. This method also enabled us to get a parcel if a prisoner had been prevented from collecting it for some reason or other. The parcel could be left in store and recovered later, on one of our visits to the forbidden rooms.

My wife at home in France helped us by sending us tinned food which had gone bad, so that when it arrived at Colditz it was in such an advanced state of decomposition that the tins containing it bulged. The German guard noticing this, would cautiously pierce the tin with his bayonet and a terrible stinking gas hissed out. The sickened guard thrust away the tin and told the owner to get it thrown into the rubbish at once. But the swollen tin contained a smaller one full of contraband. This scheme was very useful and was never discovered.

I had ordered from France, by code, an electric generator which could be operated by hand, to enable us to use our secret radios when the main supply was switched off. The code name for our generator was *La Moulinette* and I asked for it to be sent to me at Colditz. Before it came, however, we were transferred to another prison camp at Lübeck. It was forwarded to us there and we used it during the last months of our captivity.

Earlier, on 1st October 1942 the Germans had transferred thirty-one French prisoners, including myself, to a camp at Munster. Le Petit and Le Conscrit, who stayed at Colditz, inherited all the secret information and the cruciform and universal keys.

At the Munster camp I escaped once more, exactly two months after our arrival. There were eight of us and three made home runs. Among those recaptured were my friend Pierre Boutard and I. We were caught, strangely enough, by being overrun by a wild boar hunt. We were taken to hospital at Soest in Westphalia and in due course we found ourselves back in Colditz.

"It took you a good while to return to us. We almost despaired of seeing you again," said my friends as they greeted me. They told me that the radio sets that had been installed by L'Ouragan, Bébert and I in our bedroom on the top floor of the Cellarhouse had been discovered by the Germans and confiscated. It was quite clear to me that this loss was the result of treason. But that is another story.

My friend L'Ouragan who escaped with me from Munster was one of the happy ones who made a home run. It took him eleven days to reach Paris. He was already as lean as a skeleton when he left but after eleven days on the run he had lost twelve kilogrammes. Madame Boutard cared for him in Paris and provided him with false documents. He died in hospital in 1944.

When the French group of Colditz prisoners were moved to Lübeck we took one radio set with us, hidden in one of our packs which, before we departed, were stored in the parcels office to await a thorough search by the Germans. During the search period which lasted a day or two I made my last visit to the parcels office and transferred our radio sets into one of the packs that had already been searched.

When the French company left Colditz in July 1943 I bequeathed my whole stock of escape material, including the radio station with a new radio, in the attic of the Cellarhouse, and all the keys*, to Captain Richard Howe, the British escape chief.

One of the radio sets we left at Colditz had a defective valve. I had ordered a new one from France and it caught up with me at Lübeck. We were able to return it to Colditz through an Englishman who had changed places with a Frenchman. The Englishman attempted to escape, was caught and returned to Colditz, taking with him the new valve, probably concealed in his creeper.

News Bulletin Service for Prisoners

In the summer of 1942 I had succeeded in securing a complete three-valve radio set through a dynamite parcel. We code-named this set 'Arthur I'. As an insurance against its discovery by the Germans, I ordered another set from France, but this time not in a single large parcel, but in thirty-five parts, distributed in the tins and boxes of our dynamite parcels. The second set, Arthur II, was

---

* The special keys which permitted us to open all the doors in Colditz Castle had been hidden in the side posts of our wooden beds, which had been hollowed out with wooden stoppers corking the apertures. The camouflage was of the highest perfection. Even if a searcher put the bed upside down it would not betray its secret.

just ready when Arthur I was discovered and confiscated by Captain Eggers himself. So on 15th December 1942, the very same evening that Arthur I was taken, my friends who had remained at Colditz (among them Le Petit and Le Conscrit) were able to get Arthur II working, and there was no break in our radio service.

Arthur II had initially been hidden in the dentist's room, and was used in the evening, except when the dentist had an unexpected visitor, so I was told after my return to Colditz. The officers who knew where the radio was hidden could be counted on the fingers of one hand – an excellent precaution, as I admit that in the case of Arthur I, I had not done all I should to keep where the radio set was hidden a secret.

Arthur II was later hidden in the attic over the rooms 303 and 304 of the Cellarhouse, not far from the spot where the Germans had found Arthur I. In order to make a second discovery more difficult, we covered the set with a big heap of broken tiles.

At about this time, another batch of French escapers arrived from other camps. Their chief was Paul Dugardin, known as "Popol with the dirty hands" – to distinguish him from Paul Houdart, the seminarist, whom we called "Popol with the clasped hands".

Popol with the dirty hands was an extraordinary type from every point of view. Le Petit and Le Conscrit joined his team. As for myself, I decided to explore the attics of the Cellarhouse to find a blind spot where we could set up a permanent laboratory and radio station in which our experts could work with all our material, undisturbed by sudden invasions, not only German ones.

One day, during one of our tours of exploration, Le Petit and I were very nearly caught in the attics. In spite of our being warned that a German search-party was on the way up, we found ourselves cornered, having not left ourselves enough time to return to our quarters. Where could we hide? The attics were immense, but they did not serve as lumber-rooms as is often the case in less orderly establishments. The floors were absolutely bare, and above our heads there were only the great roof beams. It seemed to us that we were caught in a trap, until one of us had the idea of climbing up into the beams, which we did at once and soon lay clinging silent and motionless to the main timbers high in the shadows of the roof. Within seconds, the German riot squad, under the command of a sergeant known to us as Le Grand Noir, quietly entered the attics. The Germans need only have lifted their heads to see us, but they were too occupied in studying the floor. We watched them, in particular Le Grand Noir who took a two-metre rule from his pocket. We wondered why. There was an old rag lying on the floor and Le

Grand Noir, helped by his squad, set about measuring its distance in relation to the door and the wall. We had noticed the rag before, but I had ordered that nobody should touch it – an intuitive instruction which was almost a luxury in precaution. I was thankful that I had given this order.

The German riot squad then examined the floor of the attic near the door and the unavoidable passages, looking for fingerprints in the dust, but we had taken care of this too. On every one of our visits, we powdered the floor with dust taken from the roof beams. I could now see that this precaution too had not been in vain.

I do not know how long we had to wait on those beams, with our nerves strained by the fear that we might at any second become pistol targets, but at last the Germans left. I still remember the faces of our friends when they saw us return safe and sound from that mousetrap.

The German sergeant of the riot squad, Le Grand Noir, suspected me particularly: twice we had had a little story without words.

One night at a late hour I was on duty watching the German guards from a window in our quarters on the ground floor. I was standing just above the punishment cells, so that I could watch the main door to our inner courtyard. I saw a group of German searchers wearing track suits and soft shoes. I watched them moving about until they disappeared around a corner. Fearing they would invade the room where I was, and wishing to explain my presence there, I went to a cupboard, opened it and took out a mug as if to get a drink. At that moment, Le Grand Noir came in, so I pretended to drink from my mug, but as I did so he shone his torch right inside the mug, exposing its emptiness and my pretence.

A few days later, in the same place and under the same conditions, feeling that the searchers would again enter the room where I was, I went to the urinal to give the impression that I was going to satisfy a call of nature. At the critical moment, Le Grand Noir came in and directed his torchlight exactly on my *pipi*. Alas, it was not possible for me to get a single drop out of it, so I had to re-arrange my *zizi* and return, crestfallen, to my room.

We later chose for our laboratory site a long triangular hole under the roof formed by a vertical wall, the roof and a floor, which was the ceiling of the small dining room 303 on the third floor of the Cellarhouse. The entry to this spot was in the highest point of the triangle under the roof. Only a very slim man, wearing thin clothes, could slip through the hole which was opened by lifting two floor boards. Luckily at that time, we had no tendency to corpulence, the German rations were distributed with such thrift.

We carefully planned a camouflage for our new laboratory, as we knew the German methods of searching a building from long experience. Our lab was already inside a zone (which included all the top attics of the Cellarhouse) prohibited by the Germans and shut off from us by an iron door fitted with a cruciform lock. But did the Germans really believe that we could not overcome their barriers? They checked their own safety measures as we well knew, for they often came to inspect* those attics which were completely empty.

Our lab was hung with blankets to insulate it from cold, light and noise. Then we did not forget our escape route. We cut the rafters in our floor which formed the ceiling of the room below to make a hole of about 50 centimetres in diameter, just above the laths below and just big enough to allow a man to break through the laths and plaster of the ceiling of room 303 in an emergency. On top of this escape exit we put a part of a beam taken from the floor of the chapel. This gave support to our feet, but its second purpose was that of a battering ram to enable us to break through the ceiling of the room below and disappear in seconds should the Germans take us by surprise. We should have landed on top of a cupboard placed there for that purpose.

To furnish the lab we had stolen a door from a WC on the first floor and made it into a table. We also had two stools. Our electricity was taken from the cables in room 303, the small dining room below, and we arranged a switch so that we could put on and off the lights in our lab or in the dining room as required.

Our alarm system was operated from the room containing the airpump for the chapel organ, a safe distance away from our laboratory and radio station, so all signalling had to be done indirectly. The other prisoners, however, who knew of the existence of the radio station but not its exact whereabouts, thought it was situated near the signalling post and were forever warning us that we should soon be caught.

Within a few weeks, the lab was completely furnished. Pierre Boutard, who being a man of fine taste designed the interior decoration, Le Petit, Le Conscrit and I were the only four who actually used the lab. Only a few others knew where it was – such as the brave Aigouy, who would never see France again and our Commandant Cazabat, chief of the escape organisation of the French company, who by his position was entitled to have the honour of visiting us. His visit – the only one he paid – was a frightening one. We were side by side in the lab and were listening in to the BBC: "Here is London. The French are speaking to the French. . . ." All

---

* This was a strict regulation in view of possible air raids. – *Reinhold Eggers.*

of a sudden, the lights went out. I thought that our warning team, code-named PET, had played us a prank in bad taste. But it was not so, as we clearly heard the well-known noise of a search going on above our heads in the attic. We kept perfectly still, but as you know, when anxious, one starts swallowing one's saliva and this kind of gulp, coming from the base of the mouth, seems to produce an infernal noise. I crept under the table, disengaged the trap-door and was ready to break through the laths when the light came back. The Germans had gone. Commandant Cazabat behaved very well, but one has to admit that on his first visit he had been extraordinarily lucky in not being caught.

We followed the course of the war with great hand-painted wall-maps. At first the Germans were shown as flooding eastwards and then later the ebb tide became evident. It was at the time of the German retreat through Russia that we had the opportunity of receiving a Russian broadcast. Alas! We could not understand a single word, but one of our friends whose father was a Russian was asked to help us. He understood what was going on and what he told us filled us with hope. The reception had been good and we had found the exact wave-length, but our interpreter was not needed during one part of the broadcast, for all we could hear was an odd noise, incomprehensible because no word was spoken. The noise we heard came from a column of the first thousands of German prisoners in Moscow. . . . A great multitude of men dragging their legs painfully. The noise diminished in character and changed into a shouting, intermixed with the noise of motor engines. Then followed an immense laugh; the laughing of an enormous crowd rising like a high tide. Then we heard that after the passage of the German prisoners, municipal water carts came along and sprinkled the road with disinfectant. When the crowd saw this they laughed again. I shall never forget the laughing of that crowd.

On another occasion, we again appealed to our translator. It was another broadcast in Russian. We heard a German speaking, reciting his name, rank and other details for about half a minute. Then followed a silence, broken by the sound of machine-gun fire. The Russian speaker told another German officer to mount the podium and ordered him to tell his listeners his name, rank and so on. When this was done, there was another burst of machine-gun fire. Whether this was an act or not, we did not know.

Twenty years afterwards, I joined a party of about thirty-two of my friends, some of whom brought their wives and children on a visit to Colditz Castle. In the attic I found our old lab still intact. The British had used it to the last minute.

Captain R. H. Howe, MBE, MC

Dick Howe in Colditz

Educated at Bedford Modern School. Short spell in the Royal Tank Corps. Worked for radio firms of Kolster-Brandes Ltd and Cossors, then started own radio manufacturing company, Truphonic Radio Ltd. At outbreak of war rejoined 3rd Battalion Royal Tank Regiment. Captured at Calais in May 1940. Imprisoned in Oflag VIIC/H Laufen. Escaped, recaptured and sent to Oflag IVC Colditz, where worked as British Escape Officer 1942–5.

IV

The Forgers

BY R. H. HOWE

(For over three years Dick Howe was in charge of all escaping; Colonel Guy German's choice of him was justified for with the exception of Airey Neave, all the British who escaped and made a home run did so during his term of office. He worked under four senior British officers: Guy German, 'Daddy' Stayner, Tubby Broomhall (for a very short period) and Willie Tod. He made a deal with Guy German that he would not escape himself until ten British officers had made home runs. It was a sort of benevolent dictatorship, aided by such sterling characters as 'Lulu' Lawton (his first mate), Kenneth Lockwood (in charge of all money and maps), 'Bush' Parker (the ace lockpicker), Rex Harrison (the chief tailor), 'Checko' Chaloupka (bribery and corruption), Ralph Holroyd (photography), Grismond Davies-Scourfield (the chief stooge), Jacques Houard (the nom-de-plume used by one of the world's leading stamp forgers in peace-time) and many others who were continually on call for a variety of activities.)

Every man in Colditz had a set of false documents made out for him, which were held by Kenneth Lockwood, in case they were needed for a snap escape, together with maps, money, concentrated food and railway timetables. Such was the anonymity of this team that on various occasions when I met Eggers in this country he confessed to having no idea I had been the main thorn in his flesh; the others he regarded as good prisoners, with the exception of Peter Tunstall who, by virtue of his speciality of creating noisy diversions at my behest, spent the best part of 400 days in solitary confinement. I myself was fond of music and played in the various bands and orchestras in Colditz as a drummer. The four main bands were the Dutch Hawaian Group, the Hill Billy Group, the Big Jazz Band and the Symphony Orchestra – in which I played the timpani. My evident involvement in this music helped to mislead Captain Eggers as regards my real job as escape officer.

I had a splendid liaison with the French (Lieut. Guigues) and the

Dutch (Captain van den Heuvel) and I still see Guigues fairly frequently. In my view, Guigues was the best and most complete escaper I have ever met, as he was highly intelligent and fearless, an expert lockpicker and forger and he had the facility of disappearing into thin air which I found most intriguing. When he left Colditz, he bequeathed to me the most ingenious radio installation, a method of getting into the German parcels office and many other helpful devices.

Vandy, Guigues and I were the escaping organisers of the castle, each backed by a most efficient team of selfless people who would have liked dearly to go on every scheme in which they were inevitably involved in some way or other.

Not much has been written about the forgers, who started as a collection of enthusiastic amateurs and ended up with a highly professional approach to the subject.

The earlier papers which were supplied to all escapers were based on documents mainly obtained from French orderlies who had created a misdemeanour when working on the land or in factories in Germany. Some of them were sent to Colditz and had managed to retain their *Ausweis*. These were copied by the dozen until every British prisoner had a set of papers in case he had to make an immediate escape. They were hand-made in every respect and any photographs were usually cut out of a picture taken by the camp photographer. They would pass muster in a random check of papers at the normal control points, but when examined closely the printing could be seen to be the work of a free-hand draughtsman.

Towards the end of the Colditz story the work of the forgers had become a very professional activity. Hardly any of the later forgeries survived, or else are still hidden to this day in the most secure hides. The switch to professional forgery occurred with the arrival in the camp of one of the world's leading stamp forgers, coupled with the acquisition by one means or another of the right equipment to help him and his staff.

The professional forger carried on a lucrative business before the war by repairing damaged postage stamps of high value, by means of grafting on paper to the exact thickness and completing the design work to make a perfect stamp. He was one of the cloak and dagger people picked up in France and there is no point in giving his name as that was false too!

By one means or another the forgers were supplied with all the equipment they asked for. We made a typewriter from wood, with accurate type on the type bars; the Australian officer Ralph Holroyd (a professional photographer) made a camera by utilising prisoners' spectacles; film and printing paper was obtained to make perfect passport photographs, a wide variety of inks and paper obtained and all the paraphernalia which a good forger needs.

The standard became so good that the following example will illustrate the expertise of the forgers. Every German sentry had a pass which allowed him to enter Colditz Castle. For good security reasons, these passes were changed from time to time by the Germans so the prisoners always had to have the latest pass in their possession if they wished to attempt an escape disguised as one of the German guards. We were aware on one occasion that the passes had been changed, so an arrangement was made with a helpful German sentry to lend us his pass whilst he was on sentry duty in the courtyard for a period of two hours. Within that time our master forger produced a copy which was so accurate that the forgery was handed back to the sentry and we kept the original, having transferred the sentry's photograph from one to the other.

The patience and dedication of the forgers was most praiseworthy. It is unfortunate that not one of them was ever able to put his handiwork to practical use to his own advantage as they were not encouraged to escape for obvious reasons.

Entering the German Parcels Office

The entrance to the German parcels office where every prisoner's parcel was opened and examined for contraband was from the prisoners' courtyard through a door which was in full view of anyone in the courtyard, including the German sentries permanently on duty. The door had two locks, one tumbler lock and one cruciform lock. Both were independently wired to an alarm system which operated in the German guard house if they were opened by an unauthorised person. The cruciform lock used a four-sided Yale-type key with a varying combination on each side, but happily a foolproof method of picking these locks had been devised by the Dutch officer Lieut. Commander van Doorninck.

Before the French left in July 1943, Guigues managed to conceal himself in the parcels office for the whole of one night, being locked in when the Germans left.* In spring 1942 he had tapped the alarm system and taken the wires through the ceiling up to the French quarters immediately above, where they were connected to two switches under the floor-boards, using a long, thin screw-driver which connected with a slot in the top of the switches. The holes hardly needed camouflaging as they took some finding even when one knew where they were. The control of the alarm signal now

---

* The luggage of the French was stored there. Guigues had a second radio which he concealed in the luggage which had already been checked. Thus he took the radio to Lübeck undiscovered – *Reinhold Eggers.*

meant that the prisoners could enter the parcels office at will, sub-ject only to the difficulty of putting someone in and getting him out in broad daylight in full view of two sentries. The raids had to be carried out in daylight as it was not possible to use a light in the par-cels office without its being seen from the German guard house.

The favourite method of diverting the sentries in the courtyard was to organise a game of stool ball. This had the effect of giving the sentries something to watch and also removed them from the parcels office door as it was a dangerous place to stand when this extremely rough game was in progress. Once the game was under way, the alarm switches on the first floor would be neutralised and three or four prisoners would stand and sit around the parcels office door. The key man, who was invariably the late Bush Parker, would unlock both locks acting on the instructions of two or three stooges who surrounded him. When the door was unlocked, Bush Parker would be told when to open it and slip inside, locking the door after him. He was then free to examine the parcels waiting in the office and identify those which contained contraband. When he was ready to leave, he knocked on the door and unlocked it. At the right moment he would find the door opened and he slipped out and passed the contraband to five or six prisoners who happened to be passing. There was then just the matter of relocking the doors and reactivating the alarm systems to return the system to normal.

Several raids were made without any suspicion being aroused in the German parcels office staff. The main difficulty was in persuad-ing the authorities in England (by way of coded letters) to send out parcels full of contraband and advise us when and to whom they were addressed. There was the hilarious occasion when such a parcel arrived without any warning and it was grabbed by Lulu Lawton when it was opened in front of an astonished German par-cels office staff.* On that occasion Lulu managed to get away with

---

* This was how the scene was set for Lulu Lawton to seize the parcel. A few weeks before, one of the German Parcels Office staff asked me to draw his portrait in pastel. I agreed to do this and reported his request to the British Escape Committee who told me to go ahead with the drawing – which I did in the German Parcels Office when it was closed. The German was pleased with the drawing (About 15 inches × 20 inches on dark green velvet mat pastel paper bought from the Pelikan Works). He sent it home to his wife.

Now when the contraband parcel arrived unexpectedly from England, the Escape Committee, remembering "Watton's pet Goon" as he was called, asked me to collect the parcel by queuing at the counter-hatch manned by this German who, knowing me, would not shut down the wire mesh grille between us as he should have done. I was told to look out for Lulu Lawton who would be queuing behind me, and to make room for him to come to the counter when the parcel was opened by the German. No one knew what would happen; that was up to Lulu.

As the German began to open the parcel, its unconcealed contents were revealed – files, money, maps, false papers and other contraband. But before the German could slam down the grille, Lulu had stepped into my place, seized the parcel, wrapping

most of it, in spite of spreading German money around the court-yard as he ran for cover with the open parcel under his arm. Possibly the authorities in England could not appreciate that we had unhindered access to the parcels before they were opened, as Colditz was probably the only prisoner-of-war camp where that applied, thanks again to Guigues and his merry men.

Radio Contact with the United Kingdom

When the French contingent were moved from Colditz to Lübeck, they handed over to the British the radio installation which was located in the attic over the French quarters. The entrance to the attic (which was out of bounds to the prisoners) was through a locked door adjoining the clock tower, but the lock presented no difficulty as it was of the simple tumbler type for which we had an ample supply of home-made keys.

Apart from the stooges who watched the Germans in every part of the castle as a matter of routine, the team needed to operate the radio consisted of two master stooges, a key man, a camouflage man, an operator and a shorthand writer. The master stooges made contact with the regular stooges and advised if there was sufficient time to let the operator and shorthand writer into the radio cabin with safety and allow the camouflage man time to return – a period of five minutes in all.

Once the chief stooge had given the signal to proceed, the key man opened the door leading to the attic and immediately relocked it after letting in the operator, shorthand writer and camouflage man. These three made their way through thick dust on the floor to the far end of the attic (the Saalhouse end). The camouflage man removed the loose floor-board, exposing a pile of brick, rubble and a beam. He got right down on one ear to stretch under the fixed floor-boards and loosen a thumbscrew which allowed the exposed beam to slide back. The rubble and brick was then pushed to one side revealing a trap, which could not be opened if the beam was in position. When the trap was lifted it revealed a cavity which had been hollowed out of the castle wall, large enough to allow the operator and shorthand writer to drop into. The camouflage man then closed the trap, replaced the rubble, slid the beam back into position, replaced the loose floor-board, relaid the dust and returned to the locked door covering any signs of footprints in the

---

and all, with one sweep of his arms, and was gone.

Happily no reprisals were taken against my Goon, no longer a pet, for the whole affair was hushed up by the German parcels office staff as they knew they would be blamed for their lapse in security. – *John Watton*

dust as he went and, finally, the key man let him out.

From the cavity into which they had dropped, the operator and shorthand writer then removed a very well-camouflaged wooden trap to allow them to enter the radio cabin itself, which consisted of a small room sufficiently large to allow the operator and shorthand writer to sit side by side facing a bench table backed by a control panel covered with power supply indicator lights and warning lights. These were keyed to various locations in that part of the castle in the vicinity of the radio cabin so that the master stooge could alert the operator of the movements of the German patrols. Although all listening was done through headphones, it was the operator's responsibility to shut down if the patrols got too close, in case they carried sensitive detection devices which could pinpoint the receiver. The receiver sat on the bench table with a collection of spare parts and tools, as well as a notebook and an ample supply of sharpened pencils for the shorthand writer.

The radio cabin created by Lieut. Guigues and his team would have been a masterpiece, even if it had been built without the continual interference of the German patrols, who searched endlessly to find the receiver they knew we had. Every contingency had been considered, such as the alternative power supply necessary when the Germans blacked out the castle during an air raid. Guigues overcame this by utilising the remaining live side and using the lightning conductor which was immediately adjacent to the radio cabin on the external wall as the earth side. This merely reduced the power from 220 volts to 110 volts which the operator could quickly action as the normal working voltage of the receiver was 110 volts. Another refinement was the escape hatch immediately under the seats of the operator and shorthand writer. If by some remote chance the Germans discovered the radio cabin from the attic whilst the two occupants were entombed, the occupants merely had to jump into the escape hatch under them which was the plaster of the ceiling of one of the rooms on the floor below, taking with them the receiver and any other immediately portable bits and pieces. Yet another escape route was used in the event of a snap search by the Germans whilst the operator, camouflage man and shorthand writer were in the attic, either going to or coming back from the radio cabin to the locked door. This was the old clock weight shaft which the Germans had thoughtfully opened up in the attic and on the first floor when they found the French tunnel. All one had to do was jump into the shaft and descend at a rapid rate, breaking the fall by expanding the shoulders against the wooden sides of the shaft when the hole of the first floor appeared. This escape route was used many times, particularly by the camouflage man who found himself marooned after letting in the operator and his mate.

After the French left the castle, the radio was operated by the same team for many weeks. It consisted of Grismond Davies-Scourfield (master stooge), Lulu Lawton (camouflage man), Micky Byrne (shorthand writer), and myself (operator). It was later decided to form a relief team who worked on alternate days, with Jimmy Yule (operator), Jim Rogers (shorthand writer), and Norman Forbes (camouflage man).

The radio remained undiscovered until after the British left the castle. When Guigues revisited the castle of Colditz after the war ended he found the installation exactly as it had been left, still functioning, still perfectly camouflaged.

The escape which Pat Reid got home on was thought up by Billie Stevens and Ronnie Littledale. When they first discussed this with me, they had not carried out any reconnaissance of the German cook-house where it was all going to start. Solly Goldman*, very wisely, had appointed himself as chief British orderly in the cook-house which he more or less ran in conjunction with a German NCO. I asked Solly to help me carry out the reconnaissance at some time when the kitchen would be empty (we had our own keys). He told me that the German always went out between two and three in the afternoon, so it was arranged that I would pick the lock and Solly would come with me to show me the geography of the place, which we as officers were not allowed into. At two o'clock on the due date I opened the locked door, which was supposed to be a sure sign that the German had gone. We were walking about inside, having locked the door behind us, when to my astonishment, I turned into the German's office area to see him fast asleep in a chair with his head cupped on his arms resting on a table. I made a move to retreat back through the main door which I started to reopen when I was nearly made to jump out of my skin. Solly, who was standing right in front of the German, let out a tremendous bellow of "*Achtung!*" which brought the German out of his chair in one leap and standing stiffly to attention. He was naturally furious, but Solly gave him a lecture, in his appalling German, on the terrible state of the German army and how mad Hitler would be if he ever heard about the way his troops went to sleep on duty. The resultant clatter and diversion gave me the cover I needed to open the door and slide out, whilst Solly emerged with the German, telling him that if he wanted to go to sleep on duty why didn't he lock the door

* Solly Goldman died in America in June 1972.

first. It was a superb piece of quick-wittedness, and needless to say we repeated the sortie a few days later, having got my stooges to check that the cook-house was empty this time.

Brigadier E. G. B. Davies-Scourfield, CBE, MC

Lieut. Grismond Davies-Scourfield photographed at Laufen shortly after his capture in 1940

Born 1918. Commissioned into The King's Royal Rifle Corps 1938. Wounded and captured at Calais 1940. Served in Palestine (1947), Malaya (1949–51), BAOR (1951–5 and 1960–1). Commanded 1st Rifle Brigade (1960). British Joint Services Training Team (Ghana) (1964). British Troops Cyprus (1966), Commander H.Q. Salisbury Plain Area (1970).

V

A Load of Rubbish

BY GRISMOND DAVIES-SCOURFIELD

(The Germans recognised Grismond Davies-Scourfield as one of their more dangerous prisoners. He was not only an experienced escaper but had worked with the Polish Underground Army. The following story describes how he was loose in Germany for seventeen days after escaping from Colditz. During his absence Lieut. Mike Harvey, RN, who had been a Colditz ghost, stood in for him on parades.

When the German Commandant of Colditz was informed by telephone of Grismond's recapture, he denied that any of his prisoners were missing.

"We had an Appell two hours ago, and the count was correct," he said.)

The Castle stood high above the little town, floodlit by a ring of many searchlights.

"Look out of the window, Herr Leutnant," said the *Feldwebel*, as the train began to slow. "Now you can see Colditz Castle. Beautiful, is it not, just as I told you?"

Thus I first saw Colditz from the window of a train on a dark winter evening in the early part of 1942.

It was said that Colditz Castle, the birth-place of Marshal de Saxe, had been used before the Second World War as a lunatic asylum, and some people felt that the switch from lunatics to prisoners-of-war had probably brought little change! As far as comfort and atmosphere went Colditz compared favourably with my two previous prisons, but it was certainly rather a mad place.

The inmates, at the time of my arrival, were mainly French and Polish officers, but there were representatives of most allied countries, and the whole place was a veritable League of Nations. Life went on against the background of a never-ending contest between the prisoners and the Germans. Apart from physical violence by the inmates, no holds were barred. The prisoners' aims were first to outwit the Germans and escape, secondly to harass and annoy the Germans as much as possible, and thirdly to demonstrate their absolute confidence in Final Victory. The Germans' aims were firstly to prevent the prisoners escaping, secondly to avoid becoming annoyed, and thirdly to demonstrate their own absolute confidence in Final Victory. This all-in contest raged unceasingly. Sometimes the prisoners were successful, sometimes the Germans. I do not know who really won the game.

I never played a particularly major role in all these activities, but like most people I became mixed up in many plans and schemes of escape. I did manage once to get away and, although I was subsequently re-caught, the incident was not without some adventure.

This particular episode of mine began after I had been in Colditz for some fifteen months. The idea was suggested to me by one of the British soldiers employed in the camp as orderlies, an excellent young Scot by the name, if I remember right, of Hamilton. He and another orderly were responsible among other things for cleaning out the parcel office rubbish and were prepared to conceal me in the little hand-cart used for the purpose. I was immediately interested and felt that the idea had great possibilities, albeit great complications too. I consulted the king of escapers, Michael Sinclair, who thought the idea a good one, so I went ahead with Hamilton to produce an outline plan for Escape Committee approval.

The plan, as it eventually emerged, was going to involve a great deal of preparation. The parcels office was normally cleaned twice a week by the two orderlies under the supervision of a German *Gefreiter* (Corporal) known to the prisoners by the nickname 'Dixon Hawk' or simply 'The Hawk'. They carried the rubbish, mostly paper, cardboard and straw-packing, through the gate of the prisoners' quarters and down to a cellar under the German Sergeants' Mess in the main part of the castle where the handcart was emptied. I would have to be smuggled into the parcels office and be packed into the cart while the Hawk's attention was distracted. He would also need distracting while I was emptied into the heap of rubbish accumulating in the cellar. Hamilton and his friend felt they could do this and told me (reassuringly?) that the Hawk only used the long French bayonet, which he sometimes carried to stab into the handcart, about one trip in four. After a suitable interval I would emerge from the cellar, using a special key to let myself out, walk through the main castle area to a gate in the perimeter wire, unlock it and disappear into the countryside. I would therefore need some form of dungarees for the first stage to keep myself clean, German uniform for the second stage and civilian clothes for my subsequent journey. I would also need two vital keys.

The Escape Committee approved the plan and offered every assistance. They miraculously obtained a spare key to the cellar, but the gate in the wire was a different matter. Fortunately the daily "walk" to the park, where a heavily wired-in and guarded area was set aside for prisoners' exercise, was routed past this gate. An ingenious Dutch officer undertook to manufacture from milk tins a complicated device which, if momentarily fitted against the key-hole, could gauge the inside of the lock and make a key from the measurements.

While these problems were being considered I started to make my clothing. This obviously was a lengthy process, particularly when it came to the uniform, and in fact took me nearly four months, even with the help of a number of self-made experts. Cloth had to be obtained, cut, tailored, sewn and, of course, dyed. But prisoners can do anything if they get together and pool their enthusiasm and skill, and the final results were quite good. The first attempt to dye the uniform field-grey, however, shrank the corporal's tunic which I had made with such labour and loving care to about half size, and I had to start again on a new one.

Problems over the gate key were also overcome. The Escape Committee stage-managed a small disturbance near the gate as prisoners were being escorted to the walk, and in the ensuing confusion the attention of all the guards was successfully diverted, so that my Dutch benefactor was able to step up to the gate unobserved and measure the lock with his contraption.

"Here's your key," he said a few days later, "and although I make no promises I believe it will open the gate for you."

By October all was ready. Michael had been wounded in a recent attempt to escape and was in the sick bay. In his absence I chose Tony Rolt of the Rifle Brigade to manage and coordinate all the complicated arrangements which are automatically connected with almost any escape. It was his job, which he readily undertook, to get me to the start line, so to speak, properly prepared in all respects, with the best possible conditions and timings to give the attempt a reasonable chance of success. He proved to be an excellent choice.

On the great day I attended morning roll call as usual and then disappeared to get dressed up, protected as I was doing so by the normal system of stooges or look-outs to warn of approaching Germans. First I put on my civilian clothes, then the German uniform, then the dungarees and finally covered everything up by wearing my British khaki overcoat. Into a small case I packed my food for the journey, my civilian cap and a small civilian overcoat to keep out the cold of a German autumn. I also secreted about my person such things as maps, extracts from railway timetables, German money and specially prepared travel and work permits, as well as my faked identity document. Everything, including the case, had to be concealed by my khaki overcoat for the short journey across the courtyard to the parcels office.

Any prisoner hoping to leave Colditz in an unauthorised fashion needed a great deal of luck to overcome all the many precautions which the Germans took to keep their charges inside. I prayed that fortune would smile on me that morning and give me at least a chance of the freedom for which I had worked so hard and for so long. I slipped into the parcels office unobserved, while the Hawk was engaged in some deep conversation in the courtyard. Hamilton and his friend packed me into the handcart. It was not easy, and I ended up on my back with my knees somewhere round my neck and carefully covered over. I felt like a trussed chicken and have never before or since been so uncomfortable. Could I endure the short journey to the cellar? To make matters worse the Hawk then appeared and ordered Hamilton to put the cart down in the centre of the courtyard, while he went off on some short errand. Through a crack in the side of the cart I could see some of the prisoners walking round the yard. I was assaulted by the agonies of cramp and confinement as the long minutes passed. At last the Hawk returned, and I was carried through the gate. No stabs from the long French bayonet! On we went, tramp, tramp, tramp over the cobbles. I heard Hamilton gasp, "I can't hold him", and his comrade's reply under his breath, "For God's sake keep it up, man. We're nearly there." I was set down and the cellar door unlocked by the Hawk, who remained outside, as was his wont, to enjoy the morning air.

They tossed me out onto the pile of rubbish and once more covered me up completely. "Good luck," whispered Hamilton. "Remember me to Blighty." The Hawk came in, glanced at the pile of rubbish which concealed me, and then they all went out. The key turned in the lock, and I was alone.

For a full ten minutes I lay completely still. I then emerged quietly, stretched my numbed and aching limbs, took off my dungarees, put on my German soldier's side hat and, using a comb, tidied myself up, stuffed the dungarees into my case, smoothed over the pile of rubbish and prepared to move out.

One often hears people say, "I remember it all as if it happened yesterday." Yet, strangely enough, that walk from the cellar to and through the gate, which was the most crucial and for me the most difficult part of the escape, I scarcely remember at all. I can see myself doing it, passing among the German soldiers dressed just like me, stepping along, hoping no doubt that I looked just like the others, suitably carefree, but I cannot feel it any more. The anxiety and embarrassment which I must have experienced, the resolve not to hurry or look in any way like a British officer escaping dressed as a German corporal, I can imagine but cannot in any way recall. I can see myself playing the part, just as one watches some character in a film, but that is all. I reached the gate, I opened it with my miraculous key, relocked it behind me, no doubt I resisted a strong temptation to glance over my shoulder, I walked across the park and out over the wall and disappeared into the woods.

And then it all springs once again to life. The sudden feeling of freedom and achievement comes flooding back over the years into my mind. I can feel again the fresh air on my face, smell once more the woods and grass and earth, and hear the shooting.

Mike Sinclair, on his sickbed, also heard the shooting and sat bolt upright, full of anxiety for me. Several shots rang out in the woods to my right and after a pause one or two more. Shotguns, I realised at once. A large hare came running past me, and I waved him on, thinking he and I were in the same boat. Some Germans were evidently enjoying a morning's sport, and I smiled to myself as I imagined them totting up the bag at lunch time. "*Ja, ja, wunderbar* sport today. Forty-seven hare, three pheasants and one British officer." But they must do without him, so I hurried on up the hill until the sound of the shots died away behind me. I took off my German uniform and buried it in a ditch under a pile of leaves (it was October). I became a Belgian civilian worker and hoped I looked the part. I walked on up the hill.

I reached the railway station late in the afternoon, and now it must be explained that the Escape Committee had arranged to cover up my absence from the castle. This is no longer any secret, for the Germans found out all about it as a consequence of a later escape. It is a long story and could be retold to advantage, but suffice it here to say that we had two ghosts in the castle. Not real ones, they were flesh and blood all right. They were in fact two supernumerary prisoners who we had led the Germans to believe had escaped some months before. They had volunteered to be hidden away and used as substitutes on roll-calls for prisoners working in tunnels or who had escaped and needed a little start before the hue and cry began. I was thus able to plan on catching a train in the neighbourhood fairly soon after leaving Colditz without fear that the station would be watched.

There was no difficulty in catching a train for Leipzig, the train I had selected before leaving Colditz. No one took the slightest notice of me, even when it was necessary for me to speak. This was most encouraging, as it meant that my foreign accent and home-made clothing was causing no comment. Germany by 1943 was teeming with foreign workers from almost every country in Europe, and I was meant to be one of them with my faked documents showing me to be a Belgian on transfer from Saxony to the area of Rheine, not far from the Dutch frontier. I knew all about the job I was supposed to be going to do and was fully prepared to answer questions about it.

So far all had gone remarkably well and according to plan. I intended to travel by train as far as I would find it safe to do so, and I hoped to reach Rheine in this way. Walking and boy-scouting across the countryside would be too slow and too conspicuous a business for so long a journey. This meant where possible travelling by fast, long-distance trains via Leipzig, Nordhausen and Hildesheim. My regimental motto is *Celer et Audax* (Swift and Bold) and this was how I intended to proceed.

I left the train at a small station just south of Leipzig. If my escape had been discovered the main station would certainly be watched for me and must therefore be avoided. Clutching my small case I walked through the darkness into the city, which was, of course, blacked-out completely. I was hoping to find a suitable train at another small station in the northern suburbs and was trusting to a town-plan, which I had with me, and to the North Star to help me find it. The night was clear and the star unmistakable. Whenever I see the North Star now, I remember how it guided me through the Leipzig black-out! I reached my station in the early dawn and found a train.

I walked the last few miles into Nordhausen (I cannot now remember why) arriving at the main station about 7.0 pm, which should have enabled me to catch the night express to the north, if there had been one, but learnt from the lady at the ticket office that my train to Hildesheim would leave in the morning. This posed a problem, as no escapee likes to be seen hanging around. There was, however, an excellent waiting room with a coffee bar and some form of heating. I bought coffee (of a sort) and biscuits and settled down for the night. It was extremely warm and comfortable and I must have dozed off, for I was rudely woken at midnight and told to clear out – the station was being closed for the night. I wandered off into a small park or garden nearby and went to sleep behind some bushes.

At 3 am the intense cold woke me, and further sleep was impossible. Neither before nor since have I ever felt so cold as I did during the next three hours, and I still remember that cold these days as I lie cosy and snug in bed. The morning express, however, was hot and stuffy and as crowded as any modern commuters' train. I stood jammed up against the end of a compartment as the miles slipped beautifully and rapidly by. Colditz was receding satisfactorily into the distance. "I'm taking you home, I'm taking you home, I'm taking you home," rattled the train, and I began to believe it might be true.

We slowed down and came to rest in Halberstadt station. People got off and others got on. Among the newcomers was a small party of policemen, who ordered all passengers to produce their documents for inspection. They worked with maddening thoroughness, examining papers carefully and asking questions, as they worked their way slowly up the compartment towards me. At last only one elderly woman and myself remained to be examined. They chose her first, and an argument immediately began. The police started shouting, the woman shouted back and the train began to move. The police immediately abandoned their task and, much to my relief and no doubt to the old woman's also, turned, ran from the compartment and jumped down onto the platform. The train gathered speed and rumbled on its way.

It was somewhere around midday when we reached Hildesheim, and I would have the rest of the day to hang around for my next train to take me towards the west. I had intended to leave the station and return later. But I received such an inquisitive stare from the ticket inspector at the barrier as I passed through that I did not dare return and instead set out on the next stage of my journey on foot. I could catch a train further along the line.

There is no doubt it was an unfortunate decision which led me to leave the station. It was prompted by a natural desire not to be seen hanging about, but I would probably have done better had I gone straight from the train to the waiting room and stayed there. Yet at the time it seemed more sensible to leave, and after all the escaper, alone in a whole world of enemies, cold and hungry, can only do what seems to him best at the time and under the strange circumstances which inevitably surround him.

The main road stretched out endlessly before me. The sun shone, and the country looked beautiful. But I was beginning to feel tired and hungry. Many years later I would drive down the same road with my wife beside me in the car. Now I was very much alone. I walked down into a cornfield which had not yet been harvested and, hidden by the tall, strong German rye, I shaved and washed and slept.

The two policemen were sitting on their motor-cycles at the entrance to the village. They were chatting together and took only a casual interest in me as I passed them. We exchanged a brief 'good day' and that was all. A few minutes later, however, they started up their engines, came swiftly alongside me and asked to see my papers. I explained about being a Belgian worker who had missed his train and was hoping for a connection in the next town, which I believe was called Elze or Elzen. They seemed happy enough and were on the point of handing me my papers back, when something on one of them seemed to catch the Sergeant's eyes. He re-examined it slowly, glancing at me from time to time. He then straightened up and drew his pistol.

"You are under arrest," he said.

"Under arrest?" I replied. "Why should I be under arrest? I have done nothing wrong. I have come from Belgium to work for Germany, and now you arrest me. Why?"

"Where did you get these papers from, and in particular THIS paper?" He waved the offending document under my nose. "This is a false paper."

They were quite obviously not going to let me go, and at the police station in the village they explained that the document contained an obvious spelling mistake. After a lot of questions and argument I realised I must try a new line. I told them I was Sapper Brown of The Royal Engineers and that I had escaped from Lamsdorf in Upper Silesia. They locked me up for the night.

Although this was really the end of my escape I had some further adventures as Sapper Brown and will recount them briefly. I was escorted by train to Fallingbostel near Munsterlager, joining en route a large party of rather prosperous looking prisoners in smart civilian clothing. These turned out to be Italian officers, whom the Germans had rounded up during the first days of the Italian armistice. They were the first Italians I had ever seen.

The camp at Fallingbostel was mainly for Russians, but I saw little of them during my fortnight's stay there, as I was kept firmly in a cell the whole time. The only prisoner I was able to talk to at all was a very charming, rather elderly Russian from Smolensk who was allowed to come every three days to shave me, as all my belongings including my razor were removed. The cell was freezing, and the one blanket allowed me was most inadequate at night. I was interrogated frequently and after a week I was informed bluntly that no Sapper Brown had escaped from Lamsdorf: I would remain in the cell until I gave my true identity. And this was exactly what I did do. After about a fortnight the ghosts would certainly have been withdrawn from representing me on the Colditz roll-calls and so I gave my true identity as a Colditz escapee. This at least would solve the impasse and get matters moving once again.

Sure enough a few days later I was told to get ready to depart. Imagine my surprise, however, when I found that one solitary old German soldier had arrived to fetch me. Colditz people were usually honoured by a large, heavily armed escort, on the assumption that they were all either dangerous, or desperate, or mad, so that a guard of one, though highly convenient, was tantamount to an insult. The reason soon became apparent. As we walked out of the camp and along the road towards the station, I opened the conversation.

"Well," I said brightly, "how was Colditz when you left it yesterday?"

"Colditz?" replied my guard, "And what is that?" I cottoned on immediately.

"Where are we going?" I asked.

"Lamsdorf," he replied.

Obviously the rigid, efficient German administrative machinery had proved almost more inflexible than usual and had been sparked off into action by my first mention of Lamsdorf and would take some time to slow down, stop and get into reverse. "Hast thou appealed unto Lamsdorf? Unto Lamsdorf shalt thou go," and on we went. I was still Sapper Brown with my ridiculously inadequate guard.

We caught a train for Berlin and had a long wait at the Charlottenburg Station. My guard proved friendly and cooperative and took me to a large waiting room full of soldiers bound for the Eastern front, some no doubt returning from leave, others perhaps reinforcements for the crumbling southern sector after the German disaster at Stalingrad. He bought me the usual *ersatz* coffee and biscuits. It was warm and comfortable, and soon my friend became drowsy. Finally he fell asleep, for the poor fellow had been on the go since leaving Lamsdorf two days earlier.

I got up very quietly and left the waiting room. To leave the station without any documents proved too difficult, however, and while I was still trying to find an unwatched exit my guard raised a hue and cry. After much dodging about I was arrested once again and returned to my understandably aggrieved guard.

"I buy you coffee: I am nice and friendly: I treat you well: why you do this to me?" I could see his point of view.

Late that night we boarded a large and crowded troop train, and off we went, heading, I suppose, south-eastward. The night wore on. I tried a very old trick.

"May I go to the lavatory?" I asked.

"Yes, down the passage," I was told, and to my amazement was allowed to wander off on my own. I walked slowly down the corridor, pushing my way past sleeping soldiery, until I was almost at the far end of the train. Once in the WC I locked the door, opened the window and waited for the train to slow down. But we hurtled on, and as the minutes passed by, so the calls of nature brought others to my door. They knocked, they rattled, they shouted, they banged and finally they heaved until the flimsy lock gave way. My guard stood furiously among the soldiers without.

Back in the compartment, wedged between two large soldiers I watched my guard as he sat opposite with drawn revolver. Late on the following day we arrived at Lamsdorf, and once again I was under lock and key. I slept extremely well.

My first visitor arrived after breakfast. We spoke through the door. He left me a parcel of food and other necessaries and went off with my request to contact the NCO in charge of escaping. My next visitor was a real surprise, our ex-groom from Sussex. I did not even know he was a prisoner. We had a long chat through the spy-hole in my door. My third visitor was a sergeant.

"I understand from your message," he whispered through the door, "that you have come here as Sapper Brown but that you are actually an officer and wish to talk about escaping."

"That is correct," I replied. "I understand I am allowed to walk in the courtyard for a short period each day. I believe I can escape from there into the main part of the camp. If I do this successfully, can you hide me and help me to escape from the camp?"

"We can do this without difficulty. Supervision in the camp is not strict and we have three tunnels under the wire."

"Three tunnels? Do many people then escape?"

"Not really. One or two have got away, but the tunnels are mainly used by soldiers who visit the Polish girls working in a nearby factory. They meet the girls and then return through the tunnels."

"What about tomorrow afternoon?" I said. "I can make a recce today and let you know if it's on. I shall need food, documents, money, maps, anything you can let me have."

"We can do all that, Sir, but there is one difficulty. Can you wait for two or three days? There is one of our chaps locked up here who has been court martialled for sabotaging some industrial machinery, and he is under sentence of death. We are planning to spring him during the next day or two and hide him up permanently in the camp. We would like to get him away first."

Naturally I agreed. His need was infinitely greater than mine, and nothing must jeopardise the plan to save him.

The very next day they came for me from Colditz, a large and formidable-looking posse, and on the following morning, very early, I was marched away. I never heard what happened to our gallant saboteur.

My last memory of Lamsdorf was surprisingly a very happy one. Some thirty members of my own regiment, The King's Royal Rifle

Corps, and of our sister regiment, The Rifle Brigade, had turned out to cheer me on my way. Dressed in their best battle-dresses and all wearing smart green side-hats, they were lined up like some guard of honour. I was allowed to walk down the two lines and say goodbye. The Germans were visibly impressed and talked about it all the way to the station. I have been granted quite a number of quarter guards and similar honours since then, but none has given me such pride and pleasure as this one.

Back at Colditz I was relieved to find that the ghosts who had stood in for me had been safely withdrawn in the nick of time and were once again hidden away.

And so it was all over. Yet though it may seem to some just another tale of wasted time and useless endeavour, a catalogue perhaps of errors perpetrated and opportunities lost, this is not really so. The 'escaper' must always escape. The war of wits between him and his captors must always be waged. He is driven by some inner force. He does not count the cost, has no illusions about the odds against him and suffers no regrets. He does what seems best at the time and accepts the consequences. And thus it is with me: I am not tantalised by might-have-beens.

Flight-Lieut. Jack Best

Flight-Lieut. Jack Best photographed after his capture

Jack Best was one of the builders of the Colditz glider (*below*), a 32-by 20-foot aircraft constructed in the castle attics behind a dummy wall, built from wooden shutters, hessian palliasse-covers and mud. The mud was made from the deep attic dust, specially mixed by Jack Best who drew on his knowledge of how African mud huts were built. (He had been a farmer in Kenya and now farms in England.) The dummy wall of the glider workshop was discovered by a German who reported his find to the British. All he asked for were 500 Players No. 3. He later died from natural causes but the British suggested he had died from nicotine poisoning. The glider was never flown but was broken up after the war. All that remains of it is the rudder, now preserved in the Colditz museum.

VI

Black was Un-German

BY JACK BEST

(Jack Best and Mike Sinclair were devoted to their duty to escape. Later in the war Mike Sinclair was shot and killed while attempting to escape over the barbed wire surrounding the park walk area.

The following story by Jack Best tells of their recapture three days after he and Mike escaped out of a Colditz Castle window at night, down a rope to a terrace below, from which they cut through barbed wire and reached the back yard of a nearby cottage.)

As soon as we got into the back yard of the cottage we hurriedly tidied ourselves. I had such a large tear in my overcoat that I had to try to cover it with my brief case. As it was dark, we walked out into the street and turned right to cross the bridge over the River Mulde. The sooner we were over this bridge the better, as it was an obvious place for guards to be sent to catch us when we were missed, which might have been at any moment.

Once over the bridge, we went into a wood to repair our clothes which we had both torn on the barbed wire. I had seen a guard* come onto the terrace from the guard room, so speed had been more important than caution at that moment. We also saw a woman look at us from the back of the cottage and were thankful that she had not shouted out. We took some time sewing our clothes as it was not easy threading a needle by the light of a cigarette. My overcoat was so badly torn that we had to use safety pins when we had used all the cotton, but my brief case was useful to help cover up the rents. Later on I noticed that the locks had "Made in England" stamped on them, which might have been seen by a German and could have been enough to give us away; in fact it was not even noticed when we were recaptured.

While we were in the wood I removed the naval buttons and braid from my uniform; then, wearing my home-made coat buttons, I became what I imagined to be a perfect German civilian, and

---

* The guard had come out of the guard room because one of the escapers had accidentally pressed the button which sounded an alarm bell. He saw the rope disappear and alarmed the camp – *Reinhold Eggers*

was ready to go.

With the aid of a compass we set off across country for Grimma, a mile or so from Colditz, where in spite of the darkness and our walking straight into several fences, we managed to get to the railway station. There had been a railway timetable in the camp, so we judged our arrival at the station so as to give Mike time to buy our tickets before the train which we had planned to catch was due. All this was particularly risky, as we felt that at any moment our escape might be discovered, but it was obviously impossible to walk the whole way to Holland, so the sooner we were out of the district the safer we would be. Also we hoped that the Germans would not expect us to go north, or even catch a train so close to Colditz.

As far as we could see there were no police in the ticket office, so we went in, and no one paid any attention to us.

Mike spoke almost perfect German and could even put on a local dialect, so he did all the talking and bought two tickets to Eilenburg; then gave me my ticket to make it less likely that we should be recaptured together. On the train, we kept apart as far as possible, but in sight of each other; always in the same compartment, but on opposite sides when we were lucky enough to get seats.

We got off the train at the station before Leipzig, as we were sure that the hunt for us would be up and that the police would be on the lookout for us. We only had a short wait before we caught the next train from Leipzig to Eilenburg, where we arrived about midnight. As the train went no further, we continued our journey on foot.

I went first, as I had the compass and luckily found the correct road to Bitterfeld first time. Only one or two cars passed us on the sixteen miles to Bitterfeld. We hid ourselves as they passed. It was about 5.30 in the morning when we got there and people were just starting to move about.

As we saw no signpost to the station and as we did not wish to draw attention to ourselves by asking for directions, it took us an hour to find the station, where we also found a train which would be leaving in a few minutes for Magdeburg.

We had just enough time to buy our tickets and get aboard. Unfortunately, the train's direction signs were incorrect and we found ourselves going in the wrong direction, in an unheated train full of Poles. Luckily, Mike knew some Polish and found out we were on a workers' train to a factory. The Poles advised us to jump off the train just before the second station and hide in some woods. We did this and luckily were not seen. We now had an hour's walk back to the town and then a long wait before the next train. A very annoying waste of time and energy.

We only travelled on the slow trains, as on the fast ones the railway police usually inspected passes. Although our forged passes were good, it was not worth taking the risk of using them for the sake of some extra speed, as an expert could easily detect the forgery.

By midnight, when the slow trains stopped running, we had reached a station a few miles from Osnabruck, having been through Brunswick, Hanover and Minden. It was dark by now and there was an air-raid which damaged the railway line. Buses were provided for the passengers, but as we were the only civilians in our bus, we were very glad to get out of it as we felt most conspicuous.

We decided to walk the remaining few miles to Osnabruck, but as we got ourselves completely lost, we took to the field and luckily arrived at the town in time to catch the first train. We were tired and cross after having walked for such a long time and yet covered only a short distance. At Rheine, we listed the times of all possible trains to our next destination, in this case Bentheim and then walked away from the station to have a talk.

As it was now about ten in the morning, we did not want to leave until late afternoon so as to arrive at Bentheim at dusk and then have the whole night to cross the frontier into Holland, so we walked into the country and had a good rest under a hedge. My feet were very sore, as not only had I been unused to walking at Colditz, but my shoes were too small, causing, one of my little toes to be covered with a large blister. In spite of the discomfort, it was most important not to limp which would draw a second glance from people and it was essential for us to remain as inconspicuous as possible all the time. That second glance could easily be our downfall, as it might reveal something which was not German in us or in our clothes. Although our passes were Flemish workers, we wanted to be taken for Germans as then we were less likely to be asked for our passes.

We had been eating the German bread, margarine and cheese that we had brought with us, but it was now finished, so we returned to the town and went to an inn and had some ration-free soup and beer, both very welcome. We now had to wait until evening to catch our train, so we went to a cinema, hoping we would be able to pass the time, have a comfortable seat and possibly even some sleep. Unfortunately we were not allowed in as the film had started. Some soldiers too, were kept out and they were making a row about it so we hurried away quickly as we did not want to be involved if the police were called.

The only thing left for us to do was to walk about the town until our train was due to leave, and look as though we were going somewhere and not just filling in time. Suddenly a civilian appeared and

Mike Sinclair's false pass

said, "*Woher kommen Sie?*", to which we replied, "*Von* Leipzig". This did not satisfy him, as he said, "*Kommen Sie mit*". As his hand was in his coat pocket, presumably to hold a gun, we obeyed and were ordered into a building – the police station.

We were pushed into a room into which about half a dozen policemen came and shouted at us in an extremely unfriendly way. I realised they were telling us to take off our coats. I started to take off mine but put it on again when I saw that Mike was refusing to take off his. This resulted in a clout on the back of my head. (Mike told me later that I went white with anger and he was frightened that I was going to hit back.) By now, the room vibrated with hate. The police shouted at us to take off our clothes. This time we obeyed. They soon found Mike's pass and with great joy declared it to be "*Falsch*'. I was then asked for mine. This gave me a chance to go through all my pockets and crumple up and eat two sheets of lavatory paper, on which we had traced details of the Dutch frontier. I felt a lot better after this, in spite of being ordered to stand in the corner of the room with my face to the wall. Treated like a naughty schoolboy when I was thirty-one years old made me burst out laughing, which was not appreciated by the Germans. I know it was not at all tactful, but I just could not help it.

As the police had enough evidence to send us to a concentration camp, there was no point in pretending any longer, so we admitted to being escaped British prisoners of war. At once the atmosphere changed, and the police became friendly. All through the war, the Germans had respected the British. We were even more thankful for our nationality when we were put in the cells for the night and saw how the walls were covered with blood and the mattresses caked with it. We were given a meal in the evening and our breakfast in the morning. Then we were asked to pay for our night in the cells, as we were not the property of the police, but of the German Army, who sent an NCO and four guards to collect us. They took us to a French prisoner-of-war camp almost on the Dutch frontier where we remained in the cells for two nights until we were collected by our Colditz guards.

We made at least four errors in our attempt to escape:
1. Pressing the warning bell on the terrace.
2. The brief case having "Made in England" on the lock.
3. Getting into the wrong train at Bitterfeld.
4. My wearing all black clothes.

We were amazingly lucky in our first error, as the guard wore spectacles and did not see properly when he came from a lighted room to the dusk. Our second error was never noticed. Our third error meant that it took us thirty-six hours to get to Rheine instead of twenty-four, so we were a whole day longer in Germany before we attempted to cross the frontier. Obviously the longer we were in Germany, the more tired we would be and greater the risk of detection. Getting in to Holland was still a long way from making a 'Home Run', but it would have been a big hurdle behind us.

The last error was our downfall, as my all-black clothes accentuated my un-Germanic appearance, especially in that part of Germany where most of the people are fair. I am tall, thin and dark with a long face, and at that time I was very white – being a ghost*. I had hardly been in the open air for many months. I think that the plain-clothes policeman who collected us was sitting in his office, looking out of the window when we walked past. Evidently he thought we looked suspicious characters.

On my return to Colditz, I sent an SOS for a naval hat, buttons, braid and cotton. I converted my coat back to regulation uniform, as I now posed as Lieut. Barnes, RNR. It also enabled me to return a uniform with many thanks, which I had borrowed from Lieut. Davis, RN.

---

* As a Colditz ghost, Jack Best had to keep indoors at all times and to hide in a cupboard during parades. He lived this twilight existence for a whole year while the Germans thought he had made a successful escape.
The advantage of a prisoner being a ghost was that if he could leave the castle without getting caught, he would not be missed on subsequent parades, when the prisoners were counted. Jack's escape with Sinclair meant that the Germans would be one short instead of two.
Jack Best and Mike Sinclair escaped on 19th January 1944. When the Germans found traces of their escape that evening they called a special *Appell* and deduced that three officers were missing. Next morning a thorough recheck told them that Sinclair and *Barnes* were missing. When Best and Sinclair were recaptured the former did three weeks' solitary confinement as Barnes. It was not until that March that the Germans found out the truth about the Colditz ghosts. (See Dr Eggers' *Colditz: the German Story*, pages 130–33 and 135–6) – *John Watton*.

Brigadier J. R. E. Hamilton-Baillie, MC

J. R. E. Hamilton-Baillie in 1945

Born 1919. Served in India (1945–7). Honours degree in Mechanical Science, Cambridge (1947–9). Staff College, Camberley (1950). DAAG War Office (1951–2). BAOR (1953–8 and 1967–70). Lieut-Colonel (Chief Instructor, Army Apprentices School) (1959–62). AWMG Aden (1962–4). Ministry of Defence: Colonel (1964–7) and Brigadier (1970). In 1947 married Lettice, sister of Laurie Pumphrey (*ex*-Colditz). Two sons and two daughters.

VII

A Successful Burglary but a Failed Escape

BY J. R. E. HAMILTON-BAILLIE

(In 1942 when a prisoner of war in Germany, Lieut. Hamilton-Baillie, Royal Engineers, designed the scaling ladders used in a mass escape over the wire by forty-three officers in the prison camp at Warburg. The Germans imprisoned him in Colditz after he had taken part in the escape of sixty-five prisoners from Eichstätt, through a tunnel, in 1943.)

Over the years many prisoners of many nationalities had tried to get through the division between the part of Colditz occupied by the prisoners, and that occupied by the guards. Doors, walls, floors and ceilings had been tried, and after each attempt the task became harder. All likely places were protected on the German side by burglar alarm wires, doors were solidly walled up, and so on.

In the spring of 1944 Frank Weldon and the writer decided to have one more try. Our main object was to see if we could find an escape route from the south (German) end of the castle. Though we did not have any very certain information on this, it was likely to be much less closely guarded than the more accessible parts. A secondary object was to see what useful articles we could steal.

The route was clearly going to be elaborate and there was no question of making it on a single occasion. Each time we worked, during known quiet periods of activity of the guards, we made a little more of the route, then worked back again to the start camouflaging each part as we left it. I do not remember how many periods of work were involved, but it must have been spread over a good many weeks.

The start was in the ceiling over the spiral staircase of the south-east corner of the courtyard. A ladder, which consisted of slates on the underneath of a wash-room duckboard, wedged on top of the central stone column of the staircase and rested against the curving wall high above the last turn of the stair. Working from the top of this we cut a big plank in the ceiling close against the wall. By sliding the plank along an inch or so it would stay in place, but by sliding it back it could be dropped out. Distemper carefully matched in colour, made from blackboard chalk and applied with a shaving brush concealed the dirty end and edges of the disturbed plank. It was possible to replace the plank, apply the distemper and remove the duckboard ladder in less time than it would take a guard to enter the courtyard, cross it and come up the stairs. Our entry was therefore fairly safe. While we were working further on the route the entrance was closed behind us.

Above the plank we found ourselves, as we had hoped, in the narrow triangular space under the roof and behind the attic wall. Crawling a short way along this space we then turned upwards and wormed up the sloping ceiling of the attic in the space under the tiles of the roof and between two rafters. From here we emerged into the larger space under the ridge of the roof, over the flat part of the attic ceiling. Looking down through a heavily padlocked grill into the attic room we had a pleasing view of the burglar alarm wiring on floor and walls, all of which we had by-passed.

The next stage was to get through into the end of the rather less ancient building of the Kommandantur that abutted at an angle on to the medieval building under whose roof we were. The Kommandantur building being higher, the place in its walls most likely to lead into yet another space behind an attic wall was outside above the sloping roof of our building. After some careful thought we concluded that an area on top of our roof and against the Kommandantur wall could not be seen from the ground. We therefore cut, in a way that made it possible to replace them, one or two of the battens supporting the tiles, and lifted a few of these off. Climbing out we could sit in the valley of the roof and examine the wall which, unlike the prisoners' part of the castle, was of brick.

Returning on yet a further expedition we cautiously scraped out the mortar in an area two or three bricks long and three courses high. First the outer layer of bricks came off, and then we made a small hole to see through. To our disappointment we were looking into an open roof space with no attic rooms, and so no wall to hide us. We therefore stopped work, measured the hole and came back next time with a wooden frame to fit it, camouflaged to look right both on the outside and inside. We could now safely complete the hole and crawl through, closing it with our wooden frame behind us.

The next stage was the journey along the full length of the Kommandantur building. Here there was some risk we would be found by a patrol but we were lucky. One or two partitions with locked doors gave us no trouble as our skeleton keys opened them easily. At the far end the roof of the workshop building joined the roof we were in at a right angle on our right. This was the building we wanted to reach, but our way was blocked by our next obstacle, a big iron door.

The heavy, old-fashioned lock was on our side and fairly easily unlocked, but to our disappointment the door remained fast. To find out how it was fastened on the far side we made a little gadget that could be threaded through the keyhole. This was a little piece of mirror mounted on two wires. By manipulating these, once through the keyhole the mirror could be tilted to any angle. By doing this and turning the mirror around the whole of the back of the door could be inspected. We saw that it was fastened with a big iron hook dropped into a hasp. To undo this, we brought with us on our next visit a long curved piece of stiff wire with a hooked end. Threading this through the keyhole we could, after a fair amount of fishing, catch the hook and lift it from the hasp. By putting the hook on the end of the wire while the door was open, it was possible to shut the door and drop the hook back into the hasp on return journeys.

Now began the most exciting part of our expedition, exploring the workshop building. The time available on each visit was now rather limited due to the proportion of each safe period taken up in opening and reclosing the various obstacles on both the outward and return journeys.

We passed along the empty loft, down some stairs and back along a lower floor. Here we found a curious collection of articles, perhaps left behind by previous occupants of the castle. There was a crossbow, which we resisted the temptation to take. For some reason we did take a quite useless little machine that appeared to be intended to peel apples or perhaps potatoes. Next we explored some rooms in the tower over the entrance gate, making in one of them our most exciting find so far, a store of uniforms and equipment for the guard unit. Thinking of the endless hours of work put in by prisoners making imitations of such things the value of them seemed to us immense. However, again we resisted the temptation to take anything for fear its loss might prejudice the escape attempt we still hoped to make. Perhaps, we thought, there would be a more appropriate occasion to rob this store at some later time.

Finally we found our way down another staircase and into the workshop on the ground floor. Here we found cupboards full of tools, and especially files. I have always wondered why there were so many; they must have been far beyond any reasonable need of the castle. Among so much there seemed little chance of some items being missed, so we filled our swag sacks with these highly desirable things.

Our plan for the next visit was that we should explore a small locked room with a window opening on to the outside of the castle, as a possible escape route, and of course collect another load of booty. The lock on this small room did not open with any of the skeleton keys we carried, so we would need to pick it, or find a suitable key among the hundreds in the workshop. All this would take time, so we needed a day when we would have the best chance of a long period undisturbed. A promising date seemed to us to be the Whit Sunday public holiday.

That day, therefore, we set out again with an extra member in the party to help with the exploration and theft. We worked uneventfully through all the obstacles and came to the door of the locked room, at the foot of the staircase, and inside the entrance from the courtyard to the workshop. I went on into the workshop to look for a suitable key. Then to our horror we heard the outer door open. The others could retreat up the stairs, but I was cut off and could go no further than an inner room of the workshop. Unfortunately the old locksmith, who it was, coming unexpectedly to his workshop on this holiday, came on into that room and saw me. I must have looked a curious sight dressed in a dirty vest and long underpants. "*Posten! Posten!*" he yelled, threatening me with a big bunch of keys. Quite soon a sentry from the courtyard hurried in. The others were by that time safely on their way back, but for all of us it was the end of this adventure, and for me fourteen days in the cooler.

Giles Romilly

*Giles Romilly
at Colditz, 1941*

Daily Express reporter in the Spanish Civil War and later at Narvik where captured by the Germans in April 1940. Interned in civilian camp of Wülzburg, Bavaria; whence escaped disguised as a woman. Recaptured. Ultimately reached Colditz, where Captain Müller noted in his diary on 25th October 1941: "Today two officers in a car brought a civilian internee to the camp. He is the reporter Giles Romilly, a nephew of Winston Churchill." Given the cover name 'Emil' and placed under special guard by order of Hitler, who regarded him as one of his most valuable hostages. Two attempts to escape from Colditz failed. On 13th April 1945 Romilly and the other *Prominente* hostage prisoners were taken to Oflag IVA Königstein. Later, when they were moved to Tittmoning, Romilly escaped with the Dutch Lieut. Tieleman and succeeded in rejoining the Allies in Munich.

Code-Name 'Emil'

BY REINHOLD EGGERS AND BY GILES ROMILLY

Fragile, with Care

On 25th October 1941 Giles Romilly, a nephew of Sir Winston Churchill, was transferred to Colditz Castle, by special order of the German High Command. He came from a camp for civilian internees at Tost near Breslau in Silesia, where he had spent about a fortnight after his escape disguised as a woman from the Internees' Camp in the Castle of Wülzburg, near Weissenburg in Bavaria.

Colonel Schmidt, the Commandant of Colditz Castle at that time, had strict orders to keep his prize prisoner in a room to himself and under a close guard. At night, his door, fitted with a spyhole, was locked and a guard posted outside. A blue electric light burnt in his room and the officer in charge had to check at irregular intervals whether Emil, as Giles Romilly was code-named, was present. The High Command frequently telephoned to enquire if Emil was in his cell. Agents from Switzerland had warned the High Command that in England, plans for the liberation of the valuable prisoner had been prepared. So although he could move freely within the section of the castle allotted to the other prisoners, from morning roll-call until half past ten in the evening, the special guard was instructed to trace him at least once every two hours to make sure he was present and also that he did not take part in the park walks.

The first three weeks of this regime passed normally, but on 28th November, when some Polish orderlies were loading a wagon in the yard under the supervision of a guard, Emil managed to mingle with them, disguised in a Polish uniform. He wore a pair of spectacles and made his face darker-looking with soot so as to deceive the guards who had previously been ordered to familiarise themselves with his exact appearance so that they could recognise him by day or by night.

By some mischance however, the special guard detailed to check Emil's movements, happened at this time to be searching the castle for him. As he was nowhere to be found in the castle, he was soon discovered among the orderlies and reported to Captain Priem, an officer who enjoyed a little joke. Captain Priem went into the court-yard at once and told Emil, "But Mr Romilly, this is no work for a nephew of Winston Churchill. Please don't make your hands dirty with such a menial task. And since when have you been a Pole?" One of the guards then led Emil to his room, where he had a wash and soon reappeared in English uniform. I don't remember whether he was punished at all for this attempt.

In July 1943 Emil played another trick that brought him a good deal nearer to freedom and the German Security Officer, Captain Lange, into arrest.

The German High Command, trying to overcome the notorious indiscipline of the Colditz International Bad Boys, had ordered all non-Anglo-Saxon prisoners to be moved to camps appropriate to their nationality. The big French contingent was sent to Lübeck in two batches, the last one on the 12th July. One week earlier, the first transport arrived at Lübeck without a single loss. Captain Lange, the security officer and his staff took this as evidence that their methods were escape-proof, so he decided to keep to the same system. The heavy baggage of the prisoners was prepared for trans-port by being assembled in the castle and was checked by Captain Vent and Captain Müller, two German officers of the Security Staff and Sergeant Grunert, known as 'Le Beau Max', the parcels office chief. After the baggage had been checked, the trunks, kit-bags and various bundles were brought through the main gate into a small intermediate yard in front of the guard-room. From there, trucks took them to the station where the baggage was piled up in railway wagons. Guards watched at the station as well as in the small yard. So much for the heavy baggage.

The prisoners themselves, who were allowed hand-luggage only, were marched to the Schützenhaus, our secondary camp, where, in the garden, a long row of tables was set up behind which Cap-tain Lange's helpers awaited to check the identity of the prisoners who were paraded before them. Other German staff searched the prisoners' hand-luggage and clothing. It took hours to do this, for more than two hundred officers had to be dealt with, so it can be understood if some of the searches were a little skimped.

When the search was over, the contingent was marched to the station, where their train was waiting, with properly prepared coaches having only one door at each end and with their windows secured by barbed wire. The luggage wagons were put at the ends of the train.

"What prisoner could escape from here?" I thought. I had no definite job to do at the time, so I was just strolling about keep-ing my eyes open. I found myself standing in front of a big pile of luggage in the intermediate yard of the castle, when I saw a bundle of woollen blankets suddenly begin to move, and out rolled a man who had almost suffocated inside the bundle. It was Lieut, Klein, one of the Gaullists. He tried to hide something in another bundle, but the guard saw him and retrieved a packet of money – ninety-six marks. I took Klein to be searched and found on him escape maps, false passports and a pair of pincers.

In a room upstairs in the Saalhouse, the senior prisoners' quarters, there was a big French collection of books which had been packed and nailed into large wooden Canadian Red Cross boxes. A German corporal had supervised the packing. In another room on the same floor were some British officers who had nailed down a similar Red Cross box, but inside this box, crouched and compressed to the utmost degree, was Emil, our most precious prisoner.

The German corporal in the library sent the nailed boxes, carried by Polish and French orderlies, down the staircase to a hand-cart. There were no German soldiers guarding the staircase, so it was easy for the British to smuggle an extra box into the number brought down. Oddly enough, the guard at the handcart and the corporal in the castle did not count the boxes and compare figures.

When this rather tiring work was done, the handcart was taken outside, where the orderlies loaded the heavy boxes directly on to a truck which was driven straight to the station. The unloading party managed to put the box with its living contents in the upper row of boxes. Lieut. Price, who had nailed down the lid, had drilled a hole into it to give Emil a little air to breathe. But the day was hot and the narrowness of space in the small box – about sixty centimetres in each direction – caused its inhabitant such pain that he tried to get more air by lifting the lid of the box a little. All was quiet, but Emil did not know that there was a guard waiting for the next load. This man heard the noise, saw the moving of the lid and helped Emil out of his prison. But what a surprise! Who was it but Emil! The guard called for help and so the valuable prisoner was kept safe till a lorry came with the next load. It did not return empty this time.

Emil was brought before the Commandant, then Colonel Prawitt, who raged with fury. Captain Lange, the Security Officer responsible, was sent for and asked how this gross breach of security could be possible. He did not know, of course, and promised to investigate. In the meantime, Emil was safely returned to his solitary room, the window of which was now marked with a broad white border. There was enough breathing space there at any rate.

The Commandant punished Captain Lange with three days room-arrest for not having taken sufficient care to stop Emil from a near-escape. Later, the General at Dresden gave the unlucky captain another job at a Stalag in Mühlberg.

At Colditz, Emil gave us no further trouble. The other *Prominente*, little by little, profited from their position and secured some extra privileges from us. Three times a week they were granted walks in the country around the town; they were not obliged to attend parades, but were allowed to remain in bed or in their rooms, where a guard counted them separately.

But on their way to the Alps, during the last fortnight of the war, Romilly managed to escape from the castle of Tittmoning, together with the Dutch Lieut. André Tieleman. This happened on 20th April, when far away in Berlin a man on his last birthday had to think over what he had done.

Thanks to the help of the Dutch Captain van den Heuvel, the attempt was successful and both escapers reached Munich in safety.

(The following three articles by Giles Romilly describe life as a prisoner in Colditz. The first two articles are reproduced by courtesy of the Daily Express)

Search Me!

On the morning of a search one feels thoroughly disorganised. The external disorder created by the searchers seem to reproduce itself internally, in stomach, liver and intestines. Creatures of an unvarying routine, we have become sensitive to the smallest disturbances.

Groups of prisoners of war, released from the search, walk round the courtyard. They are unshaven. The sharp morning air aches on their unwashed eyes. They have a clammy feeling in their shoulders which they manipulate against the roughness of their clothes.

What is happening?

They don't speak much, because they have seen so many of these things before. Later all will be known. In the meantime each one is guarding his private store of energy and resistance.

Of course there are the sensationalists and attention-seekers, who will tell exciting stories and invent others. They will have some listeners for everything is news in prison, and news is food. But the majority will disregard them.

The common experience of the search makes faces, staled by familiarity, a little more interesting to each other. But the more important question is that of the cup of tea. Where is it, and who is making it? Each person salvages a cup which he keeps in readiness, hoping to hear word or catch sight of the steaming urn.

In bad cases of search tea is the only remedy.

The green-clad searchers appear across the courtyard, walking briskly, with boxes of confiscated goods.

By noon the worst symptoms are over, but the period of convalescence is slow and irritating. Nothing has been cooked for lunch. The rooms are in dreadful disorder. The floors are littered with rubbish, including single torn socks and frayed, dust-coated shoes, dragged from their hiding places under beds.

Disconsolately, the prisoner peels himself an unappetising boiled potato, which he eats with a little salt, accompanied by chopped swede from the rations. Dry biscuits and cheese and a cup of lukewarm and ill-mixed cocoa increase the indignation which his stomach is already suffering.

Afterwards he cannot settle down. He leans against a stove or cupboard, smoking cigarettes without enjoying them and exchanging banalities. The atmosphere is heavy with dust and listlessness.

But the waters of time are obliterating the episode of the search. By tomorrow there will remain no trace of it.

(Daily Express, 25th September 1943)

Bader Sees a Play
Oscar Wilde's satirical comedy *The Importance of Being Earnest* has just been acted here before an audience of Englishmen, Irishmen, Scots, Canadians, Australians, New Zealanders, Frenchmen, two Czechs, and a Dutchman.

Producer, cast and audience are prisoners of war in a German castle. The castle has a real theatre, dusty yet imposing, whose walls are painted with laurelled names in Literature and the arts. The only non-German name besides Rossini, is Shakespeare. (Not that his name is everywhere regarded as non-German.)

Production – I speak as a member of the cast – took place under difficulties. Dresses were made out of paper, which tore at any rash movement, scenery and furniture out of paper, cardboard and wood, handpainted.

Twelve thicknesses of cardboard, glued together, were used in the manufacture of a high heel. The rubber bulb of a scent spray became the knob of an umbrella. A garden set was decorated with armfuls of branches fetched from a nearby zoo. These were real, if not exactly realistic.

Prisoners of war are, perhaps, easier to please then other theatregoers. They enjoyed the glamour of a theatrical evening, which makes them forget the unattractiveness of daily existence.

They know that complete sophistication is unobtainable (there are no programmes, no preliminaries) and are happy to suspend criticism.

They like to see their companions costumed and grease-painted, for here the removal of a familiar moustache, or even a mere change of jacket are minor sensations. They enjoy also tea-party scenes, introductions, and anything else reminiscent of the intimacies of family life.

Helped by this circumstance, by its own merits and by a most convincing Lady Bracknell (acted by a young naval officer), the play had a very long run of two nights to packed houses of nearly 150 people.

All seats (hard chairs) cost one mark each (about 1s 3d) in prisoner-of-war currency. A band – piano, drums, double-bass and guitar – played 1890 tunes in the intervals.

Reactions were unexpected. The audience laughed where laughter seemed a miracle, and stayed silent where silence amounted to an insult.

A loud laugh was prompted by the remark: "I don't think you will require neckties, Uncle Jack is sending you to Australia." It probably came from the Australians.

The Frenchmen, Tunisian prisoners, were appreciative afterwards and so also were the two Czechs, who are pilots. One of these said: "Very vitty. The biggest figures what struck me most was the ladies."

A Canadian enjoyed the jibes at aristocracy, "because we haven't got them in Canada." An English colonel considered it "a very slick sort of play."

Perhaps the most sympathetic member of the audience, from the actors' viewpoint was Lord Arundell of Wardour, who regretted that there wasn't a third night, and discomfited those critics who judge works less by their merits than by their date, with the observation: "If anyone says that play is dated my reply to that is – so am I."

Wing-Commander Bader (the legless pilot who was captured in August 1941) was also uproariously enthusiastic. "It was written a hell of a long time ago" he said "but it made me laugh a hell of a lot in places." As a matter of fact he laughed all the time without stopping.

There were however "Average Englishmen" who found Wilde paradoxes either not amusing anyway, or unpleasing. An Army chaplain, who in peacetime is a Cambridge don, considers them "not really amusing" and the play itself as "amoral, the plot appalling."

One difficulty for a modern audience is that the dialogue outstrips the situations, and the remarks are frequently laughable in themselves without reference to their context. "Her hair has turned quite gold for grief", "Divorces are made in Heaven" – these are typical.

'Ballet Nonsense', example of British theatre at Colditz

An audience accustomed to modern comedy, and therefore unaccustomed to witty dialogue, is often uncertain whether it ought to be laughing or not, and tends to practise silence as the safest policy.

I may mention that the coming production, now already in rehearsal, is *French Without Tears*. The cast will display French accents acquired during captivity.

(Daily Express, 24th February 1944)

After You

(Romilly's notes for this article were found in a search by the Germans. The original manuscript was destroyed after having been translated into German by an interpreter. The following version is a translation back into English. Therefore it will be appreciated that only the story is Romilly's.)

At one end of his bed hung a roll of toilet-paper; at the other end he had pinned up a photograph of his wife. Both would go with him for both were, each in its own way, necessary. There, too, was his shelf – a fine piece of handicraft – which he had made himself. It could remain here for the next prisoner who occupied the bed. He packed quickly, for soon he would be locked in a cell until 5 a m next morning, when his slow train journey would begin, to another castle. He had lived in Colditz for nineteen months as a prisoner and now the military authorities were having him transferred.

He was glad of the prospect of a change, as was every prisoner. And yet he regretted leaving all those whom he knew so well. They were good fellows and besides this he had got on well with them, for he enjoyed the company of men who had succeeded in not being depressed by their captivity – at any rate, not externally. He sighed when he thought of it.

Well, he would have to get used to another set of people who might well be less congenial. Discipline could be stricter; polished buttons on parade and so on, with not at all the same Colditz spirit, where all were easy-going, good natured and prepared to help when help was needed. Someone put a hand on his shoulder and said: "I say, Dickie old chap, I am sorry you're leaving, but I should like to bet you're damn glad about it."

"Yes, I could do with a change. There might even be a chance to make a break for it."

"A damn good chance I should say. By the way, you have a nice little lifeboat here. Do you think I could inherit your bed?"

"As far as I am concerned you can, but I hardly believe it belongs to me any longer."

"Anyway, I shall stake my claim. Do you want your bed any more?"

"No, I've finished packing."

"Righto then, I shall dump my kit here now."

Dickie made a final bundle of his soiled linen, tied it by the sleeves of his khaki shirt and put it into his kitbag. He looked at his watch. It would soon be teatime and the British prisoners would be assembling in an upper room used as a dining hall, to wait for the tea cubles.* Five or six members of his mess stood around their table. One cut the black bread into slices; another spread them with margarine.

"You are cutting too many slices," said one of them. "Only twenty-one today not twenty-four."

"Why?"

"Dickie's going."

"Yes I know, but he would like his tea rations, wouldn't he?"

"I don't believe he'll have time enough for that. Anyway, he can help himself to his bread if he wants it."

"Anything but that," said an anxious voice. "You know he takes far too much. I know our Dickie."

"Buller asked me if he could join our mess now Dickie's going. I told him I'd let him know. What do you think about it?" The mess members exchanged glances, showing their indecision. Nobody wanted to speak first. Eventually, someone said, "I think it would be better for us to be a mess of seven instead of eight. For one thing there'd be more room, and for another, we should get an advantage with rations as they won't reduce our marg. and jam ration if we are only one less." This seemed to satisfy everyone.

"I shall tell him," said the fellow who cut the bread. "Anyway, I am sorry for Buller, he's a nice chap, but really I don't see why we should take him in. We've been a bit short on most things recently. But it's a pity they couldn't keep Dickie here until Thursday, instead of moving him today."

"Why, I don't see that two days of his company will make much difference after he has sat at our table for nearly two years."

"I am not thinking of that, but tomorrow the week's issue of Red Cross parcels is due, and if he were still here, we should get rations for eight and next morning he would not be here any longer to share them." Their faces became long when they became aware of this dreadful truth.

"But yesterday we got German sugar and margarine as well, so at least we're well off for this." Just then, the tea was brought in and Dickie joined his mess. They slapped him on the back and said, "Hello Dickie, you blear-eyed old ——. We were just talking about

* Aluminium containers, about the size of a small dustbin, for tea, soup, etc.

you. What a pity it is that we shall lose you. But he's not sad, look at him. He's pleased. I think it is rather mean of him."

There was a shout of "Goons up!" and a German corporal came into the room, approached Dickie, saluted and asked him to leave.

"Have you got to leave now? Don't you want your tea first? Make him wait a minute."

"No, I am not hungry. Cheerio everybody!" He grinned and waved to the whole room, before he was pushed outside with a lot of good-natured chaff. The prisoners then devoted themselves to their tea with voracious concentration.

Two minutes later, a man hurried along in the direction of Dickie's old sleeping quarters. Awkwardly he carried a rolled-up palliasse, a checkered sleeping sack and some blankets. Another man followed him, struggling under a similar burden.

"They're off to get Dickie's bunk," said the bread-cutter. "One would think they had enough manners to wait a bit longer. There certainly are some queer people about. I personally couldn't do it."

"Neither could I," said another.

When they had finished their tea, several of them got together in Dickie's old corner. Three of them claimed the bunk. They all had their palliasses, blankets and their bits of gear, producing a considerable confusion. The rest were onlookers, hands in pockets, making proposals and humorous prophecies as to what the outcome would be. The competitors were extraordinarily polite to each other.

"I am very, very sorry, old boy, but I asked Dickie personally, and he said I could have his bed. I was the only one who asked him."

"I don't know what that has to do with it. Dickie's gone. I had been waiting for six months to get into this room and I am top of the list if a place becomes vacant.

"I was the first one here. That's what counts, much as I must regret your misfortune."

"Why not all three of you take the bunk," said an onlooker. They had reached stalemate from which a decision by force was excluded.

"We can't go on like this. Here is the man to decide, the Padre. He has a legal mind. Let him decide for us."

"You only ask him because you go to the services on Sunday and sing in the choir."

The Padre joined the group, beaming. He was a man of above average size, with a kind, rosy face and a high, intellectual forehead.

"I have spoken to the Colonel about this," he declared in a judicial voice. "The corner is free from draughts and therefore he wants me to bunk here on account of my rheumatism, for which I have a medical certificate. I am sorry to disappoint you." He looked around beaming. The applicants gasped for breath and the audience burst out laughing.

"Hurrah for the Padre! Who said the Church has lost its power?"

At this moment something astonishing happened. Dickie himself reappeared carrying his washing kit. They stared at him, asking "What's the matter, Dickie?"

"After all that, I'm to stay here. They've just now revoked the order to move me as there is no room in the other camp." While everyone digested this news, Dickie noticed the confusion around his bed and asked, "Have you had a search?"

"Oh no, this is only the whole British Company trying to get into your bunk, but the Padre, with his rheumatism, has defeated them all."

The Visitor by Reinhold Eggers
(*My acquaintance with Mr Romilly and the other hostages at Colditz Castle became a danger to me in an unexpected way. I was suspected of being a spy by the Russians who were the occupying power in my home town, Halle/Saale, after the Americans had left them Saxony and Thuringia. So in September 1946 the GPU decided to arrest me. This was done by the ingenious method of asking me what I had talked about with Mr Romilly, Churchill's nephew, and to the other British and American prisoners of war at Colditz? Whatever I replied was taken for a lie, and so I had to atone for my Colditz activities by ten years' forced labour.*)

Released from my imprisonment by the Russians in 1956, I settled down in the small town of Sigmaringen, beautifully situated on the banks of the Danube, in the midst of enormous woods and steep rocks through which the river had gnawed its way to the east.

I soon began to renew friendships with my former prisoners who gladly responded with letters and visits. But Mr Romilly did not answer. In his book he described me as "A called-up schoolmaster with manners of the treacly kind which makes pupils wary". Perhaps he had had enough of schoolmasters.

Because of my arrest by the Russians in 1946 my wife and I were still very wary whenever our doorbell rang. We would first of all open an upstairs window (we lived in the upper part of a small two-family house) and would ask, "Who's there?" If the person was not known to us, we at once shut the window, sometimes not even listening to any explanation given from below.

One fine summer morning I went shopping in the town, which took me about two hours, as we lived in the suburbs. My wife, who suffered from arthritis, stayed at home. While she was waiting for me to come back there was a ring on the bell, so she opened the window and saw a taxi standing outside the house.

"Who's there?" she called. The man who had rung the bell looked up but she did not know him. When she again asked him who he was, he stammered something which clearly showed he was not a German. My wife shut the window, thinking that the Russians had sent some agent to arrest me a second time.

The visitor, not to be put off, found the landlord and begged to be allowed in; so the stranger came upstairs, knocking on our door. My wife opened it a bit and again asked what he wanted. He stammered something about a surprise but refused to give his name. My wife felt that after all he was probably an Englishman and asked, "Were you at Colditz?" He avoided a direct answer and again mumbled that his visit should be a surprise and asked, "When may I see Dr Eggers?"

"At four o'clock," she replied and pushed him out into the hall. Her heart hammered with anxiety as she watched the taxi go back to the town. Now she was tormented with the idea that this was perhaps some agent or other who would meet her husband in the town, invite him to get into the taxi and then smuggle him off to one of the Eastern countries as had happened about twelve years previously. So she asked the landlord to go into the town to warn her husband about the suspicious visitor. In her anxiety, my wife forgot that the nearest Eastern frontier was at least 350 kilometres away and that it would take about seven hours' hard driving to get there.

Eventually I came home, having met my landlord who told me of my suspicious visitor and how he was possibly a member of the NKVD who were trying to find me, so I hurried home to reassure my wife.

"Heaven be thanked, you're back," my wife exclaimed in relief. Now she told me about the visitor and of her fears. I calmed her, promising solemnly neither this time nor in the future ever to get into a car whose driver was in the least suspicious. There was no afternoon sleep for us that day. Punctually at four o'clock the taxi re-appeared. We watched from behind the curtains and saw a man leave the car and slowly come down about ten steps to the door – our house was situated on a slope.

"I certainly know this man and he is most probably from Colditz," I said. "There is no risk, so I'll let him in." With these words, I went downstairs and reached the door at the same time as the visitor rang the bell. When I opened the door, I saw a man who was a bit under middle-size, rather stout, well-dressed and who greeted me in English, "Good afternoon, Doctor Eggers, how do you do?"

"Good afternoon," I replied. "How do you do? But I am sorry

that although your face is familiar, I cannot recall your name."

"I'm Giles Romilly, your special prisoner at Colditz," he said. At
once I recognised him, both by his face and his voice, which convinced me of his identity. I led him upstairs, calling to my wife,
"Here's Mr Romilly. He too has come to see his old jailer!" I said
to him, "I am very glad to see you. Please come in and meet my
wife. We shall do our best to entertain you in our modest home."
He wore neither hat nor coat, as if it was a fine sunny day, so we
went into our drawing room. I offered him a chair and asked, "Tea
or coffee?" He promptly answered, "In Germany, always coffee."
My wife went into the kitchen to prepare it. Meanwhile, I excused
my inability to recognise him at once. I remembered him as a rather
slim young man and now I saw a stout, seemingly satisfied, well-
kept looking gentleman.

"I am glad that your last attempt to escape was successful," I
said, "after I had done my best to foil your earlier attempts at Colditz. Certainly you will never forget the occasions when you imper-
sonated an orderly working on a lorry and, in July 1943, when you
were carried to the station by our own men, hidden in a Canadian
Red Cross case when the French contingent left Colditz for Lübeck.
As far as I personally was concerned, I was not responsible for your
failure as security matters were not my business at that time."

He smiled and recalled his earlier attempt when Captain Priem
had ordered him to leave work on the lorry, to change his clothes
and get back to his role as our most prominent prisoner. So we went
on talking about details of Colditz life. My wife brought the coffee
and, as she knows some English, she took part in our conversation.

"I hope that this coffee is better than at Colditz," she said. When
we lived in Colditz my wife had often watched the prisoners from a
window in the Witches' gallery high above the prisoners' yard, and
had seen Romilly going to his room in the middle of the buildings
on the eastern side of the yard.

Mr Romilly praised the coffee, and we apologised for the rather
poor quality of the cake. I asked him why he had not written to announce his visit. He replied that he preferred not to write but to
come as a surprise. I congratulated him on his being able to judge
how others would react to this.

Another subject we talked about was my imprisonment by the
Russians. He was amused to hear they had asked me what I had discussed with him when we were in Colditz. But he could hardly believe I had gone through ten years of a captivity far worse than that
in Colditz, and yet survived so well. Probably he doubted the hardships I described.

Sometimes during our conversation I had the impression that my

partner was slow in remembering some of the details and personalities of Colditz life. I was at least over twenty years older than he,
and had gone through double his time of captivity. But people are
different; though I remembered how quick and vigorous his reactions had been in captivity.

I did not ask him how he earned his living. Probably he belonged
to a rich society and could work at his ease. I wondered if he still
worked as a journalist, but I did not find out as he had ordered his
taxi for seven o'clock. My former prisoner, Emil, the first
Prominente at Colditz Castle, had indeed acted in an unusual way
by coming out of the blue to visit his jailer and discuss the tragic
events which happen to men on this earth.

Sidney Smith

Sidney Smith (left) before his capture at El Alamein

Born 1922 in Dulwich, London. Joined the Home Guard 1940 and Royal Sussex Regiment 1941. Egypt 1942 with 44th Infantry Division. Captured at El Alamein October 1942 and sent to PoW camps in Italy. Recaptured when attempting to reach Yugoslavia. Worked in copper mines. Moved to prison camps Oflag IVA Königstein and IVC Colditz. Joined Metropolitan Police in 1959.

IX

An Orderly Talks

BY SIDNEY SMITH

(*In Colditz there were about a hundred orderlies – English, French, Polish and Belgian. They were prisoners who had volunteered to do the cooking, cleaning, and so on, for their corresponding Allied Officers. Their orderlies became experts in negotiating with German guards, trading with German civil workers and dealing on the Black Market. They were thus of great help in furthering the escaping activities of their officers, to whom they supplied contraband material and extra food. Not infrequently, orderlies would make their own escapes, sometimes with surprising success, as they had a knack of being able to mix and communicate with all manner of people without drawing attention to themselves.*)

I was captured by one of Rommel's tank units during the battle of El Alamein, on 28th October 1942. With me were many of my colleagues of the 4th Battalion, The Royal Sussex Regiment. After we had been taken back through the German lines, we were handed over to the Italians for safe keeping.

For a year we were prisoners of the Italians, until they surrendered, leaving us free. Most of us broke camp but were eventually recaptured by German patrols and taken to Germany. After going through various transit camps, we came to Stalag VIB, where about a hundred of us were formed into a party and put to work in a copper mine with some of our Russian allies.

After nine months in the mine, I and five of my friends were moved to Königstein Castle, where we were housed quite comfortably in rooms built into the castle walls. As far as we knew, we were the only prisoners there but a strict guard was kept on us, which was ominous, as we did no work. We were all concerned about our fate and our anxiety increased with the arrival, about a month later, of some sergeants from the Special Air Service, who had been captured a year before in Yugoslavia. Since then they had been subjected to constant interrogations. They were not classed as soldiers, but as bandits, for they had been captured while wearing civilian clothes. They had been told they were to be shot.

Three or four anxious months passed while we played cards and chess or just slept. Then, in November 1944, we were ordered to assemble in a room to hear a special announcement from the German Army GHQ. It was with a certain amount of relief that we learned that we were all to be moved immediately to the notorious Colditz Castle.

At Colditz, after a searching individual interrogation by the British Security Officer to ensure we were *bona-fide* British soldiers, we were invited to volunteer for various duties as orderlies. I was offered the job of being batman to a group of special prisoners known as the *Prominente*. They had a higher hostage value than the rest of us, as they were either related to, or connected with, royalty or high state officials. (Some were of exceptional importance in their own right. For example, General Bor-Komorowski, Commander in Chief of the Polish Army and of the Polish Underground Home Army, had at one time been a Colditz *Prominente*.) I found them to be particularly interesting people and well remember those for whom I acted as batman.

Their senior officer was Brigadier Davis, a short, rotund, bald-headed man, who had been captured in Yugoslavia after being parachuted straight into enemy hands. The Germans had found out that fires were to be lit by the partisans to guide Allied aircraft which were to drop supplies and personnel, including the Brigadier, who had dropped right in it, as you may say. He had also been badly wounded for his efforts. He seemed to me (I was only twenty-two) to be rather old to have been floating around in a parachute. We used to chat together freely and he often showed me his wounds of which he was quite proud.

One of the more important *Prominente* was Lord Lascelles, who sometimes amused me (I am Cockney born and bred) with his efforts to swear. His swearing sounded as if he were speaking normally, with no particular emphasis on the consonants. It was as if a London docker had said nothing but "Bother!" when a crate dropped on his toe. I believe that his serenity came from his love of music. He constantly listened to classical music, played on a gramophone. I listened too, while I swept his room. My work was made pleasant and I was given a taste for culture.

Captain Lord Haig, son of the Field Marshal, was another of my charges. He seemed to me to be the least soldierly figure of them all; the antithesis of his father – possibly because of him. He was tall and thin with a pronounced stoop. He felt the cold badly and during the everlasting roll-calls he wore a blanket draped over his shoulders and stood on a box to keep his feet warm. He loved painting, which I am sure was of great help to him during the long days of captivity, as he spent hours working on his canvases. He once told me I had a perfect Greek profile and would like to paint my portrait, but he never did.

Another of my employers was Captain the Earl of Hopetoun, who wore wire spectacles and looked like an intellectual egg-head. As a leader of the Conservative prisoners, he arranged weekly political meetings, which I attended for want of something better to do. Once he spoke to me about his powers of concentration. He said he could make himself go into a trance and told me I could do the same. "What you have to do," he said, "is to take the figure one and divide it by three. This gives you .33333 and so on, to infinity. Concentrate hard on that, and you can go into infinity with it, but for God's sake, Smith, if you do try it you must know how to come back." I noticed he had a half-empty bottle of hooch by his bed. I never reached infinity, possibly through lack of the right spirit.

Giles Romilly, a nephew of Sir Winston Churchill, was a highly prized prisoner, who had been captured while performing his duties as a war correspondent. He was small, with a boyish face and light blue eyes; an unassuming quiet man, but easy to talk to. As unlike his illustrious uncle as one could get. Giles Romilly's politics were different too, for he held secret Communist meetings to which I was allowed to go. I went for the same reason that I went to the Tory meetings. I remember Giles telling us that he considered the United States would be a bigger obstacle than the Russians to peace in the post-war world.

There were other *Prominente*, too. Some before my time; but I shall always remember with pleasure those who I knew personally in Colditz.

Captain Michael Farr

*Captain Michael Farr
in 1939*

Royal Military Academy, Sandhurst, and 2nd Battalion Durham Light Infantry. 1939 to Belgium with 2nd Division of B.E.F. Captured at Dunkirk. After various attempts to escape from prison camps, sent to Colditz. After the war, appointed a Staff Officer on the War Crimes Commission. Left to join old family business of wine merchants.

X

Chateau Colditz

BY MICHAEL FARR

Having done a tour of several prison camps including the Special Security Camp at Poznan in Poland and having attempted to escape and been recaptured on numerous occasions, I was sent to Colditz Castle.

Escape from this sinister fortress was extremely difficult to achieve, so I wrote home and asked for books on wines to be sent to me. My mother sent books by such famous personalities as M. Andre, L. Simon, Berry, and Warner Allen. As I was then able to study wines and get extra help and advice from some of the French prisoners who owned vineyards, I soon received requests from my brother officers to help them make wines and spirits.

There had been several attempts at making potable alcohol or wine, chiefly amongst the Polish officers, both in Colditz and in other prison camps in Germany, where crude alcohol drinks had been brewed which were not altogether good.

Towards the end of 1943, and early 1944, after my study of wine making in Colditz, I evolved a very simple recipe which consisted of putting dried fruits, such as prunes, apricots, raisins and sultanas, etc. into a gallon jar of water. This was then put down behind one of the large stone stoves in Colditz, where an even temperature was maintained during the whole of the fermentation period. We had been able to get a small amount of yeast, which we kept alive all through our wine-making operations. The fermentation period of the wine in the jars lasted from four to six weeks, by which time all the sugar in the wine had been converted into alcohol. At the end of this period the contents of the wine jars were put together into a bucket-like soup container which made the main part of a successful but rather crude still. The first two or three stills were confiscated, but in the end Captain Eggers allowed us to continue brewing and in fact helped us by giving us rough clay wine jars which were most suitable for making wine. The still worked admirably and was in fact fairly clean, giving out a very potent alcohol probably at around 120° over proof. As we were very short of food we were unable to drink such a high-strength spirit, so to make it more palatable, we broke it down with water and cleaned it with charcoal to produce a high strength pure white Schnapps! Sometimes we flavoured this spirit to make it into a sloe gin, a popular and a very old English drink. We were unable to obtain genuine sloes as the Germans were suspicious that this was another method of escaping. Nevertheless when Christmas came, quite a potable Schnapps sloe gin was put on the table. I also made rosé wine and a remarkably good sparkling wine, which for a joke we called 'Farsac' and 'Champenoise' respectively. The sparkling wine was done as in France. The wine was made in jars, fermented in the usual way with selected raisins, water and sugar and put down behind the stove. Afterwards, the wine was allowed to rest, was clarified and filtered and put into bottles which were laid, cork down, on end for a week or two so that all the sediment in the bottle fell on to the cork. The neck and cork were then put into a mixture of ice, snow and salt so that the cork and the first inch of wine in the neck of the bottle became frozen solid, as is done in the *pupitre* method in France. The cork was then taken away, the icy sediment withdrawn to leave behind a perfectly bright, clear wine with all the yeast removed. A little liquid sugar was added before the wine was re-corked. An excellent sparkling wine resulted which was served chilled.

The rosé and white wines were made from varying dried fruits in just the same way, except that they were bottled later, fermented out more, and were thus less sweet.

My good friend and mess-mate, Colonel Moir of the Royal Tank Regiment, made an excellent hydrometer, and took regular readings on the progress of the wines during their fermentation period. We both felt we were following the great Louis Pasteur who had made a life study of the process of fermentation of wines.

We also made a very rough form of spirit from our ration German synthetic jam but we stopped this as the jam spirit was highly dangerous to our health, especially so because of our lack of food.

Whilst our distilling activities in Colditz, which Captain Eggers allowed, were beneficial to us, it is also true that some of us had headaches afterwards! But a lot of merriment and high spirits resulted, and we forgot where we were for a short time. Nobody suffered from the effects!

Alain Le Ray, Général de Corps d'Armée

Lieut. Alain Le Ray
in 1940

Born 1910. L'Ecole de l'Infanterie et des Chars. Troupe Alpines (Sections d'Eclaireurs-Skieurs). 1939–40 Commandant de Compagnie. Wounded and captured. Escaped from PoW camp in Pomerania. Recaptured and imprisoned in Colditz. Made the first successful escape attempt on 11th April 1941. Founded the first Comité de Combat at Vercors. Chief of Vercors, Chief of the Forces Interieures of the Isère Department after May 1944. Commandant of the 7th half brigade of 'Chasseurs Alpines' (Mont Cenis 1944–5). From then until retirement with the rank of General de Corps he held various senior appointments in the French Army, including those of military Attaché in Bonn (1959–62) and General Inspector of Territorial Defence (1968).

XI

My Good Friday

BY ALAIN LE RAY

It was the disgusting Pomeranian winter of 1940–1 when I was back again, a prisoner in Germany's comfortless sheep-fold. I had escaped and had been recaptured.

First, I was subjected to a cunning interrogation by a German security officer but I stubbornly refused to reveal the secret of my escape. There followed twenty days of solitary confinement, when I was lodged far from my comrades, except for Tournon, who had been my partner in escape. We were like people caught in a plague. On roll-call, we had to stand twenty paces in front of our comrades and a special jailer followed us closely wherever we went.

Yet all the time I was working, working at high speed on my new escape-suit. My new trousers were already washed and ready. I had even succeeded in bribing a corporal to buy me a watch for a few marks.

Then one fine morning, three German guards came to us and announced, in their usual roaring voices, that we had ten minutes to pack our things to go to a new camp.

My trousers were not yet dry; my suit not yet complete, so I had no hope of escaping during the journey. I prefer enterprises which are carefully prepared beforehand.

When I found out we were travelling to the west, I felt that at least I was gaining distance and that I should have time in my new camp to prepare more thoroughly for my second attempt.

Tournon and I started this new trip in the highest of spirits. From the train we watched the well-known place names pass before our eyes. We changed at Stettin and Berlin, crossing them like beggars burdened under the weight of the luggage we had to carry. We went on to Cottbus and then to Leipzig where we slept on the tiled floor of a police station.

We left Leipzig by a local train in the early morning of 24th February 1941. I was careful to remember the direction we were going and the names of the stations we passed through. Eventually we reached a river in flood, its grey water filled with sheets of floating ice. The railway followed the river up a narrow valley, flanked by rocks and snow-covered forests.

Then we came to Colditz. High above the town, on the right bank of the river Mulde, was a castle with an entanglement of pinnacles, small clock-towers and steep roofs like those of a cathedral. Seen against the bright sky, the fortress appeared gigantic.

Our guards led us up through the town, up a steep and narrow lane, through the castle's heavy gates, which were closed behind us. This marvellous castle became just another prison. Farewell delight and hope.

Now we penetrated deeper through a tunnel which led to the guard-house at the end of a terrace, where a battery of search-lights shone at night in all directions and through every possible angle. Their beams swept along the walls without missing the smallest corner. The windows overlooking the approach-yard were secured by enormous iron bars.

The many guards at this time were young soldiers, not the second-line troops usually used for guard duty. A sergeant-major with an enormous bunch of keys opened the wicket gate in the door leading to the inner courtyard, which was not so much a yard as a pit, about fifty metres deep and paved with stones.

In each corner of this yard was a small door which led to a hundred winding stairs past four floors to the attics. On one side of the pit, a chapel had been built into the castle.

Although the castle had a certain grandeur, it was nevertheless a place of punishment for us. There was no doubt about that. We were isolated, searched and interrogated before we were allowed to join the other prisoners who lived there. At that time, there were twenty-three French, eighty Poles, twenty British and, in the attics, a contingent of Jews. These prisoners were the aristocracy of escape experts and enemies of Germany.

At Colditz I passed some extraordinary weeks which, although filled with despair, gave us hope too, for a precious solidarity reigned here. In spite of all the restrictions, we felt we were recognised as officers. This was because of the respect which our guards had for us. But our lack of freedom became more evident than at any other prison I had been in.

I observed my surroundings, an exercise which gave me not the slightest glimmer of hope of escaping. After a fortnight I felt ill with frustration. My sense of powerlessness so overwhelmed me, I was almost prepared to jump from one of the towers and was determined to attempt the impossible, even if it led nowhere. My examination of the walls and roofs remained disappointing as the castle was surrounded by steep precipices to the north and west. To the east, the slopes were gentler, but there were double rows of barbed wire along the guards' cat-walks.

The Germans in Colditz, respecting the Geneva Convention, let us out in the castle grounds from time to time to walk around in a wooded park surrounded on three sides by a fence of barbed wire and on one side by a wall. But it was such a nuisance to get ready for the park walk – assembling in the courtyard, being counted and recounted – that many of the prisoners could not be bothered to go.

Apart from the wired-off section reserved for prisoners, the park was not particularly well guarded. On the other hand, the castle guards could survey the whole area including the path down to it.

For the walk, our guards counted us twice in the inner courtyard before we left. Then again after arrival in the park, and the same on the way back. This was done although the walk down took us only four minutes. In spite of these precautions, I felt that this was a weak spot in the castle's defences and made my plans accordingly.

Until the spring of 1941, no one had succeeded in escaping from the castle. The prisoners had tried tunnelling, hiding the spoil in the attics, and climbing the walls, but always in vain. They were caught and caught again to be punished and threatened, so I decided to do it alone. I planned to escape through the park, telling no one until the day of my attempt. In the meantime, I manufactured a new civilian suit, much better than those I had made before and in due course I was ready. I chose Easter to execute my plan to escape on the park walk, for my observations of the route down from the castle showed that when we left the castle gate on the way to the park, we went down a small path past a big house known as the Terrace House. At the corner of this building, where there was a door, the path curved slightly. One day I noticed that the door was half-open. That was all.

Now the curve in the path by the corner of the Terrace House was of tremendous importance as I realised that if the marching column were to close in to the house, there was a moment, as a result of the curve, when the accompanying guards could not observe all the park-walkers at once.

Friday 11th April was a glorious day. The hills showed the return of spring and the light blue sky was like a promise of joy. The river Mulde was brown and almost in flood as it raced through its winding course. I looked at the forest and beyond to the horizon, but as I was still looking from behind the iron bars of my prison window, I hoped that this look would be the last one from my captivity.

It was half-past two; in about ten minutes we should be assembling for the park walk. I wore my uniform, but only for appearances as my white stockings were covered by blue trousers which

Colditz Castle: the route down to the park

reached to my shoes and my light cardigan was hidden under a thick chestnut-brown pullover. On top, I wore a wide khaki great-coat to cover my small parcel of baggage, which, though concealed, made me look a little fatter than usual. Three of my friends had been let into my secret, together with our doctor (I had to ask him how to insert my creeper – a tube filled with money – into my alimentary canal).

Now the Germans had opened the wicket gate and we began to pass through, one at a time, while we were counted twice. As I went through the wicket, my luggage was not noticed by the guard commander in charge of the walk, a sergeant with a scarred face who counted us automatically. As with all professional jailers, he could count prisoners and be quite certain his figures were correct, even though his mind could be on other things.

On the other side of the gate, we were counted for the second time. These mechanical precautions did not alarm me in the least, as I knew it would not be too difficult to confuse such an arbitrary count, should there be a prisoner short.

At last, the column of park walkers started to move. Our steps echoed under the first vault, through to the sunlit German yard where a squad of guards took positions around our column.

As it was Good Friday, no one was about except for the guards and the prisoners. At 3.0 p m we passed the Terrace House and I noticed that the little door in the basement was still open. This looked good.

But no, I could not escape today as the guards along the sides of the column would be too dangerous. I weighed this consideration like an athlete who has signed a contract for a contest in an arena. So far, I had hardly started the game, but already I sought excuses to drop out. Do such excuses cause discouragement? I do not know. But the day was not over yet. I again contemplated success, even if today should begin only the first of a series of escape attempts. Perhaps I am like one of those musicians who refuse to play because the air is damp or because the position of the piano is not exactly right. Sometimes I felt like this on the sports field when competing in the long jump – imagining I had started on the wrong foot, I would stop and begin the run again.

Soon we reached the barbed-wire enclosure in the park, where we spent the next hour or so walking around. When it was time to go, we formed a column, were counted and began the march back. I was resolved to make my attempt before we reached the castle, if I possibly could.

I threw my coat over my back and marched on the left side of the column with my friend Tournon beside me. As we walked up the path, Tournon whispered, "Now?"

"Impossible! No chance yet."

I was in the third rank behind the colonels and other senior officers. Behind me were some Jews. None of them had the slightest idea of my intentions. One of my friends was in the front rank; the other, who was near the German sergeant, had agreed to start a diversion if need be and in the case of any shooting, to turn aside the sergeant's gun.

We crossed the bridge over a brook and started to climb the steep path. Tournon had whispered to the senior French officer, Colonel Le Brigant, "Slowly". The colonel, cunning as a fox, at once slowed the pace of the march. He did not know why, but he was anxious to co-operate as much as he could with any conspiracy his comrades had planned.

Now we had only about a hundred metres to go before we reached the Terrace House again. Tournon whispered once more, "Now?"

"No!" I repeated furiously. I trembled with excitement. The guard at the head of the column was still looking ahead. I watched the guard on our flank. We were now close to the house. Another guard was ten metres behind me. I should have five seconds to act.

"This is it!" I whispered to Tournon, who, without turning, warned those around him to take no notice of anything, but to keep marching normally.

My heart was beating as if it would break. Tournon grabbed my coat; then with a single jump I reached the grass slope and fell. Was all lost? Would I be shot? I was on all fours and almost in despair, but I got up again and with two more jumps I reached the darkness beyond the little door.

For some seconds my universe was upside down. Little by little my awareness returned.

Where was I? In a vaulted cellar stored with beds and straw mattresses. I had scarcely time to grasp where I was, before I knew I had to get out and get away before the next count would reveal my absence. Then it would take only two minutes before the guards would be on my heels.

Still trembling with shock, I turned up the lower parts of my false blue trousers, so that they looked like plus-fours, revealing at the same time my white stockings with their decorative garters. I took off my pullover and my linen waistcoat. This changed my appearance in such a way that it would be improbable that I should be recognised. Indeed I looked elegant enough, with the collar of my open blue shirt falling down on my cardigan; my cap with buckle and flap and a small suitcase, completed the picture of a German traveller. This change took me about one minute. Now I had to get out to the walls of the park. I had already planned what to do. I worked like clockwork. On the tips of my toes I crossed the flagstones of the cellar, out through the door and up the grass slope in a single jump. I felt weightless as I reached the path. There was no one to be seen. Quickly, quickly. But no, I must not show haste. Somebody may be looking down from the castle. I went back down the path, with nerves strained to the utmost. There in the park were three Germans playing football inside the barbed wire enclosure. There was nothing for me to do but return to my cellar hiding place. This time, my excitement had gone. I knew that within moments an armed group of German soldiers might break in and catch me. If I should try to escape they would undoubtedly shoot.

I was becoming desperate, but my reason calmed my fears. I realised I must have enough patience to wait until dawn, when the park would be empty. My faith in doing this lay in my friend Tournon, who I believed would succeed in causing a diversion at the count. The German guards, trusted their own counting efficiency and disliked having to report any irregularity for which they were responsible. If the count could be fixed, I should win some hours of respite, at least until the evening *Appell* at 6.0 p m.

Time passed without any alarm being raised, so Tournon had succeeded after all. Then I saw three German officers pass the cellar with an Alsatian dog. Time was going and I felt I had to get out of the cellar at any price. All was clear outside, so I departed; my rubber-soled shoes made no noise.

For the second time I went quietly down to the park. There was no one there now, but eyes might be watching me from the windows of the Terrace House where a watcher could have followed my every step. I went to the small bridge over the brook and hid for a while in some bushes and ferns. Should anyone see me there, it would be quite clear what I was up to, so I hurried to a fallen tree lying across the brook; a few more steps and I had reached the other bank and was near the barbed wire fence which surrounded the ground of the park walk, near where the soldiers had played football about twenty minutes before.

Everything I did now I had already planned in detail days before. I felt like a guide to a party of mountaineers, leading them up a dangerous route which led only to the summit.

The whole park was like an immense eye watching me as I went along the barbed wire fence, to where it joined the wall and grasped the upper strands of wire putting my foot on the end of one of the wooden wire supports fastened to the wall. I stretched out my hands despairingly, until they felt the round top of the wall to which

I clung tightly, whilst my crepe rubber shoes groped the wall to find a foothold somewhere. With a tremendous effort I succeeded in swinging myself to the top of the wall and down the other side, out of the castle grounds.

I had only a little money, yet I managed to travel by train as far as Nuremberg. I was tired and stiff with the cold. I badly needed money and a coat, so I decided to commit a brutal act of robbery with violence against a German civilian. My victim, chosen carefully, resisted me at first, but I was successful in striking him with two well aimed blows with my fist, which left him lying dazed on the ground. I justified this act* to myself with the Jesuitical casuistry that I was acting in self-defence under conditions of warfare, as I could have been shot at any time.

From now on, my voyage became a pleasure trip. I went through Stuttgart – Tuttlingen – Singen. On the evening of the Easter Monday, I was only ten kilometres from the Swiss frontier, near Schaffhausen. During the Monday night, I made my way through woodland paths to Gottmadingen, the last station before the frontier and customs-control, where I waited hidden in the bushes. A train passed at about 11.0 p m and the locomotive stopped five metres in front of me for the train to be searched. When the doors were shut again, I crept up to the engine, and when the engine driver gave the whistle signal to start, I sprang up onto the front of the locomotive between its headlights, where I hid. The driver opened the throttle and the train roared through the fresh air of the

---

* Prisoners-of-war lived in a state where moral values seemed to be different from normal. The Germans at Colditz once tried to bring a charge of theft against a prisoner who had stolen a bicycle. He was acquitted because the prisoner's German defence lawyer pointed out that a German prisoner of the Allies had stolen a motor car, which had helped him escape home to Germany. This theft was considered to be a perfectly legitimate escaping act. Prisoners could also carry false papers; give false information to the police and commit similar crimes for which any ordinary German civilian would have been heavily punished or executed. The recaptured prisoner of war could expect nothing much worse than a period of solitary confinement in the cells of his prison camp. On the other hand, he could also expect to be shot while escaping. – *John Watton*

Article 50 of the Geneva Convention states that a PoW can be punished for an attempt to escape, but only with a disciplinary punishment, not by a court martial. In articles 51 and 52 the nations signatory to the Convention declared that they would be as indulgent as possible when deciding when a trial by court martial would be necessary for a violation of the laws which protect persons and their property. Generally it was the rule that crimes against property were included in the disciplinary punishments, but for cases of murder or of wounding, a court martial would be justified. Article 54 sets as a limit for arrest of a normal disciplinary punishment as 30 days.

At Colditz and generally in District IV, the commandants were allowed to give sentences of up to 14 days of arrest. If they believed a more severe punishment was necessary they had to appeal to the General at Dresden. For him the Convention limit of 30 days arrest was the utmost he could give. – *Reinhold Eggers.*

spring night. Five minutes later we passed the red lights of the enemy guard post; on under a bridge, and then into Switzerland. I had reconquered for myself the right to freedom.

Lieut. Pierre Odry

*Lieut. Pierre Odry,
Colditz, 1941*

Born 1911. Ecole Militaire de St Cyr (1930–2). Captured by the Germans 1940. Escaped from a transport. Hoyerswerda hospital to Colditz in October 1941. Campaigns in Tunis, Italy, France, Germany (1942–45). Later in Indo-China and Algeria. Now a retired colonel.

XII

Fourth Time Lucky

BY PIERRE ODRY

(*Lieut. Odry had made two escape attempts from his former camp VIA at Soest in Westphalia. During his second escape he reached the Franco-Belgian frontier and was caught there by a forester near Verviers. When he returned to his camp at Soest, he was first sentenced to twenty-one days in the cells and then sent to Colditz. There on 18th June 1941 he tried his luck again.*)

Colditz Castle was a special prison where the Germans kept their most dangerous officer prisoners-of-war of the Western Allies – French, Belgian, Dutch, British and Polish. In 1941 there were about 500 of these specialist prisoners who were so well guarded, escape was almost impossible.

Because the castle yard was so small, the German Commandant, Colonel Schmidt, allowed the prisoners a daily walk from about 2 to 4 pm in the castle grounds. There they walked around a walled and barbed-wire enclosure in a wooded park. Before the park walk began, the prisoners, between sixty and a hundred on each walk, were carefully counted twice. Then they were marched down to the park, accompanied by numerous guards.

Within the recreation ground there was a park shelter, where a man could hide in the roof beams, provided he was not spotted by the guards. On the other hand, should he reach his hiding place, and if the count were found to be one short, the Germans would make an immediate search of the area and easily find the escaper, as one of the first places to look would be among the roof beams of the shelter. It was therefore essential if a prisoner were to hide in such a way, that the count should be falsified in the first place. This was how it was done.

During the counting, before we left the castle for the park, one very small prisoner would conceal himself under the greatcoat or cloak of a large one. For the count, we would assemble in three rather disorderly ranks before the guard house with the two-in-one man surrounded by the biggest men of the company who carried blankets on their shoulders and formed a compact mass by standing close together. The Germans would check us by counting the files from the front and if they did not notice anything suspicious, we would reach the park with one extra man.

The next thing was to arrange a diversion such as a dispute in a rugby game – just sufficient to attract the guards' attention without arousing their suspicions. At the same time, the would-be-escaper had to climb unnoticed under the roof of the shelter. When the Germans counted the park walkers for their return to the castle, the number would be correct, according to their records.

Now the escaper under the roof had only to wait until there was nobody in the park before he slipped down from his hiding place and over the wall.

When it was my turn to try this trick – two of us had already succeeded in doing so – a civilian saw me when I climbed over the wall. He at once called the guards, who alerted as many motorists and cyclists as they could find and I was caught eight kilometres from the castle. My punishment was twenty-eight days' solitary confinement.

My cell had a grille of two rows of iron bars in front of the window which overlooked a path which was not well guarded. One of my friends smuggled a small saw into my cell, so I was able to cut the first bar. Unfortunately, I had to leave the cell before I could get through the second bar which was much thicker. I do not know when the Germans discovered the damage, but at least I was not charged for it.

My Escape on 14th October 1941

When in Colditz, I and twenty of my friends had dug a tunnel which the Germans had discovered. This was most discouraging and I could see no way out of the castle until, curiously enough, I was given fresh hope by a kick on the ankle I received when playing football.

This kick gave an excuse to report to the sick-bay for treatment. Fortunately, the German doctor had recently been alarmed when one of his patients was found to need an emergency operation, so, to be on the safe side, the doctor had been transferring more of his patients than usual to the local hospital. I and several of my friends hoped to take advantage of this by reporting sick with sprains, bruises and pulled leg muscles. To my surprise, the doctor told me that my ankle had been broken, so there was no question of my going back to the castle. I joined a few others who were sent to the hospital of Oflag IVD at Elsterhorst, about 150 kilometres away, in Western Silesia. This hospital was guarded like a normal camp, but it was easier for us to get money or civilian clothes there than from our Colditz prison.

A prisoner who worked outside the camp, provided me with a new cap and an old pair of trousers. I had a coat made from a blanket by one of the patients who was also a tailor. Two of my friends who had planned to escape with me equipped themselves in the same way.

While we were there we agreed to try to persuade the Germans to discharge us from the hospital, so that we could try to escape on the way back to our camps. Two other Colditz prisoners joined us, which made us a party of five. We planned to make our attempt during the nights of 13th to 15th October 1941.

The two guards took us the five kilometres to the station where we were to catch the first train very early in the morning, when it was cold and still totally dark. The guards did not notice we wore extra thick clothes, not only to protect us from the cold, but conceal the civilian clothes we wore under our uniforms. We knew that this night march to the station should give us the best chance we might get to escape, so we were all ready to go at a second's notice from an agreed signal. A chance came as we marched past a wood which we could just see as being even darker than the night. I gave the signal, and three of us plunged out of the column of prisoners, crashed stumbling through undergrowth and into the blackness of the trees. We caught fractional glimpses of the guards' rifle fire flashes, but the darkness saved us and we got clean away.*

As I had been able to study my route, thanks to a map I had borrowed from a friend in the hospital, I resolved to walk the seventy kilometres to my first goal, Dresden. Our escape would result in a general alert for the whole district, meaning we would have to avoid stations and main roads by making a long detour through forests. The extra caution was well worthwhile, as I was able to reach Dresden after a thirty-hour non-stop march over open country, except for the last few kilometres when I followed the railway line from Schwepnitz.

At nine o'clock in the morning of the 15th October I reached the suburbs of Dresden, where a tram took me to the city centre. I was in a tattered-looking state after my long march through the woods and fields, badly needing the wash and brush-up I enjoyed in a nearby cafe. I made myself sufficiently presentable to do a little shopping in the city, where I bought a compass. My train was not due to start until half past three in the afternoon, so I spent the time

---

* The other prisoners who escaped with Lieut. Odry were Lieut. Navelet, who reached France, and Lieuts. Levi and Charvet who were both caught at Aachen and were returned to Colditz. – *Reinhold Eggers.*

in seeing the town from a tram which took me on a circular tour.

I had to get to the escapers' Mecca, the heavily guarded frontier city of Aachen, but there was no direct train so I bought a ticket to Kassel instead and arrived at one o'clock in the morning. Convinced that the station was strictly controlled, I decided not to take the next train to Aachen, but to catch one going in a westerly direction, simply to keep myself on the move. This brought me to Frankfurt-Main. I spent several hours touring the city and noticed that the devastation caused by British air-raids was not yet too serious, though there was bomb damage everywhere, especially around the cathedral.

I had to move on again. This time I risked buying a ticket to Aachen, but to avoid a possible police check I left the train at a suburban station, covering the few miles into Aachen by tram. The station was strictly guarded and my provisions had come to an end so I went into a teashop and ordered coffee and cake. When I called for the bill, the waitress asked me for ration-coupons for the cake. I had none. Happily she did not insist on my giving them to her when I explained that I had forgotten them and offered her a good tip.

When I was ready to move on again, I caught a tram to Eupen, from where I had to cross an immense forest extending from Dueren to Verviers. In a night of total darkness, I stumbled through the thick woods blindly guided by my compass alone and following neither road nor path which could be patrolled. On the following day, the 18th October, at one o'clock in the afternoon, quite exhausted, I reached Verviers, where I thankfully took refuge at a certain address that had been given me. I was received marvellously and rested there for two days, to give me a chance to mend and clean my clothes which had got into a deplorable state after my long struggle through the woods.

From my Belgian friends I was transferred from one family to another until I reached the Free French zone. My route was Verviers–Dinant by train; I crossed the Belgian–French frontier on foot; Mezières–Besançon by train; Besançon–St Laurent by car. At St Laurent I missed finding my guide across the demarcation line into the Free French zone so I had to cross the border alone, before dawn, again guided by my compass. On 23rd October, after a journey of nine days, I reached the non-occupied French zone.

Looking back on those nine days makes me wonder why I was not arrested on sight. Although I spoke German well, my appearance was bad enough to arouse the strongest suspicions in all who saw me, and plenty of people stared most curiously. My badly shaved face covered in patches of stubble; my strange clothes and dirt-darkened skin, made me an obvious man-on-the-run – a caricature of an escaping prisoner, not the peaceful German civilian I had pretended to be.

Junior Lieut. Jacques H. Hageman

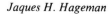

Jaques H. Hageman

Born 1918. Graduate of the Royal Military Academy; assigned to Royal Netherlands-Indies Army. After Dutch capitulation in 1940 was one of Dutch officers who refused to discontinue active opposition to Germany and was imprisoned in Colditz. 1945–50: Dutch East Indies Combat Patrol, Combat Intelligence and Staff Intelligence Officer. 1950–5: trained at European Command Intelligence School in Oberammergau; assigned as Chief Instructor of Dutch Intelligence School, Holland. 1955: emigrated to United States. Present position Engineering Supervisor with Boeing Airplane Co. Married with two children.

XIII

The Most Dangerous Tunnel

BY JACQUES HAGEMAN

I was one of the younger members of a group of about sixty Dutch officers imprisoned in Colditz Castle. We were there together with smaller and larger groups of five nationalities – French, English, Poles, Belgians and Yugoslavians. After a brief time in a transit camp, we had been transferred to Colditz, where we spent most of our captivity. In the later part of the war we were transferred and united with prisoners of our own nationality. At the liberation a large part of the German camp administration fell into allied hands. Among the documentation were the individual personal records of the bad boys of Colditz – Oflag IV C – accurately kept up-to-date, complete with photographs, physical descriptions, characteristics and lists of all their evil deeds. Following are some of the entries and the memories surrounding these statements:

> Good military attitude. Hostile towards Germans. Except for escape attempts has caused no other problems.

This was the first entry in the individual record that the Germans kept about me. Basically the statement was correct and could, as a matter of fact, be applied to all the prisoners sharing the hospitality of Colditz Castle. Some of them were there because there was something special about them, such as having high-ranking relatives in the free world. They were called the *Prominente*. Most of them were considered to be bad boys because they had made a nuisance of themselves by repeated escape attempts or otherwise, and had therefore been transferred mostly from camps of their own nationality to this *Sonderlager*, or special camp with maximum security.

There was another entry of a somewhat general nature:

> The Dutch prisoners of war are Anglophiles and hostile toward the Germans. They have a strong desire to be free, which makes it mandatory to establish special security measures to prevent escape attempts.

– a statement very typically German. It showed their born respect for a proper military attitude, which enabled them to consider the Dutch to be model prisoners in spite of our continuous escape attempts.

The Dutch were indeed a well disciplined group. Our Commanding Officer, Major Engles, strongly supported by the other senior Dutch officers, was of the opinion that there was only one kind of military attitude; which was not to be influenced by the circumstances, nor by contacts with allies or enemy. It was also the only safeguard against deterioration of morale, he believed. The Dutch were properly dressed and maintained a rigid discipline during parade; meals were a joint affair, quarters were kept clean, beds were made, and so on.

There were also other arrangements equally rigid. Escapes were a prime concern, but they had to be organised. For that purpose Captain van den Heuvel was assigned to be the escape officer. All plans had to be submitted to him. He was responsible for the development and the execution of the plans which everyone had to assist. The other nationalities were organised along the same lines and all escape officers kept each other constantly informed. Captain van den Heuvel was respected by everyone for the restless, energetic and determined way in which he carried out his assignment.

Who was going to escape was established by priority; those who were considered to be of immediate and best use for the free Dutch forces were to go first. Since the Netherlands still had a fleet on the seas and a small air force in England, the pilots and naval officers had first priority. The best plans went to them, the plans with a slighter chance were divided among the others. This was felt by all to be very just; besides, it left plenty of opportunity for the rest of us. He who came up with a plan was almost assured that he would be added to the escape team when the plan could take on several persons. Also, there was always the possibility that a young officer with a low priority would be given an excellent opportunity to participate in a top-rated escape plan by being assigned to team up with someone of high priority. In such a case the young officer was to do everything possible to assure the escape of the other, including any risk for his own safety. A senior Dutch Air Force officer, Major Giebel, whose presence in England would be of great importance, was therefore teamed up with Lieut. Drijber, a gallant young officer who was known to carry out assignments at all costs. Both made it.

Also, sometimes the plans rated as having only a small chance, and therefore given to the less important ones, turned out to be a near success. The German records note:

> Hageman and Geerligs, dressed as German workmen, attempted to escape from the camp.

As the entry indicated, the attempt failed, but it had been a near miss. Two German labourers had for a couple of days been busy with filling up a recently discovered tunnel. A close observation of the work habits of the labourers was made, including their comings and goings through the main gate. My closest friend, Geerligs, a junior lieutenant with an indestructible morale and a fine sense of humour, and I decided that it was worth trying to impersonate the two workmen. The workclothes we put on were a near-perfect imitation – including the blue cap, made from a navy cap minus its ornaments. Even the yellow armband with the German eagle was there to complete the outfit.

Shielded from the sight of the two hardworking Germans by a group of other prisoners, I picked up the wheelbarrow that the two had been using and went to the main gate while Geerligs knocked on the big door just like the real ones had done. We fully expected to be stopped right there, in which case we would drop the wheelbarrow and run back to safety, speculating that the guard would not leave his gate post. Great was our surprise when the guard let us out. The guard stationed on an outer wall looked at us but showed no sign of concern. After that, we met at least half a dozen other German guards, apparently off duty, lingering around their quarters adjacent to the castle. Finally the two of us reached the bottom of the hill on which the castle was located. The only obstacle now was the bridge over the moat which surrounded the castle grounds. The last guard there would certainly not have any suspicion – but somebody else did – a small camp electrician and handyman by the name of Willi who was heading back towards the castle from downtown. About to say something to the two 'workmen', he hesitated and then yelled, "Guard! those two are not our men – they are prisoners!" The guard levelled his gun and said, "Do you have a pass?" He apparently wanted to be sure, but probably would have done nothing, if we had not been challenged by Willi. After all, we had come through the main gate.

I snapped back in my best German, "Nonsense. We don't need a pass." Of course that did not help. In the meantime, Hauptfeldwebel Gebhard had been summoned. This German senior NCO was a very capable opponent. He constantly searched all the quarters and knew nearly every prisoner by name and face. With a big grin he remarked, "*Ach so, der* Hageman *und der* Geerligs." Geerligs, who was no more than 5 feet 8 inches tall, coldly replied, "For you, Oberstabsfeldwebel, we are Mr Hageman and Mr Geerligs." Gebhard did not bother to react but instead invited us to follow him back home. On the way up we met the duty officer, Captain Püpcke. Gebhard saluted him and reported, "Herr Hauptmann, these two here wanted to go for a walk." Captain Püpcke looked somewhat puzzled, not quite understanding what this was all about.

Only after Gebhard introduced us by name, rank, and nationality, did the Captain realise what was going on. He then remarked, "That was bad luck gentlemen." We must really have looked very genuine.

The German camp security certainly had no easy task in dealing with this small allied force in Colditz. We all had a common goal, and our escape organisations worked together closely. The Dutch were especially close to the English, where Captain Reid and later Captain Howe were the master minds behind their escapes. A combined English–Dutch escape was not uncommon.

What must have been somewhat confusing for the Germans was the difference in attitude and temperament of the nationalities. It was obvious that the Germans preferred the Dutch attitude, due to our disciplined military behaviour. The irony was that this often turned out to be very disadvantageous for the Germans in many ways. The fact that we stood motionless during roll-call parades enabled us to use dummies – which misled the Germans by impersonating the missing.

To meet our housewifely request to scrub and clean our quarters and wash our windows, the Germans provided us with the necessary materials – which were often not used only for scrubbing and washing. In one instance, the material requested for hygienic purposes played a key role in a major escape attempt in the Dutch tunnel.

Digging a tunnel in Colditz Castle was not an easy operation. Several had been started, only to be discovered sooner or later. A major difficulty in addition to the constant surveillance by the Germans was disposing of the debris. The possibilities of doing so were extremely limited in this old castle. The most difficult part of all, however, was the entrance to a tunnel which had to be opened and closed frequently to let the diggers in and out – this had to be done in the shortest time possible, and each time it had to be camouflaged invisible to an inspecting eye. Every nationality had tried to tunnel at least once, except for the Dutch, it seemed. The Germans didn't trust this situation. The Dutch had a high escape attempt rate, yet a tunnel, at least one identified with us, had never been involved. Didn't we believe in digging tunnels, or was it impossible for us to start one, being located on the third floor?

Yes, we had a tunnel too, and what was more, it met all those difficult requirements. The digging had been going on for quite some time and the Germans had been standing many times within a few feet of its entrance without ever even looking in its direction.

Captain Eggers did not trust the situation and therefore continued to search persistently. Finally he was rewarded with the discovery of the Dutch tunnel. However, it was not by finding the entrance that the Germans scored their success. That was too well camouflaged – due to the material provided by the Germans themselves. A pot of tar and a brush.

The Dutch occupied the third floor on one side of the castle where the outside wall was several feet thick. About in the middle of that side was a small balcony. It appeared to be ornamental because there was no connection with the inside, at least, so it seemed. However, in line with the balcony, a thick wall ran across the whole width of the Dutch floor with the exception of a large opening in the middle where two rooms connected. It was not logical for a dividing wall to be that thick! It was more likely that the thick wall consisted of two thinner walls – one side enclosing the hallway to the balcony and on the other side possibly a stairway to another floor. Anyway, they were plugged up, but what about the enclosed cavities? Had they been filled up? As for the balcony itself, this was supported by a protruding part of the main wall. It could be possible, however, that this support consisted of three walls attached to the castle wall thereby leaving a hollow shaft between them and the main wall.

If the most favourable conditions were true, we would have a

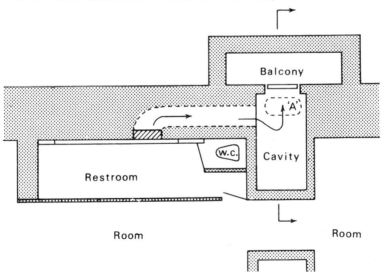

tunnel half ready, constructed for us by the Germans. The cavity in the thick wall on the floor could be used as a hiding place for contraband, at the same time providing a starting point for a descent into the hollow shaft under the balcony. Once at the bottom of the shaft, all we had to do was to dig horizontally to a point outside the barbed wire.

The main problem now was to decide where to have the entrance. There could be no experimenting. If discovered, this would give everything away. We considered it impossible to start the entrance in the thick dividing wall because there was no adequate way to camouflage a hole in a white cement wall – certainly not when the hole would have to be opened and closed frequently. To cover a hole in the wall with a poster, curtain or any other ornament would really be underestimating the intelligence of the Germans. The floor consisting of wooden boards presented the same problems. Although the Germans inspected the walls and floors occasionally, they did not seem to be overly concerned. They must have been convinced that the thick dividing wall was solid, or that no camouflage of holes in the floor or walls could withstand a close inspection.

One thing was sure: this unique chance had to be exploited but where to start? Walls and floors were undesirable, as to camouflage a wall it would have to be painted, time and time again, in exactly the same colour. And it was impossible for paint to dry instantly or very fast. Then came our brainwave: what if a wall was not *supposed* to look dry – as a matter of fact – was *expected* to be wet most of the time! Such a wall was available and fortunately enough, very close to the thick dividing wall. In a very small enclosed area adjacent to the thick wall, a part of the inside of the castle wall served as a urinal, providing room for about three men at the same time. This wall was indeed kept pretty wet most of the time. Then even a better idea was born, what if the wall could be painted with approval of the Germans! So we asked the Germans to provide us with some thick black tar, if possible with some disinfectant in it; this would assure much more hygienic conditions and would eliminate the unpleasant odour in this small area. The Germans nodded approvingly. In the meantime, could they also spare more soap? Also agreed. After all, we were setting a good example of how quarters should be kept clean and tidy.

Soon material was delivered – a big pot with tar and a brush; the soap would come later. Oh, there was no hurry, we said. First we cleaned the wall by scrubbing and flushing it down. Then, under the approving eye of the German who had delivered the material, the surface was painted with a nice black layer of tar. "Yes, it looks very good and it smells much better now," the German agreed. Yes, we could keep the pot and the brush to repeat the treatment when required.

The idea was to enter the wall in about the middle of the urinal surface and to make a connecting tunnel in the castle wall, leading to the thick dividing wall and the expected cavity. Digging down from this cavity would lead into the area under the balcony and hopefully a hollow shaft.

The entrance would have to be a square hole about 18 inches square, this being the minimum for an average-sized man to get through. A wooden frame of thin board was made to shape a cement slab several inches thick. The frame was placed in a hole in the wall flush with the surface, the cement slab providing a tight-fitting lid for the hole formed by the frame.

We had all the ingredients needed for the job: a chisel, a hammer and cement – all stolen from the Germans. Although German work and repair crews were always guarded, the prisoners often managed to snatch something from them. Distracting the guard's attention, two prisoners would start an argument and exchange blows very close to the guard. The guard would tell them to stop fighting; other prisoners would rush to the scene trying to separate the fighting men, thereby placing themselves between guard, fighters and work-men. At that moment an assigned individual would pick the desired item.

The other ingredients required, the clayish soap to be used as putty and the tar could be obtained legally. Making the initial hole was a crucial time. Singing and music could drown out the sound of the hammering, but how to camouflage an unfinished hole at a moment's notice if the Germans should decide on a surprise inspection of the quarters? At this stage the camouflaging was done by filling up the holes created by the removed cement with the putty-like soap and a coat of tar. Finally the frame was properly in place, providing a neat square hole in the wall. Putting the lid in place was a matter of a few seconds now and after a little patch-up job only those who knew could point out the exact location of the hole in the black tarred cement wall. From this point it was just a few feet to the thick dividing wall. We were triumphant when the thick dividing wall indeed turned out to be the former hallway to the balcony! No time was wasted in breaking through the floor in a diagonal direction to investigate the suporting wall of the balcony.

Again, good luck – the wall was hollow, providing a long narrow shaft all the way down. A rope was soon made out of sheets. One more pleasant surprise was waiting: the bottom of the shaft was several feet below the outside terrain level, deep enough to start digging horizontally. The chance for a breakout was only some twenty-five feet away.

Breaking through the foundation of the wall, however, turned out to be a very tough job. It consisted of big rocks bonded together

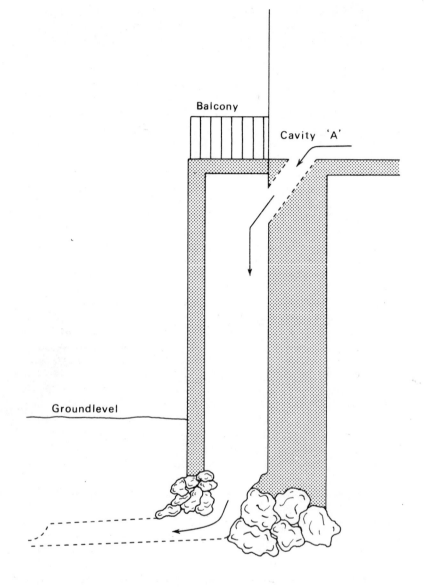

with a kind of rough cement. The Germans had a guard posted between the castle wall and the barbed wire because Giles Romilly's room was nearby, and while working in the bottom of the shaft, one could hear the guard's footsteps. The cement had to be scraped away from between the rocks before they could be removed with a crowbar. Sometimes it took a week to remove one such rock because the work had to be done without making a sound. Fortunately, there was enough room in the shaft to stack up the removed rocks.

Digging was going on as usual one day when Dames and I were on duty. Dames was resting at the bottom of the shaft while I was in the tunnel digging cautiously. The job of the one resting was to signal the digger to stop when the footsteps of the patrolling guard outside came close. Suddenly we received the signal to stop, this time followed by the order to crawl back out of the tunnel.

"Something's wrong," Dames whispered. "There's a lot of commotion going on outside the shaft." He had hardly said so, when a loud hammering noise indicated that the Germans had decided to find out for themselves what this supporting wall for the balcony really looked like on the inside. Later it turned out that Captain Eggers had been pondering this for quite some time.

The hammering went on and small pieces from the inside of the shaft were dropping down on our heads. Since no alarm was given from upstairs it was obvious that the Dutch had been ordered to clear their quarters. Most likely roll-call had already revealed that two were missing and also who those two were.

Dames decided that it would not make sense to wait down there any longer so we both climbed back up into the cavity upstairs. We had barely made it up there when shouts of excitement indicated that the Germans had found the shaft – including a rope dangling down. Their attempt to grab the rope, however, failed – we had just pulled it up. As it would still take some time for the Germans to enlarge the hole in the wall and work their way up in the shaft, Dames and I decided to try to destroy the cache of contraband. We managed to burn it, which developed a lot of smoke and dirt in the small space.

The guard working his way up had his share of misery with all the débris which we shuffled down the shaft. When the climber was only a few feet away from the cavity, Dames decided that he didn't want to wait to welcome the guard aboard and that we should find out how the situation was in the Dutch quarters, so I crawled into the small tunnel and with a hard push shoved the cement slab out of the wall. The Germans by now knew that the tunnel entrance had to be in the vicinity of the restroom – and had stationed a guard there.

Imagine the expression on the face of this guard when all of a sudden a cement block popped out from the glistening wet wall of

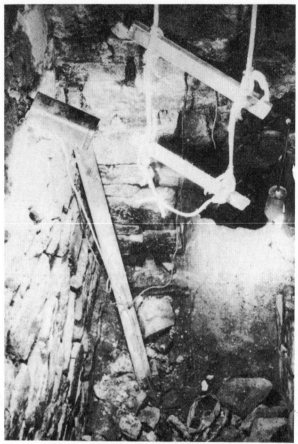

The tunnel where Hageman and Geerligs
were discovered

the urinal and a dirty face became visible. For a few moments he just stared, then he yelled for his Captain. "There he is," the Captain remarked happily, followed by the obvious question: "and where's Dames?" "He's coming," I mumbled, trying to wriggle unaided out of the hole. I was more accustomed to being firmly but gently extracted from the wall by friendly hands.

There we stood, two dirt-covered captives surrounded by victorious Germans who did not hide their admiration for the ingenuity of the tunnel entrance. A new note for the record:

The end of February, Hageman and 1st Lieut. Dames involved in escape preparations by means of digging a tunnel below the Dutch quarters.

Then the penalty – three monotonous weeks of solitary confinement in one of the castle cells. Every morning starting in the same identical fashion. The firm loud footsteps of the corporal in charge. His loud but not unkind voice asking us to rise. Then the sharp metallic click of the opening of the small door of the Dutch oven that kept the cell lukewarm for the day. The sound of sweeping out the old ashes and of the coal bricks put in place. Then a monologue, "*Jetztein wenig Roten Hahn* [Now some 'Red Rooster' starter]", followed by the lighting of a match, the slamming of the open door and concluded with a contented sigh, "*So dass klappt wieder prima* [So that's in good shape again]".

Yes, for the Germans at least everything was in good shape again. The Dutch tunnel had been added to the list of victims.

Then came the day when we Dutch were informed that we were going to be transferred. Somewhere someone must have decided that it was not such a good idea after all to have all the bad boys concentrated in one place.

The trip was one of several days to somewhere in the southeastern part of Poland. The Germans were not going to take any risks and secured the transport with more guards than there were prisoners. Even so, we did it again, and one of us managed to get out during the trip. Regretfully it was not for long. Lieut. van Lynden was captured a few days later.

The place of arrival turned out to be Stanislaw. The camp, a large former Polish barracks, was surrounded by a high wall. Outside this wall was a two-storey building, apparently the main administration building. There, in front of the building, after a brief ceremony, the new camp command took over and the Colditz guard left.

All partings have an atmosphere of their own. So had this one. The Colditz guard should have been glad that this difficult group was now the responsibility of someone else. For the Dutch, a new environment meant new possibilities. Yet, after all those years, would we perhaps miss each other? When they marched off, some of the old guards looked back at us and seemed to smile.

We were politely invited to enter the administration building and then go up the staircase to the top floor. There we were guided into a couple of rooms facing the main street which ran in front of the building. A guard was posted in the doorway of the room next to a table where a NCO was seated ready for the registration. Incredible

– the three windows in the room overlooking the street had no bars. They could even be opened. And there were no guards stationed on the lawn between the building and the street. It was hard to believe. Didn't the Germans know what kind of people they had here? Or was it a trap? Invite us to escape! The guards unnoticed on the sides of the building could easily catch us or shoot us. This would teach us right from the start we were not dealing with fools! Well, there was one way of finding out. The drop to the lawn was somewhat high for older bones, van den Heuvel decided; now here was a good chance for the young and nimble. Two groups of three each were going to jump: Dufour, van Lingen and myself first, Geerligs and two others to follow immediately. Shielded from sight of the two Germans at the door, the first three jumped. The drop was indeed a long one; too long, as a matter of fact, except for van Lingen, who twisted both his ankles but got away. Dufour broke his heels and I an ankle. Also, the window which I jumped from was apparently rusted in the hinges. It fell loose and came crashing down after me.

This noise was enough to alarm the main guard, who came running around the building to see what was going on. So another statement had to be entered:

Escape attempt; jumped from the window of the L.F. Building, recaptured in the garden.

Van Lingen was arrested a few days later, unable to go any further. He had asked for help from a man he thought was a Pole – who turned out to be a German.

Recovering with my leg in plaster, I was visited by the number one escape chief, van den Heuvel. "Good show, son, too bad it didn't work out. The long train trip must have weakened you."

Having just inspected the camp, van den Heuvel had another small matter to discuss – terrific escape possibilities which had to be tried out right away, before the Germans got wise. However, the camp was divided into two parts by a wall separating the junior and cadet officers from the others. He thought it would be a good idea if, with all my experience in Colditz, I would set up an escape office in the cadet officers' half of the camp. What did I think about that? In the military world it is very hard to draw a line between a request and an order. So . . . Oh well, after all, the show had to go on.

XIV

The Manhole Escape*

BY OSCAR DRIJBER AND BY C. GIEBEL

Extracts from the reports of Captain Kunze, German Adjutant and Captain Eggers, German Security Officer, concerning the Dutch officers Major Giebel and Lieut. Drijber who successfully escaped from Colditz on 19th September 1941:

Roll-call. 21st September 1941: the Dutch officers Major Giebel and Lieut. Drijber were missing from the morning parade. As no evidence of a break-out could be found we presumed that they were hiding somewhere in the castle. Dutch officers had already caused us trouble by pretending to have escaped in this way. A comprehensive search of the whole castle had no results. The security officer was left without the slightest idea as to how the two officers had disappeared. Later we heard that Giebel and Drijber had crossed the Swiss frontier near Schaffhausen on 23rd September 1941, and were now beyond the reach of the German authorities.

Captain Kunze

Major Giebel and Lieut. Drijber were chosen for this attempt by the Dutch escape committee, for these reasons. Giebel was a comparatively young staff officer who could be of value to the Allies as a member of the staff officer school (Hoogere Krijgs School). He was a member of the Netherlands East Indies Army (Infantry); a qualified pilot-observer, and willing to take the risk of escaping – many other senior officers had mixed feelings about this.

Drijber was selected for his practical experience and proven ability in the field as an infantry man; his knowledge of German, French and his familiarity with the German-Swiss border near Singen. (He had spent his holidays for many consecutive years around the Bodensee, Schaffhausen, Schwarzwald and Stuttgart areas.) Also in his favour, was the fact that when he was caught tunnelling by Captain Priem, he had not lost any tools, betrayed his friends or given away any information. He accepted full responsibility and punishment for the whole tunnel.

Giebel and Drijber were given invaluable up-to-date and accurate

---

* The two reports in this chapter are of the same escape by the Dutch officers Major Giebel and Lieut. Drijber. Any inconsistencies in the stories have been left as they are reported and no attempt has been made to make the stories fit each other by editing. – *John Watton.*

information by the recaptured escapers Dufour and Smit. These two Dutch officers had escaped between 15th and 18th August. The exact time and the other circumstances were unknown to us. They were caught at Gottmadingen, the last village before the Swiss border. Two other Dutch officers, Lariva and Steinmetz, had crossed the frontier safely. Three others, Kruiminck, van der Krap and van Lynden hid in a forgotten corner of the castle for several days and were eventually found there. This whole mess caused us many headaches and never was cleared up completely.

Captain Eggers

Lieut. Oscar L. Drijber

Oscar Drijber

Born 1914. After the defeat of Holland in 1940 he refused to stop fighting against Germany. Imprisoned in Soest, Westphalia and later in Colditz. Escaped 21st September 1941 with Major Giebel. From Switzerland he went to England; in 1945 to Indonesia, and served there in the Intelligence, Paratroops, Air Force, Infantry. Demobilised in Holland in 1948. Emigrated to Canada. Became a schoolmaster. Has five sons and a daughter.

I: Oscar Drijber's Story

My personal reason for escaping may be stated as follows: "A professional officer has to serve his country as well as he can under all circumstances within the realm of his honour and the officer's oath. Hence, as a prisoner of war, his duty is to rejoin his Allies. Therefore he has the right and the duty to attempt to escape."

One of the essentials for an escape attempt is sufficient German money. This was provided for me by the English prisoners, on condition that I would return it to them after reaching Switzerland, which promise I fulfilled by means of sending them a chess-board, hollowed out and filled with German marks, files, maps and other escape equipment which reached the English prisoners undetected. A code was also arranged for them to communicate with British Intelligence in London. At the same time I wrote to Captain Priem from Switzerland, to thank him for his treatment and to apologise for escaping before I had completed my sentence for a previous unsuccessful break-out. I received no answer, but I understand that Captain Priem got my letter.

Giebel got his money some way or other not known to me. He hid it in a smooth cylindrical cigarette-lighter which was inserted through the anus into the alimentary canal. This could be done without any discomfort to speak of. We all used this method to carry money and papers out of the camp during the preliminary stages of an escape.

I obtained clothing from Flight-Lieut. Thom RAF, who gave me a pair of trousers, a jacket with civilian buttons replacing the RAF variety, and a woollen sweater. Major Giebel wore navy trousers borrowed from Commander Fraser, a black sweater and a navy coat. Giebel had also borrowed a compass which had been made by Commander van Doorninck. Our identification cards were forged by Lieut. Diederick van Lynden. The only camp material we took with us were a few photographs and a set of prisoner-of-war currency which we later gave to the British Intelligence. My orders from the Dutch escape committee and from my senior officer, Major Engles, were to take Major Giebel to Switzerland and to keep an eye on him during our escape. At the same time, I was officially under his command, but just the same, I was responsible for his escape and for getting him over the border. This order was carried out, but needless to say it created considerable difficulty.

Giebel and I were briefed before the escape. Then I was given an extra briefing on how to handle Major Giebel.

We were also assured that we would have, or rather could expect, about twelve hours without the camp knowing that we were gone, by the use of 'Max' and 'Moritz',* which turned out to be true.

This is what I remember of the escape after twenty-five years. It was, I believe, 20th September when a strong contingent of walkers went down to the park. They were asked to stage games so that Giebel and I could slip unobserved into a manhole which led to part of the castle's drainage system. This manhole was on our side of the barbed wire fence, which separated the area for walking from the rest of the park; it was covered by the usual manhole cover which was fastened by an iron bolt. On top of the manhole, van Doorninck used to conduct a prayer party to give cover to would-be-escapers while they disappeared into the hole below. This he did on the afternoon of our escape. Others of us distracted the guards with athletics and other sports.

At the right moment we went down the manhole, but not as pre-arranged. Giebel refused to go in first, so I had to go down followed by Giebel who stood on my head and shoulders. Hence my control on opening the hatch was gone.

So there we were, both in the manhole, having achieved the first part of our escape operation.

Our orders were to remain in the hole until after dark. However, as everything was quiet, Giebel became cramped and impatient and wanted to go. As his feet were on top of my head and shoulders and my feet were in the water at the bottom, I had no control over him at all. I had the iron bolt in my pocket. Our friends above had a bolt of glass which was made from an aspirin tube with wooden nuts.

* 'Max' and 'Moritz' were two busts made by one of the Dutch officers from plaster, life-size and in full colour. These busts were used to replace escapers like Giebel and Drijber on roll-call. A long wooden stick was introduced into a hole inside the dummy's head, so that it was on the same level as that of the prisoner who held it in position and who stood in the middle rank. The bust was fitted with a long military cloak and a military cap. Below the long cloak a pair of nicely-polished boots made the appearance complete. One of the busts is to be seen in a photograph in the Colditz museum which is reproduced overleaf.

The success of this impersonation depended on the Dutch contingent being by far the most disciplined of all the prisoners. The Dutch stood like puppets on roll-call, so the real puppets fitted well into the general impression of this model company of soldiers. During several roll-calls after Giebel's and Drijber's attempt, Max and Moritz fulfilled their roles perfectly. The German officers were pleased by the really Prussian exactness of the Dutch parades, so the counting was done quickly and superficially, easily deceiving the Orderly Officer. The trick was discovered however, on 12th December 1941, when two Dutch officers were hidden in the park under what seemed to be a heap of leaves. One of them should have been replaced by Max. The counting officer in the park, irritated by previous attempts to deceive him, repeated his job with the utmost care and so finally discovered the busts. Consequently, after a park search, the two escapers under the leaf camouflage were found.
– Reinhold Eggers

The Dummy 'Max' with a Dutch officer

This was almost identical with the real bolt, both in size and colour, which when fitted in place could be broken by the escapers below who could get out when all was clear and replace the original iron bolt. In spite of all my begging him not to go and risk spoiling it, he pushed up the manhole cover, breaking the glass bolt and got out. He went over to the shelter, urging me to follow him; but I had to rearrange the bolt in its correct position, clean up all signs of broken glass and to leave our surplus clothing in the rafters of the shelter. Giebel, however, ran to the stone wall at the edge of the park and yelled to me to come on. (That was an order, by the way, one of the many to follow.) It was daylight by then and I still do not know how we got away with it.

When I caught up with Giebel, who could not get over the wall without my assistance anyway, he climbed on my shoulders, looked over the wall, threw his baggage down to the other side, almost broke my neck by using my head (without warning) as a stepping stone to hoist himself over the broken-glass-covered top without getting himself hurt, and joined his baggage. (Whatever he took along for food and extras I never knew, and never will know apart from his English cigarettes and chocolates. I had one-third of a bread issue, which I had kept for escaping purposes for almost a year, eating it daily and replacing it with fresh bread).

Anyway, there I was at the foot and at the wrong side of the high wall, the top of which I could only reach by jumping for it. This I did, and thanks to the broken glass on top, I had a perfect hold, though a rather painful and bloody one, in spite of my gloves. When I got over, Giebel was on his way already and in the wrong direction at that. Anyway, we sorted ourselves out without any serious difficulties, apart from meeting one of our German corporals on a bicycle. He paid us no attention whatsoever. From this I concluded that the first parade from which we were absent, and the other count on our return to the castle, had gone well without either of us being missed.

We made our way to the railway station at Leisnig, where Giebel insisted on getting the tickets, since he had his money out already (from the anus!) and since I could not "speak German well enough". So he got the tickets and we boarded the train, which was crowded. I happened to sit next to a lovely *Fräulein*, which was rather upsetting for me after all the time in prison. But no harm came of it.

If I remember correctly (I am not sure of this), we travelled through the night via Regensburg to Munich. Just before we got to Munich, I went to the toilet to take out my money from my creeper for tickets to Singen. At Munich, we had enough time for Giebel to go to the station restaurant to order a meal. Then a lady came over and asked him to look after her children. Somehow we got out of that mess too.

We went on by train from Munich to Ulm, changed trains there; then on to Stuttgart-Tuttlingen and on to Singen. On the first stretch from Munich to Ulm, Giebel smoked, and even offered the other passengers English cigarettes and chocolates, which he ate in full view of the German passengers, who took it all as a matter of course. I couldn't stand it any longer and retreated to the water-closet.

We had to change at Ulm where a great number of German troops were being moved to the East. I had suggested to Giebel that we split up on the station and meet again on the train afterwards. Although he objected strongly to this suggestion, he was pleased we did so as he was able to run off when a German officer stopped me to ask why I wasn't in the army. I told the officer that it was the army's mistake and I was on my way to try to join up in my home district, which I had been told to do.

Later on, Giebel and I found each other on the train again, which was just as well since Giebel had insisted on keeping both our tickets. At any rate, after this incident he gave me my ticket to keep.

Everything went comparatively well until we reached Singen where we decided to separate and to meet again about half a kilometre from the station. There was a control at the station and all papers were being checked, so I supposed that our escape had been found out and that they were checking all passengers in consequence. I told Giebel about my suspicions and told him to walk straight through the exit, hand his ticket over and keep on walking. This he did, and I went right after him, ready to distract the attention of the police should he arouse their suspicions. All went well and I found Giebel at our pre-arranged rendezvous.

It had grown dark and I was afraid there might be a curfew, so we went carefully down the road to the frontier. Since the information supplied by Dufour and Smit was accurate and very clear, I knew just where we were, but could not convince my colleague. On the way, we met a man on the road whom I greeted with the old German prayer, "*Grüss Gott*". To my surprise, I received a very enthusiastic "*Grüss Gott*" in return, as I had just realised I should have said "*Heil* Hitler". This was enough for Giebel to ask the man whether the road led to the Swiss border. Naturally he was rather surprised and asked us to come with him. This was far too dangerous, so we tried to reassure him before we disappeared off the road and stayed in hiding for about two hours. At that time Giebel told me, when I asked him for the compass, that he had sat on it and smashed it. Now I had to take him over the border.

As I knew the surroundings by heart from the information we had received from Dufour and Smit, we found our way around the bridge over the railway and down the embankment, all on our bellies. Giebel did not enjoy this very much, but he saw the need for it after a German patrol and a German shepherd just missed seeing us. We crossed the railway at a suitable point and crawled up to the main road along the border where we waited for about two hours till around 2 a m. Then we crossed the road between German patrols when the moon was more or less obscured by clouds.

The happenings of the next hour topped the whole escape off with the most ridiculous incident one can imagine. Anyway, Major Giebel was not sure that he was in Switzerland, and disappeared. When we were hailed by a Swiss border guard, I answered the German challenge in French and at the same time changed my position and asked the guard to light up his face with his flashlight. This he did. A German soldier would never have done so, not only to make himself a perfect target at night but blinding himself for long enough to be put out of action, whether he was armed or not. Anyway he was evidently a Swiss so I joined him quite happily. It took us more than twenty minutes to find Giebel and convince him that we had crossed the border safely into Switzerland.

We were taken to Ramsen. In spite of the late hour (or should I say early hour, three or four o'clock in the morning) we had a wonderful reception. They gave us soup and a place to sleep in the local jail. The next day we were escorted by train to Schaffhausen prison where our identity was established. Then we were housed in a hotel. Later, we visited the Swiss Intelligence before we were finally released to the Dutch Legation in Bern and interned in Geneva.

Giebel went on to England and then to the United States. I stayed in Switzerland until January or February, working for the Intelligence Service and enjoying it immensely. After that I went through occupied France to Spain and Portugal, still working for the Intelligence, and arrived in London in April 1942. Later, in the Isle of Man, I was almost imprisoned by the Dutch as a German spy. But the British Intelligence intervened, as they seemed to know me better than my own government at that time.

Lieut-General C. Giebel

*General Giebel in 1947
as Chief of Air Staff
in the Netherlands*

Born in 1900, C. Giebel was commissioned in 1920 into the Dutch
regular army from the Royal Military Academy at Breda and at the
time of the German occupation of the Netherlands was on the staff
of the 4th Army Corps. Taken prisoner in 1940, he escaped from
Colditz in 1941 after which he had a distinguished military career in
the Far East. From 1947 to 1950 he was Chief of Staff of the RNAF
and 1951–1960 on the staff of the NDC at the Hague.

II: C. Giebel's Story

The sixty-eight Dutch officers, who arrived in Colditz on 24th July 1941, came from an Oflag in Juliusburg, Silesia, where, because of their frequent and insistent attempts to escape, they had been a nuisance to the German garrison. When one such attempt succeeded and two Dutch officers got away, the Germans decided the time had come to transfer the Dutch to the Sonderlager at Colditz.

As if it were only yesterday I still remember our arrival at Colditz in the early morning. We were escorted through its narrow streets to the mysterious, typically mediaeval castle on the top of a hill, which was to be our next residence in World War II. As I remember we had to go through several gates and cross bridges before we finally arrived before the main gate, which opened to our prison quarters and the castle's inner courtyard.

When we were let in, the place looked practically empty. Only a few officers in Allied uniforms – Belgian, British, French and Polish – were standing around, glancing with more or less distrustful looks – to say the least of it – at us newcomers, who were to be their comrades in captivity, if not in arms, for some time to come.

It took some days before we Dutch were accepted as full members of the Colditz community and were initiated into its secrets. The main secret was the existence in Colditz of British, French and Polish escape committees, who in perfect coordination worked day and night to prepare ways and means to escape for everybody who was interested.

So far, the result of their exertions had been that every three or four days there was an escape attempt. Unfortunately, not every attempt had been entirely successful. According to Colditz rules, an escape was considered successful when the PoW succeeded in staying more than twenty-four hours outside the camp. In this sense there had been several successful attempts, but as far as was known in Colditz at that time, only once had an escaper got right away: a French PoW, Captain Pierre Mairesse-Lebrun, had found his way back to France after his escape a few weeks before we arrived.*

When caught, the delinquents were conducted safely back within the castle's stately walls by German guards. It had become a Colditz habit to greet them with a respectful applause. If somebody had succeeded in staying away for several days instead of the usual few

* Actually Lieut. Le Ray had also made a home run in April and Lieut. Colin in May 1941. – *Reinhold Eggers.*

hours, the applause would be louder, in spite of the bitter disappointment that once again all efforts had been in vain, even though the long absence had fostered the hope that the Swiss border might have been crossed.

With the approval of all concerned a Dutch escape committee was established under the brilliant leadership of Captain of the Netherlands East Indies Army Chiel van den Heuvel, who soon proved to be a true genius in this rather delicate matter. The Dutch had hardly been in Colditz a month, when they produced their first achievement at the end of August 1941, when two Dutch officers, NEI Captains Smit and Dufour, managed to get out and stay away for ten days. Two days later two Dutch naval lieutenants, Larive and Steinmetz, also found their way out. They were more fortunate than their army predecessors and reached Switzerland.

Smit and Dufour's escape had remained unnoticed, but when Larive and Steinmetz disappeared, the Germans became aware that several Dutch were missing.

Van den Heuvel's escape route was very simple. As Colditz was too small for its more than 500 inhabitants, the greater part of a park bordering on the east side of the castle, had been added to the camp as a place for daily entertainment. Most afternoons from three to half past four, the PoWs were allowed to leave the castle for a walk in the park. Sometimes some eighty to a hundred of them took part in this highly enjoyable business. If the weather cooperated, it was a very pleasant pastime as the park was a beautiful spot, in spite of the barbed wire fence with which – for obvious reasons – it was surrounded. The main part was a well-kept grass-covered hillside with here and there impressive trees. The lower, flat part of the hill was used as a football pitch. A very good pitch it was too, apart from a few trees standing in the middle of it. The players as well as the spectators had become accustomed to this inconvenience and had learned to live with it. After all, when handled in the right way the trees made the game more exciting.

Another imperfection in the pitch was a manhole, also situated close to the middle. Ten feet deep, it could have been a real nuisance, had it not been closed by a square wooden cover which had been loosely laid down over the top of the manhole, so it was no more an obstacle than the trees, only a kind of *Schönheitsfehler*.

Chiel van den Heuvel's cunning mind had quickly appreciated the far-reaching possibilities of this manhole for escape enterprises. The only thing to do was to let two PoWs down into the manhole during the walk and keep them there hidden until the walk was ended. As soon as the walking party with their guards had returned to the castle, the two in the manhole would be free to go where they

wanted, provided that they could manage to climb over the barbed
wire fence and over the ten foot high wall which separated the park

*A park walk
at Colditz*

from the free world. The only difficulty standing in the way was
that the PoWs who took part in the walk were counted by the
German guards, not only once, but four times: first on leaving the
castle, second upon arrival in the park, third when leaving the park
after the walk, and fourth upon arrival back in the castle.

This trick through the manhole had succeeded twice, first with
Smit and Dufour and then again with Larive and Steinmetz.

Alas, it appeared soon after the latter escape that the Germans
suspected the manhole as having something to do with the Dutch

escape route, so they stopped the Dutch taking part in the daily walk. This was not too bad, however, because if somebody applied to take part in the walk dressed not in uniform but in gym clothes, the German guards would not notice that a Dutchman had joined the walking party. In this way van den Heuvel had been able to go to the park, where he found the wooden cover, which previously had been lying free on top of the manhole, was now firmly closed by a solid steel bolt and a corresponding steel nut. This meant – as we saw it at first – that from now on an escape attempt through the manhole would be out of the question.

So I was amazed when, two weeks later, van den Heuvel asked me if I would be willing to take part in the next attempt to escape through the manhole, which – he guessed – was going to take place next Friday, 20th September. Of course I was ready to cooperate, but I first wanted to know how it could be done.

Van den Heuvel explained that his committee had succeeded in making out of one or two pieces of scrap metal a kind of monkey-wrench to unscrew the nut on the manhole cover. So my escape could take place in the same way as Smit and Dufour's.

In addition the committee had made a pseudo-bolt from a sort of plastic and a corresponding wooden nut of the same size as the real ones. As soon as the manhole had been opened and I had jumped in, the real bolt and nut would be handed to me and the cover would be replaced and closed again, but now with the plastic bolt, so that nobody would notice that the manhole had been opened. As soon as it was all clear, I should have no difficulty in pushing up the cover from within, breaking the plastic bolt and getting out.

Van den Heuvel's plan sounded reasonable. But what about the roll-call? How to prevent the guards, when the party was about to leave the park, from becoming aware that somebody had been left behind and immediately suspecting the manhole?

Van den Heuvel promised to take care of this, but he preferred not to tell me how. He said he had planned a trick but if it didn't work, the attempt could be cancelled.

Then he told me that it was his and the committee's intention that one of the other Dutch officers should go with me. The committee knew that I happened to be in the happy possession of a hundred German marks, which on my urgent request had been sent to me by my wife when we were still in Juliusburg. (I had been told that a hundred marks were needed for a third-class ticket to the Swiss border.) But now that we had moved to Colditz in Saxony, much closer to the Swiss border, forty-seven marks would be enough. So van den Heuvel asked me to take Lieut Oscar Drijber with me.

The committee had selected Drijber because a few days before, when boring a hole in one of the Dutch quarters' walls from where a second Dutch tunnel had been planned, he had been caught out by Captain Priem, the Chief Camp Officer. Boring holes was not tolerated in Colditz and therefore Drijber was to be punished with two weeks in the cells. But he had to wait a few weeks before he could sit it out as no empty cells were available, as all ten cells were occupied and reserved for months to come. The committee would appreciate it if Drijber could be saved this ordeal.

I had not the slightest objection. On the contrary, I welcomed the idea that Drijber would accompany me. But now that it had come to a definite appointment several things had to be done. First we needed an accurate picture of Smit and Dufour's experiences. After they had left Colditz on their escape attempt they had travelled by train from Leisnig, five miles from Colditz, via Leipzig, Munich and Ulm to the Swiss border near Singen, a few miles to the east of Schaffhausen. Singen had been selected because nearby there was a piece of Swiss territory on the north bank of the Rhine. Smit and Dufour had arrived at Singen but when they were on the point of crossing the border they had been arrested. From their story two items were likely to be of the greatest importance to us.

They had left the manhole in the evening when it became dark and had to climb over three walls before they reached a public road. This sounded a bit strange. To me it seemed more likely that they had lost their way in the dark and had crossed the same wall three times. As we could see from the park, the wall indeed made several sharp turns. So it seemed to me that the right thing to do would be to leave the park before it had become dark. Moreover it appeared from their story that climbing over the wall was not as simple as it looked at first sight. It would be less difficult to do it by daylight.

Not less important was our dress. For this occasion I annexed a beautiful pair of trousers which had belonged to the naval uniform which Steinmetz had left behind. It went very well with my dark sweater. And my uniform raincoat could pass for a civilian coat.

Drijber's position in this matter was less fortunate. He had to be content with an old Royal Air Force service dress, in which the RAF buttons had been replaced by some kind of civilian buttons. Together with a khaki shirt and an expressionless necktie it was far below the standards to which a subaltern PoW, travelling as a tourist through Germany, was entitled. This apart from the highly deplorable fact that the jacket didn't fit him at all, being much too small for Drijber's massive torso and so tight he could not possibly close it. But after all it was the best he could get hold of and we could do no more than hope for the best.

There was still another item that could be useful to complete our outward appearance: a newspaper – the German *Nazi-Zeitung*, the *Völkische Beobachter*. Not so much for the news it contained but because it was decorated with an inch-wide red band, by which it was easily recognisable as one of the main instruments of the *Partei*. We were inclined to believe that by carrying this paper we would not be so likely to be interfered with, at least not in Germany, even if our dress might arouse suspicion. A red-banded paper in somebody's hands was after all an indication of some relationship with the Nazis and during our PoW time we had gained the feeling that many Germans were not very fond of their Nazi brothers.

Nevertheless we thought it safe to add a passport to our equipment. Our British friends were acquainted with the appearance and contents of the German passport issued in Germany to foreign labourers. The Dutch chief drawing master in Colditz, Royal Dutch Naval Lieutenant van Lynden, helped us out by providing us with passports which, should the case arise, made it clear to anybody who might be interested in us that Drijber and I were Dutch labourers who had been working on an air-base in Poland and were now under orders to move to Ulm in Württemberg where we had to report to the labour office to apply for a job. From the advertisements in the German newspapers we knew that we would not have to wait long to obtain a decent job in the Ulm region. So our passports did not fail to give us confidence.

At the last moment another Dutch Naval officer Lieut-Commander van Doorninck presented me with a home-made compass. As we had to go across country for a while in the vicinity of the Swiss border, a compass might be very useful indeed.

When Friday came, we were ready to leave. At three o'clock completely equipped for the occasion, Drijber and I joined the others of the walk party in front of the closed doors of the gateway. We were, however, quite amazed to see that this time the walk party numbered more than twice its usual number. Instead of about eighty there were now some two hundred. When the doors were opened, we pushed our way through to the outer courtyard where our thirty German guards were waiting for us. We became quite a throng when we tried to line up for the roll-call.

But things went wrong. Probably it was only accidentally that the Chief Camp Officer, Captain Priem, was on the spot. Confronted with two hundred park-walkers instead of the usual eighty, he at once understood that something was brooding. But he knew how to handle the situation. With an ironic smile he addressed the PoW crowd, apologising that apparently it had not become known in time, that on this Friday the walk in the park had been cancelled. He regretted that we had not been warned earlier and suggested that we should forthwith retire behind the walls of our inner courtyard.

We could do nothing but obey. Back in our quarters we learned that our escape committee had urged some of our fellow prisoners to take part in the walk that Friday because they might be needed for camouflage purposes. But it had been overdone a little bit. The committee had underestimated everybody's desire to be helpful.

The trouble now was not only that our attempt had to be postponed, but that the Germans had become aware that there was another attempt in the making and would be more alert than ever.

Obviously we should try again as soon as possible, preferably the following day. But that would be on Saturday the 21st September, the very day of an important football match played between a Polish and a Dutch team in the park. It was decided we should make the attempt so at three o'clock we joined a much smaller crowd than the day before who were waiting at the gate. This time there were no more than sixty-seven men, namely the two teams, the referee with his linesmen, plus twenty-two Polish and twenty Dutch supporters, including Drijber and me.

When the gate was opened the German Feldwebel in charge told us he had strict orders not to allow the Dutch supporters to take part in the walk, since the walk – as we all knew – had been forbidden for the Dutch by Priem. Only the Dutch footballers were allowed to go outside.

The Dutch players protested at once. They were not going to play – they said – if there would be no Dutch supporters. Playing an important match without supporters would be no fun. This argument did not at all impress the Feldwebel. "It's all the same to me," he said, "whether you play or not." This seemed to be the end. We were already beginning to withdraw when one of the Poles found the solution. He reminded the Feldwebel that he was interfering with the intentions of the Camp Commandant whose wishes were that we play Olympic Games among ourselves. He warned the Feldwebel that his refusal to let the Dutch supporters out would not be appreciated by the German authorities.

This cogent argument convinced the Feldwebel, who gave in. "All right then," he said, "you may have your game." So he let us out and the whole party entered the circle of German guards and lined up in three ranks for the roll-call. Two guards started to count our number going from the right to the left, one in front of us along the front row and the other behind us along the back row.

I had found a place in the middle row. Just as the guards approached from the right I felt something touch my feet. Looking down I saw a small-sized Polish officer disappear under the cloak of my neighbour who was a tall Dutchman wearing a Polish uniform cloak. These Polish cloaks were extremely long, so long that they almost reached the ground. Under this cloak our Polish friend climbed on my neighbour's back. It happened so fast and so dextrously that the cloak had become motionless again when the guards passed.

At once I realised that the same trick was being played somewhere else in our ranks so that the guards would count two men less than were actually leaving the castle.

Nobody had noticed anything; so we were allowed to move down to the park, where the counting ceremony and the under-the-cloak trick were repeated, with the same result. The Germans now thought that our party was sixty-five strong, while there were in fact sixty-seven. So Drijber and I would have every chance to stay behind unnoticed when the party had to return to the castle.

The match started at once. Both parties' supporters were standing along the touchline, the Dutch on one side some twenty metres from the manhole and the Poles on the opposite side, all of us pretending to encourage our players with our cheers. In the meantime from behind the barbed wire thirty German guards were looking on, wondering whether the Poles or the Dutch were going to win, if not wondering if other things might happen too.

The Dutch supporters seemed to be not content with the place where they were standing, which was muddy, so we moved forward a few feet across the touchline in the direction of the manhole. When a few minutes later we moved forward again the players objected and said we were spoiling their game and should keep off the field. But that did not stop us from moving, step by step, nearer to the manhole. Another German Feldwebel, the one who was in command at the park, seemed to distrust our intentions. He circled around our party once or twice to find out what we could have in mind, but he couldn't see anything wrong.

Within half an hour the Dutch supporters were standing right on and immediately around the manhole, from where they continued to encourage their countrymen in their desperate struggle against the Poles. Again the Feldwebel seemed to be in doubt. Again he joined our group around the manhole, by whom he was, however, completely ignored. From the expression on his face it looked as if the poor fellow was wondering if he was making a fool of himself with his seemingly unmotivated distrust.

In spite of his alertness, he failed to notice that in the middle of our group somebody was desperately trying to unscrew the nut with our improvised monkey-wrench. This was a much harder job than we had foreseen. Half-time had already passed and still the nut resisted all efforts. We began to wonder if we should ever succeed.

Time went on. At last there were only ten minutes left before the end of the match, when my persistent cheers for a Dutch victory were suddenly interrupted by one of my friends who whispered in my ear, "The manhole is open. Jump in!" Within two seconds I was hidden in the manhole, where Drijber was already waiting for me, standing on the bottom. The cover was immediately put back in its place, but now with the pseudo bolt and nut. The real ones had already been handed down to Drijber in the manhole. We found we could stand on the iron steps fixed in its walls, with our backs leaning against the opposite wall. It was pitch dark inside.

Soon the match ended and from our hiding place we could hear what was happening. First the whistle signal for the PoWs to line up for the third roll-call; a few minutes later came the signal for the guards to withdraw and assemble around the PoW group. Another few minutes and we heard from the receding sound of human voices that the whole party had gone back to the castle. Then all was quiet.

After a quarter of an hour I pushed my shoulder against the cover above my head, moving it up until the plastic dummy bolt gave way and broke. I lifted the cover slightly and saw all was clear. In the park everything was quiet and with the setting sun still shining out of a blue sky the place looked more picturesque than ever.

I had planned to rip off the badges from the collar of my raincoat while I was in the manhole but there was no time for that. The only thing to do now was to turn up my collar to keep my military insignia hidden.

Half an hour later, I decided the moment had come to leave the manhole. Why wait any longer? So we both got out, put the cover and the steel bolt back in their places, screwed the steel nut on the bolt as far as we could with our hands and climbed over the barbed wire. The wall appeared higher than we had expected and it took us some time to get over it. On the other side were vegetable gardens. There was no question of a second and a third wall. From Smit and Dufour's story we knew that not far away we should cross a road, which we had to follow to the left. Before we got far we met an aged woman, working in her vegetable garden. Answering our most courteous "*Heil* Hitler" salute, she stared at us, but immediately looked away when she saw we had the *Völkische Beobachter*. At least I thought that this was the reason why she did not want to look at us any longer.*

We got to the road and turned left. A traffic sign indicated we were eight kilometres from Leisnig, the nearest railway station.

Our walk to Leisnig was one of the prettiest I ever enjoyed. It

* The old woman was one of the less serious cases from the neighbouring lunatic asylum. – *Reinhold Eggers.*

happened to be ideal autumn weather with a wonderful sunset in a picturesque landscape. From time to time we met some local Germans standing in front of their homes along the road, all of them very nice people, though they were not inclined to pay much attention to our correct "*Heil* Hitler" salute. There was some hesitation in their attitude when they half-heartedly raised their hand and whispered back "*Heil* Hitler". Once a group of Germans hesitated a little too long and only raised their hand after I had invitingly repeated my "*Heil* Hitler" and had given them a stern look.

When we arrived at Leisnig it was getting dark and reached the station just in time to catch the last train to Leipzig. We had only to pay a few Marks to the booking clerk when we asked for "*Zwei dritte* Leipzig". We found a compartment to ourselves and arrived at Leipzig about ten-thirty, where the night express to Regensburg was waiting for us; so we got tickets for: "*Zwei dritte* Regensburg", and jumped into the train.

At first we did not find a compartment which suited us as they were all closed and dark: obviously the travellers did not wish to be disturbed during the night. We preferred not to go into an occupied compartment without having any idea of what kind of people were in it, so it took some time before we found one with the lights on. It was occupied by two ladies who were talking through the open window to two gentlemen on the platform. We decided to take this compartment. Throwing the door open, we entered, shouting "*Heil* Hitler" at the tops of our voices, as if we were addressing a regiment instead of two females. The ladies' reaction to our impressive salute was pitiable. Shudders ran down their spines and their "*Heil* Hitler" in reply was hardly audible. We sat down and started to read the *Völkische Beobachter*. It reported Hitler's victory at Kiev, where according to the paper hundreds of thousands of Russians had been encircled and taken prisoner. So Drijber and I were soon engaged in a discussion – in the immaculate German we had acquired at Juliusburg and Colditz – about the prospects which the battle of Kiev might have for an early conquest of Moscow and the rest of the Soviet Russia.

When the train moved off we had to stop our conversation while the ladies waved good-bye to their menfolk who were seeing them off on the platform. Then the ladies turned round, took their suitcase out of the luggage rack and left the compartment with the most gracious "*Heil* Hitler" I have ever heard from female lips. As soon as the ladies left we turned out the light and went to sleep.

In the early morning we came to Regensburg, where we bought tickets for "*Zwei dritte* Ulm". Nothing happened until we arrived at Munich, where we would have to wait for three hours before the train to Ulm would leave. The station and the platforms were crowded with people, among them a great many men in the uniform of Reichswehr and Luftwaffe.

Although we were talking in almost impeccable German, we thought it unsafe to continue to walk up and down the platform for three full hours. No doubt sooner or later Drijber with his baby RAF jacket, and I with my untidy raincoat collar would attract attention. So we went into the waiting room, which was full of people; it took us some time to find an empty place. Sitting down we started to read, once again, the famous Kiev story, pretending not to notice that a woman with three small children was also taking a seat at our table. A few minutes later she asked us to be so kind as to take care of her children while she was away, so we were obliged to lay aside our paper and to entertain the children, a job we had not done for quite a time. But we got ample time to work ourselves in again to the details of our new job as the mother stayed away for an unusually long time. Then at last we were allowed to lose ourselves once more in the excitement of the Kiev campaign.

Up to now everything had been most reassuring. But then something happened. From the corner of my eye I saw a man rise from his seat and move in Drijber's direction. Besides reading his red-banded paper Drijber was smoking a cigarette. I didn't like this much as in those days one seldom saw Germans smoking cigarettes and, as far as I could see, nobody in the waiting room was smoking. The German, who was moving now in Drijber's direction, passed behind me and stopped in front of Drijber to ask him for a light. Trying not to betray that I felt extreme anxiety, I looked on to see what would happen.

Drijber's reaction was beyond all praise. For a while he remained motionless, looking at the German with an air as if he was wondering where the devil the other got the impertinence to trouble a fellow-citizen while he was reading the *Völkische Beobachter*. But seeing then the other one's unlighted cigarette, he at once resumed control of himself and changed his attitude. With a broad smile he answered the request by saying loudly, so loudly that everybody around could hear, two words in the most perfect German that had ever been spoken in Germany. He said: "*Aber selbstverständlich.*" Only an individual of unquestionable German descent could have pronounced "*Selbstverständlich*" as Drijber did. Any doubt which his open-breasted RAF jacket might have raised about his identity disappeared as snow in the sun. With a charming gesture he produced the requested light. Remaining seated, he offered it, taking care to keep it no higher than just above the table, so that the other one was forced to bow, even bow deeply, to get what he had been asking for. While Drijber, complete master of himself and the situation, resumed the reading of his paper, the other stumbled back to his seat, a prey to deep humiliation in spite of his lighted cigarette. Without doubt he had learned his lesson, that in these days one should not interfere with anyone who was reading the *Völkische Beobachter*, even if they were smoking cigarettes of non-German origin and were dressed in an outfit that looked more like the uniform of the enemy than what a decent German citizen was expected to wear in wartime.

The journey from Munich to Singen via Ulm passed off without any further incidents, though the train was crowded with people who apparently were highly enjoying their trip through the Bavarian countryside. All the time we had to share our compartment in the train with German families, but nobody seemed to notice that we were not the men we pretended to be. The *Völkische Beobachter* did its duty perfectly, though I had some trouble in keeping my interest in what was going on in Kiev.

Twilight was falling when we arrived at Singen. From now on we had to be extremely careful. When leaving the station we passed the station guard at the exit one by one, so that if one of us was caught, the other one might still have a chance to cross the border.

Soon we found the road to Gottmadingen. We didn't meet anybody. When we arrived at the viaduct we followed the railway. Still there was nobody to be seen. Only a train passed by and then we lay down to keep ourselves hidden. Soon we arrived at the spot where we had to leave the railway and turn off to the south. It was pitch dark but the sky was clear and filled with sparkling stars among which the Great Bear did not fail to show us the way. So we didn't need our compass after all.

When we approached the main road we hid again to let some farmers pass by. They were not stopped by anybody, which meant that at this spot there was no German sentry. So we could safely cross the road.

We were now about half a mile from what, according to Smit and Dufour's information, should be Swiss territory, namely the small piece of Swiss territory on the north bank of the Rhine, to the east of Schaffhausen.

After a ten minutes' cross-country walk over open fields we began to wonder if we were in Switzerland. Exactly at this moment a dog barked and in front of us a man cried "Schweiz!" We ran away as fast as we could. Then the man called again. I didn't catch what he said at once, but Drijber did. To my great surprise I saw him turn round and go to meet the man and his dog. Soon I saw them shaking hands and lighting cigarettes. Then I joined them.

The man was a Swiss policeman. After he had called "Schweiz!" he called again, this time in French, and Drijber had at once understood that he had called "Suisse!"

We were escorted to the nearest Swiss village. All the policemen there seemed to be quite pleased to have laid their hands on two Dutchmen instead of French soldiers, who used to cross the border at this spot almost every night, most of them having deserted from Bavarian farms where they had been set to work.

Happy though they seemed to be, our new friends of the Swiss police did not fail to lock us up in the local jail for the night. Next morning we were escorted to Schaffhausen amidst applause and other kind gestures from the Swiss public who appeared to be strongly anti-German and very friendly towards every PoW who had found the way to their country. Nevertheless we were locked up again; this time in the jail in Schaffhausen. This was a bitter disappointment for in this jail we were much worse off than we had been in Colditz. After my protest that the Swiss should not do such a thing to us, they changed their mind and in the afternoon we were released and allowed to stay in Hotel Schwan in Schaffhausen, until the Swiss authorities had gone through all required formalities. On our way to the hotel we were joined by two English officers who, the week before, had escaped from a PoW camp somewhere in the south of Germany.

We had to stay in Schaffhausen for five days. Then we were allowed to report to the Netherlands legation in Bern.

We used these five days in Schaffhausen to write a letter to the Dutch escape committee at Colditz, as we had promised to do should our attempt succeed. For the benefit of any successors we had to send them a report of all our experiences. In order to bypass the German censor we had arranged a code, a rather intricate one it was too, so it took us four days of hard work before the letter with its secret message was ready for transmission.

Only years later did I hear that it had safely arrived and that the Dutch–English pair Luteyn and Neave had used it to advantage when they left Colditz in January 1942.

We had made yet another promise. From Switzerland we would send to the Dutch escape committee an amount of German money and some files and it had been arranged that this prohibited stuff would be hidden in a wooden chessboard. In Bern we took care of this. Holes were bored in a chessboard, wherein we put the banknotes and the files. For this occasion the files were wrapped in a newspaper, not the *Völkische Beobachter,* but an edition of *Vrij Nederland*, the Dutch newspaper that was printed in London during the war. We were fortunate enough to get hold of a special edition, containing the address which a few weeks before had been delivered over the BBC in their programme "Radio Oranje" by Queen Wilhelmina of the Netherlands.

Contraband (maps and banknotes) smuggled into Colditz in a chess set

To my great satisfaction I learned afterwards that the chessboard had arrived in Colditz. When it had been broken open and the contents had been found, the escape committee took at first more interest in the wrapping paper than in the banknotes and files. In the evening a meeting was called in the Dutch quarters. There Major Engles read out to the assembled Dutch Colditz Group, as from then on they used to be called, Queen Wilhelmina's radio message to her people in occupied Holland, testifying Her Majesty's firm and unrelenting faith that in spite of all hardships the ruthless struggle in which Europe was involved would finally lead with the help of God to a glorious end.

In November 1945, when I happened to be for a few days in Batavia (Djakarta today), I had the good fortune to see again Captain, now Major van den Heuvel, the chairman of our escape committee. We had only half an hour to ourselves; not enough for me to go far into what had happened to me since I had left Colditz, and not enough for him to tell me how Colditz had reacted to our disappearance and what had become of the Colditz Olympic Games.

It was not given to us to see each other again. Two weeks afterwards Major van den Heuvel was killed in action when on patrol at the head of his infantry company in the hills of West Java, somewhere between Batavia and Bandoeng.

Lieut. John F. Watton

John Watton in 1940

4th Battalion The Border Regiment. Captured at Incheville, France by General Rommel's Ghost Division in June 1940. During his five years of captivity he drew some hundreds of his fellow prisoners' portraits in pastel, water colour and conté. Many of these drawings were sent to his father in Lyme Regis, via Portugal, and were later published in British and U.S. magazines before being forwarded to the prisoners' relations. John Watton now lives in Windermere with his wife and five of his nine children.

XV

Goodbye Colditz

BY JOHN WATTON

It would have been too difficult for me to escape from Colditz, as I did not consider myself competent to achieve the skill and effort required, but I did make an attempt when a few of us prisoners who, being considered harmless by the Germans, were being moved to the castle at Spangenberg. There were about eight of us in the custody of a squad of guards commanded by Captain Püpcke.

We travelled by train, second class, in quite good comfort. When we reached Sangerhausen, Püpcke allowed us out on to the platform to have a cup of coffee from a mobile coffee stall. I felt that this was a favourable moment to try to escape. The platform was crowded with Germans who had just got off the train and were walking past us.

I put my half-empty cup on the coffee trolley, and walked away into the crowd.

There was an uproar among the guards, not only on my account, but for another prisoner, Captain Jim Rogers, ('the old horse'), who chose this moment to divert attention from me, by diving under the train. He was caught, but the diversion gave me time to get lost in the crowd.

I kept walking, although I longed to run. All the people I met looked past me to where the guards were still causing an uproar. My route took me haphazardly down subways, up and down platforms, until I reached the sidings outside the station where a passenger train was standing. I went to it and climbed into a third class compartment, joining a group of German civilians who made room for me.

My fellow travellers took no particular notice, as my escape preparations had included my wearing a pair of paint-stained blue trousers and a blue jersey. I had worn these same clothes for months beforehand, so that the Germans who guarded us had grown to accept them as my normal and only wear.

When the train moved off, it went through the station and, to my horror, right past the spot where I had got away. I had got back into the same train I had just left! Out of the corner of my eye, I could see Püpcke directing operations for my recapture. No one spotted me, and the train picked up speed to clear the station.

After about ten minutes, I decided to go to the lavatory to recover my money and papers which were contained in my creeper – a cut down celluloid tooth-brush holder. Although the Germans searched us before our departure, they didn't bother about creepers as it would have taken too long to recover them. One was once taken from a Frenchman who had tied a piece of string to it to facilitate extraction.

When I got back to my compartment, I relaxed and smoked a Gauloise – my papers stated I was a French worker, a painter. Apart from a splitting headache I felt that events were happening in my favour – until the Ticket Collector came.

Everyone handed him a ticket except me. It would have been bad enough to be caught travelling without a ticket in England, but here in Germany it was awful. I said I was French and wished to buy a ticket. The ticket collector summoned a French-speaking German from the next compartment. I spoke to him in very fast, very bad French, to which he replied in an equally atrocious version of the language. He seemed to be satisfied I was harmless and so were the other Germans in the compartment. "Look at the paint on his trousers," they said. "That shows he's a painter."

"All right, where did you board the train, then?" asked the ticket collector. Where? I had no idea, so I appealed to my fellow passengers.

"Sangerhausen," they all said, anxious to help me.

But by now the ticket collector was more than suspicious and called the Railway Police. I knew the game was up, so I took out a packet of twenty Players cigarettes and handed them around to my fellow-travellers who accepted them with thanks and amusement.

When we reached Nordhausen, I was escorted off the train by two railway police, who made me look more dangerous than I was. The police cleared a way for me through the crowds, who looked at me with astonishment, as if they wondered why such a harmless-looking person should be under such a heavy guard.

My guards took me to the police station where I was given a meal. After about half an hour, Püpcke arrived to collect me. He drew his pistol and ushered me in front of him out of the building, through the streets and back into a train to Spangenberg.

For that episode, Jim Rogers and I were sentenced to ten days' solitary confinement in the Spangenberg cells. But as we were allowed Red Cross food, musical instruments, books, painting materials and so on we enjoyed what amounted to no more than a

pleasant room-arrest. I painted a large self-portrait in oils and practised plain-chant, with the help of a recorder to find the notes. Jim
played his guitar. It was pleasant to paint while listening to really
excellent guitar music played in a nearby cell.

After we had been in Spangenberg for a few months, the Germans discovered, below the castle, a huge tunnel which had been
carved out of the living rock over a period of years by the regular
prisoners of Spangenburg. We, the newcomers, were credited with
this great feat of tunnelling and were promptly returned to Colditz.

It was true that we helped a little with the tunnel. I extracted
about eight ounces of rock with a hammer and chisel after two
hours' exhausting work by the light of a wick burning in a tin of fat.
On the other hand, Jim Rogers, who was a mining engineer, chisel-
led out more rock than anyone, so there may have been some justi-
fication in the Germans returning us to Colditz. We took with us
two of the St Nazaire Commandos who had escaped from Spangenberg and been recaptured after several weeks on the run.

It was comparatively good to get back to our international
friends in Colditz. Somehow it was good too, to see again the old
familiar faces of the German guards with their *Gefreiters* and *Feld-
webels*; even the German officers Püpcke and Eggers.

The Day
"*Bitte, meine Herren, weg! Es ist noch nicht schluss.*"*

That was the last German order I was given, just before American troops from General Hodge's 1st Army released me, on 16th
April 1945, from the international PoW camp at Colditz.

When we heard the sound of approaching troops, a crowd of us
prisoners rushed to the closed gates of the inner courtyard, where
we found ourselves faced by the German Duty Officer, Captain
Hans Püpcke, who stood with his back to the gates and gave us his
last order.

We stopped and waited in silence for a few moments.

Then the gates were slowly opened by a single US soldier, who,
startled at the roar of cheering which greeted him, shouted at us to
keep clear. He held us at bay with his rifle until he was joined by
other GIs whom we reassured with an invitation to have some tea
and a smoke in our quarters. We gave them a change of socks and
cleaned their rifles for them as well. I noticed a striking contrast between the strong, healthy, dusty, tanned faces of the GIs, and the
pale pink, bony faces of the prisoners, or should I say ex-prisoners.

* "Please, gentlemen, get back! It is not over yet."

The effect of the exchange of roles between ourselves and the Germans made me feel as if I had experienced an evolutionary jump, like being re-born, for I felt like a different person, especially,

German guards playing cards outside the door of the inner courtyard: sketched by John Watton as he waited to go on a park walk

when I was appointed gate-guard to the inner courtyard. My badge of office was a whistle on a lanyard. All the German staff were now our prisoners and a group of them were standing close beside me. Some of their relations from the town came up to see them. One elderly lady came to me and held out for my inspection a paper bag in which were a few sandwiches. "*Mein Mann. Mein Mann,*" she begged, asking if she could give them to her husband. I let her go to him at once. She was the first woman who had spoken to me in five years.

After my turn of guard duty, I decided to explore the German Kommandantur. The place seemed to be deserted* except for a few

* All the German staff, except Captain Püpcke and the paymaster Heinze had already been taken away into captivity by the Americans.

French officers who were tearing down racks of German correspondence files and strewing the letters along the corridors.

I knocked on a door which was opened by the German Paymaster Heinze. We exchanged greetings. He told me that the water
had been cut off and that his lavatory was useless. I expressed my
sympathy and moved on down the corridors until I reached
Püpcke's quarters. His wife invited me in to see her husband who
was sitting on the bed. She said he found it very difficult having no
duties to perform for the first time in many years. While we were
talking, Alan (Black) Campbell called to pay his respects to the
Püpckes and to ask if he could help them in any way. All we could
do was to give them some of our Red Cross supplies. I brought over
a box full of tinned meat and dried milk together with a certificate
stating that the food had been given to the Püpckes by us. This was
in case there were any questions as to where the food had come
from.

In the afternoon of the day of release, I went down to explore the
small town of Colditz. I found American troops with their tanks
and armoured fighting vehicles dotted about in the squares and
other open places. One of the vehicles, a species of armoured car
with a large gun, had the name 'Butcher Boy' painted on it in white.

As I walked down the main street, where long queues of townspeople waited outside the few shops which were open, a beautiful
little German girl of about eleven came to speak to me. She wore
pig-tails, was neatly dressed in a flowered frock and seemed very
self-confident. She asked me if I would buy her some coffee, offer-
ing me her ration book and some money.

"Why should I get coffee instead of you?" I asked.

"Because you can jump the queue to get it," she said. I had no
idea that an ex-prisoner could enjoy such a privilege. But no one
objected when I went into the shop, where I was served at once, to
the delight of the little girl. She asked me to help her again. "Come
with me," she said, and took me to her home at the other end of the
town. There on her doorstep were the bodies of two dead Germans
in civilian clothes. "Would you please have them removed?" she
asked. I went to where a group of US troops stood nearby and
asked if the bodies could be moved.

"Sorry, can't be done," I was told. "They were werwolf types
who fired on us. We have to leave the bodies there as an example." I
regretfully told the girl that nothing could be done, so she thanked
me and went back into her house.

I continued my tour of the town and decided to see if I could get a
meal. Feeling like the man who walked up and down to see where

he could dine in town, at last I found an hotel which was open. I entered it and sat down at a table in the deserted dining room. A waitress came and told me there was only potato soup on the menu, so I ordered a plateful, which tasted only slightly better than prison rations. While I was enjoying my soup, half a dozen of the hotel staff stood in the doorway to the kitchen and watched me until I had finished. When I called for the bill, they told me, with astonishment, that there was no question of my paying – the meal was free. I thanked them all for their hospitality and went out to have a walk by the river Mulde.

On the bank I found two small boys aged about five, playing together among the bushes. On the ground nearby was a German stick grenade. I warned the boys not to touch it.

"Ach, we know all about that," they said scornfully. "It's only a hand-grenade." I felt I had insulted their intelligence, so I went back into the town where I met an old man who invited me to meet two old ladies with whom he shared a flat. I could hardly understand what they said for they all spoke at once, but I believe they told me how they dreaded the future.

On my way back to the castle I was asked for some soap by two Hitler Jugend boys of about fourteen. I said I'd give them some if they asked their mother to wash an old shirt for me. They agreed, so I fetched them one of my shirts and a few cakes of soap. They told me they would bring me my shirt back at teatime, but if they did I missed seeing them.

That evening I heard how the other ex-prisoners had been out exploring the district. One had bought a car; another a motor bike. Some had repaired the damaged water-works; a Marine had acquired a sub-machine gun. All manner of goods were available, from which I had a share of several cases of excellent cigarettes – Papistratos I believe they were called. They lasted me for months.

As the British were to be taken to England, we unloaded our surplus goods on to the 2,000 French ex-prisoners who had to remain behind for a few days. I handed over my possessions to a Parisian. I took with me a few toilet articles, a box of vine charcoal from the Pelikan works, my cigarettes and a little food. I would have liked to have taken more, but only hand-luggage was allowed as we were to be flown out of Germany. I did store a crate of drawing materials in the castle attic but I have never recovered them.

On the morning of our departure we assembled in the inner courtyard, ready to march down to the trucks the Americans had ready for us in the town. Captain Püpcke came from his quarters to join us in the courtyard. The curious thing about this, was that following a few paces behind the Captain was one of our Scottish officers, staggering under the weight of a huge valise – Püpcke's baggage.

When we got to the town, we found a small crowd of Germans watching the US negro truck drivers, who were entertaining their audience with some sort of dance. We showed Püpcke to the leading truck, but before he got in, he saluted the Colditz townspeople. He saluted slowly, while he turned first in one direction and then in another. Then as if he was in command of the whole convoy, he took his seat in the front of the leading truck and we moved off.

The truck ride across Germany to our airport was nerve racking as there were still active pockets of the enemy on our route. We went fast, the negro drivers sweeping anything in their way off the road. I saw a German farmer with a horse and cart which had been driven off the road. He was bouncing up and down as if he was on a trampoline, behind his bolting horse.

Tank tracks were everywhere. Bomb damage was evident even in the smallest villages. Once we passed a battery of US gunners in action. Russians who had escaped from prison camps trudged in the ditches.

The route we followed went by the US name "Trample". This name was posted on roadside trees at frequent intervals.

Our destination was the German airport at Koelleda. The place had been badly bombed, but the staff quarters and office buildings had been cleverly camouflaged with black paint to look as if they had been bombed and burnt out. I had a look around some of the buildings and found the rooms were in good condition, albeit very untidy, with clothing and papers scattered on the floors.

In an aircraft repair section of the airport, I found the fuselage of a Messerschmitt standing on stilts. I asked a GI if I could climb up and have a look inside the cockpit.

"No need to climb up," he said, as he dragged the body of the aircraft off its stilts and sent it crashing in ruins to the ground so that I could see it more closely.

The whole airport was littered with all manner of valuable debris. I found a camera for taking aerial photographs, but it was far too large to fit into my haversack, so too were other items I would have liked to take away – weapons, radios, mysterious pieces of electronic gear and other nameless stuff which lay about under the shattered concrete hangar roof suspended in pieces by steel threads. It looked most unsafe.

After an excellent meal of American K rations, I joined the others to board Dakotas which flew us out of Germany 2,000 feet above a landscape covered with craters and tank tracks. In the afternoon, we landed in England where we were met by a small crowd of pretty WAAFs who offered to carry our hand luggage. Some of us would not part with our meagre belongings.

After a meal, we were put into trucks and taken to a main reception centre. On the way, we were cheered and waved at by children who threw sweets into the trucks for us. The only ex-prisoners who enjoyed this were the foreigners, our Turkish and Arabian Special Agents, who were delighted. The rest of us kept well into the interiors of the trucks.

It was late at night when we reached the reception centre – an old house in the country – where all the formalities of taking our names and so on were dealt with at once. After a short sleep followed by breakfast, we were issued new battledress; badges were sewn on by a team of ladies. I collected £10 and a travel voucher. By noon I was on the express from Waterloo to Lyme Regis.

The shock of freedom struck me while I was standing in the corridor, when the train was travelling at speed near Templecombe. The false freedom I had experienced after my release in Germany became like a dream remembered where one could escape the consequences of any crime – by waking up.

I wondered what had happened to Püpcke. Before we left Germany, we had asked the Americans if we could take him back to England with us. Unhappily this was not allowed. I remembered how he had collected me at Nordhausen after my attempted escape, and had marched me through the streets at gun point. I thought how lucky I was to have been collected by Püpcke instead of the Gestapo who might have ended my days in the Nordhausen Concentration Camp.

Now in England, I began to enjoy the years of peace, but somehow I felt that my captivity was not completely behind me. I was still a prisoner, albeit a more happy one. My release in Germany was from a small prison into a larger one, where I had to travel a bit further than across the courtyard to visit the French, Dutch, Belgians and Poles. Waiting five years for release from Colditz was replaced by a longer wait, for what? I asked other ex-prisoners what they were waiting for, now they were free. One said, "I am waiting for the Day."

One of the joys of peace, thirty years after captivity, has been to correspond with my old prison jailers, Doctor Eggers, and, until his death, in July 1971, with Hans Püpcke. I shall never forget his last command:

"*Bitte, meine Herren, weg! Es ist noch nicht schluss.*"

Captain Hans Püpcke

Hans Püpcke

Born 1892. A lieutenant of Artillery in World War I. Became Camp Officer at Oflag IVC Colditz in March 1941, remaining there as a captain until the capitulation on 16th April 1945. A prisoner of the Americans until June, mainly at Hersfeld. Imprisoned by the Russians in Halle prison 1946–8. The British helped his family to Hanover, via Berlin. Freed through diplomatic channels from captivity at Halle. Lived at Hanover and later Essen, managing a laundry. Eldest son joined the French Foreign Legion and died in Indochina. Two other sons live in West Germany. Captain Püpcke died at Essen in July 1971.

XVI

No Easy Job

BY HANS PÜPCKE

When I was posted to Colditz, on 11th March 1941, I held the rank of a full Lieutenant of the Reserve and had previously been stationed at Halle as officer-in-charge of the security and sabotage prevention in local factories. Before the war, I had managed a small sweet factory. My family had owned, with a partner, a much larger confectionery business, Püpcke and Berner of Halle, which had been lost in the difficult years after the inflation of the 1920s.

At Colditz, I was appointed assistant to Rittmeister (equivalent to Captain's rank) Aurich, who was the officer-in-charge of the Schuetzenhaus. Both camps were commanded by Colonel Max Schmidt who was assisted by Captain Priem and Lieut. Eggers.

Priem and Eggers were schoolmasters, both very different in character. The merry Priem liked a good drink, cigarettes and jovial company round the table, where he amused his companions with an unending succession of jokes, the quality of which rose in proportion to his consumption of alcohol. He was the only officer of the staff who dared to oppose, albeit jokingly, the martinet, Max Schmidt.

Eggers was a more ascetic type who followed rigid principles and kept himself under strict control. He neither smoked nor drank, seldom joined parties, but enjoyed a game of Skat. Both Priem and Eggers differed in their treatment of the prisoners in their charge. Priem was always ready for a joke, quick at repartee, sometimes not quite sober when holding a parade. He would salute in a mocking manner, grin knowingly at the prisoners when he counted them, and was altogether too easy-going. Priem had been at Colditz since it assumed its latest role as a prison camp and his rejection of the internationally accepted Prussian-style military discipline resulted in unmilitary rebellious behaviour on the part of the prisoners. On the other hand, Eggers tried to treat them with complete justice, but with the strict discipline of an old soldier of the Prussian kind and as a schoolmaster.

As for myself, I stood between my two colleagues. Like Priem I enjoyed, the good things of life but I disapproved of his lax discipline. Here I agreed with Eggers.

My first superior, Captain Aurich had just come to Colditz like me. In civilian life he had been a stocking manufacturer in Chemnitz, a town world-famous for its stockings. He was a much-travelled man who spoke English and French perfectly. Compared with Priem he was inexperienced but, according to military tradition, Aurich as the senior amongst us expected us all to address him in the third person, for example, "Would Herr Rittmeister like a glass of wine?" This had been customary in the German Army for centuries, but Hitler had introduced the address 'you' coupled with the rank – "Would you, Herr Rittmeister, like a glass of wine?" Priem had simply laughed at the old fashioned form of address. As for Lieut. Eggers and myself, we were definitely juniors and had to obey orders, asking our superiors' approval for the most trifling decisions.

Priem behaved as if Aurich did not exist – which provoked a conflict, so the Commandant, Max Schmidt, made Priem responsible for the castle and Aurich responsible for the Schuetzenhaus. This arrangement improved the atmosphere for a time, but in the long run Priem had the best chance of surviving as he was a close friend of the Adjutant Captain Kunze. The Commandant, too, liked Priem for bringing a bit of colour into the life of the castle.

Some months later Aurich was transferred to Stalag IVB at Hohnstein where Eggers had passed his apprenticeship as a prison officer in 1940. Since then it had become a much larger PoW camp.

At Colditz, Priem remained the first camp officer up to January 1943; that was the dreadful winter when Hitler ordered General von Unruh to find him at least half a million soldiers for the Eastern front by reducing the strength of the Home Army by about one third. From the very moment of his arrival General von Unruh had full power to act independently of any authority of the Home Army, whatever the rank of those he had to deal with. We called his men, who acted as a sort of press gang, "Heldengreifkommission [Commission for seizing heroes]". Only the doctors could free a man from being sent to the East. Priem's precarious health was watched over by a committee of doctors at Leipzig. They decided that he could no longer remain in the army, not even as a Camp Officer at Colditz. He was dismissed, went to his home near the old Polish frontier and took up his former position as a headmaster. On 17th August 1944, Priem was found in his bed, having died from an apoplectic fit which his doctors had expected.

So Oflag IVC had lost two Camp Officers: Aurich and Priem. They were replaced by Eggers and myself, thus reducing the number of Camp Officers from four to two, which satisfied General von Unruh.

It was now up to Eggers and me to guard and tame the bad boys who, since 1940, had become, to say the least, unruly.

When Eggers became Security Officer in February 1944, I was the only Camp Officer. By then the Schuetzenhaus had been closed and in the castle only about 300 Anglo-Saxon prisoners remained. Eggers and I had to fight on two fronts: against the prisoners and against our superiors. The Commandant, Colonel Prawitt, was our Benjamin on the staff; only forty-four years old, an active officer and Commandant of Colditz since February 1943. His second-in-command Major Amthor had come to Colditz in April 1943. He had been a merchant from Cologne and was an outspoken adherent of Hitler. Both Prawitt and Amthor tried to make us tame the mutinying mob in the castle by using arms. We wanted to restore discipline by military means and court martial punishments – not by shooting.

Prawitt himself tried using arms a few times, allowing the guards to shoot into the windows of the prisoners' quarters, from where they had shouted insults at him. When the shooting failed to subdue the prisoners, he avoided entering their inner courtyard and quarters as far as possible.

Amthor used to be greeted with whistles when he took a parade. To try and stop this he ordered the roll-call to be repeated, but to no avail. Each time Amthor entered the yard the whistling began again. At last after repeated roll-calls he failed to reappear. Then all was quiet.

Amthor did not order us to shoot, but he tried to induce us to do so when the prisoners became particularly unruly. We disobeyed him. He rebuked us sharply: "Do you still refuse? If I replace you with a sergeant my orders would be executed." I replied, "I am an old captain and do not allow myself to be influenced like a young recruit."

When Amthor attacked Eggers by saying, "All you are doing here is *Scheiss*!" Eggers defended himself by applying to the Adjutant for a posting to another camp. As he was the only officer who could speak French and English, Eggers was not allowed to leave Colditz and Amthor was obliged to apologise by saying that what he had meant was that Eggers' work in Colditz was beneath his qualifications.

At last, in July 1943, the German High Command put an end to this untenable situation by transferring all the prisoners who were not Anglo-Saxons to other camps according to their nationality. The British then modified their mutinous behaviour as they appreciated the advantages they had in Colditz Castle, and did not want to lose them. In spite of the evacuation of non-Anglo-Saxons, Prawitt received an enquiry from Field Marshal von Keitel of the German High Command, who sent a commission to Colditz to investigate the reasons why the prisoners were so embittered.

After July 1943 a *modus vivendi* was reached between the prisoners and camp officers as well as between the latter and their superiors. This semi-truce lasted until the fall of Colditz in April 1945. As for Amthor, the truce ended when he became Chief of an SS Unit which had the abortive task of preventing the Russians reaching Dresden. Amthor was never captured like the rest of us. Prawitt became a prisoner of the Americans at Hersfeld, together with Eggers, Ullrich and myself, and was to show what other qualities he possessed after the loss of his position as commandant, but that is another story. . . .

After this very rough outline of my Colditz career I want to describe in detail the last days of Oflag IVC from 12th to 16th April 1945.

On Friday 13th April 1945 the *Prominente* Prisoners were transferred by order of the High Command to Oflag IVA, Königstein. The General Kommando of the district, normally at Dresden, had moved to Glauchau to the south of Colditz, from where he sent two buses for the *Prominente*. Major Howe, the second-in-command succeeding Amthor, and Captain Eggers the security officer, were responsible for their transport. Captain Strauss of the Guard Company with a number of soldiers was in charge of the buses to prevent escape attempts. Major Howe and the Polish *Prominente* travelled in the first bus, and in the second was Captain Eggers with the Anglo-Saxon *Prominente*. The buses left Colditz Castle on 13th April at 1 am.

Captain Eggers had promised the British Senior Officer, Colonel Tod, to bring back a letter in Romilly's handwriting to certify that the *Prominente* had arrived safely. As soon as Eggers returned to Colditz he handed this letter to Colonel Tod.

On Saturday 14th April, our guards returned from Königstein by the very last train to Leipzig. Traffic had stopped. Soon after that morning parade (for we still kept to our daily routine), we had orders from Glauchau to destroy all documents, evacuate the castle and go eastwards, crossing the Freiberger Mulde at Tanndorf. Colonel Tod, however, ordered the prisoners to remain in the castle. Commandant Prawitt reported this to the Glauchau authorities by one of the last telephone connections available. He was ordered not to use arms to make the prisoners obey, but the Senior British officer had to take full responsibility for any casualties suffered by the prisoners during the coming battle, which seemed imminent. This Colonel Tod agreed to do, on condition that the Commandant would hand over the castle to the Americans when they came.

There were no more telephone calls after this. Late in the afternoon of the 14th, the Commandant and the senior officers of the prisoners, Brigadier Davis and Colonel Tod for the British, and Colonel Duke for the Americans, met in the Kommandantur to discuss the details of the German capitulation. (The three French generals who were imprisoned in the castle refused to participate in negotiations.) The result of this meeting was the so-called *Safe Conduct Document*, which was indeed a witness of the noble way in which prisoners may react after years of captivity, to even the sometimes hard but nevertheless correct way in which we treated them. The *Safe Conduct Document* was written in German and in English; it afforded some privileges and protection to our staff and German soldiers of Oflag IVC.

At this time, there was a large number of French prisoners in the castle, who had come from Oflag IVD Elsterhorst. They had been evacuated some weeks before when the Russians advanced into their district. I did not know how many French we had then. To the first 1,500 who came to us at that time, many more were added, brought in from the camp at Zeithain during the following week or so. These French were only housed in the castle and they had their own administration, so since their arrival our roll-calls were understandably unreliable, but what prisoner could be interested in escaping in such circumstances?

The British would soon be the real masters of the castle, yet they seemed to look at the approaching events with the coolness which is characteristic of their race. Certainly it was one of Colonel Tod's most valuable qualities. He stood firmly in the confusion of those days.

On 14th April, the prisoners handed to Lieut. Lance Pope all their receipts for private property which had been kept in our Security Department for them. In return for the receipts Captain Eggers issued all the numerous objects which had been taken from their owners at the time of capture. Besides this, he was busy burning all the staff records of the different departments. He did this in the central heating system and it proved to be very difficult. Our Paymaster distributed provisions of food and other material. Many useful articles came from Eggers' secret room where parcels for German prisoners were kept – an enterprise which ran under the name of "Ekkehard". Soon we too should become prisoners and these articles were more than welcome.

I packed a few extra necessities for captivity, helped by my wife and my youngest son who lived with me in the castle. They had been bombed out of their house at Halle during a recent air-raid. It was the same with the families of Captain Vent from Leipzig and Major Amthor from Cologne. Recently, Prawitt's wife with their baby son, a few months old, had fled from Hirschberg in Silesia when the Russians arrived there. We all of us knew that the end of our control of the castle was near.

On Sunday 15th April 1945, the night was quiet. We heard guns firing from the direction of Leipzig. German troops no longer marched singing from there into the Mulde region as they had been doing recently. Our sentries stood on guard as before, but without ammunition for their rifles. One of the surrender conditions was that our ammunition had to be deposited in a strong-room, the key of which had to be handed to the new master of the camp, Colonel Tod. With stubborn steadiness and iron discipline, he steered a course which achieved a minimum of possible losses in the castle and a maximum of quiet and safety. He agreed to my proposal to place British officers as guards at the main gate, to keep everybody inside the prisoners' part of the castle until he believed it was time to afford freedom of movement to the now released prisoners.

A perfect spring sunrise heralded this Sunday, the historic end of Oflag IVC. A blue sky, clear quiet air and a landscape absolutely without movement. No church bells called the faithful to prayer. The battlefield around the castle was as empty as the most modern commander-in-chief could wish. Were the German leaders so perfect, or was the emptiness a consequence of their lack of troops? The view from the castle to the west was limited by the forest of Colditz. In front of it, to the left, we could see the village of Hohnbach in the valley. Below the castle, the river Mulde wound its way among rocks and small woods from the south, past the village of Lastau and under a railway bridge. In the centre of the picture, we saw the fields and meadows of Hohnbach and Thumirnicht, a small suburb of Colditz on the far banks of the Mulde. Some defiles with bushes cut through the gently rising ground.

Directly below the castle was the town of Colditz, with no traffic in its streets or over the Adolf-Hitler bridge. It was time for the usual Sunday service. But that day, real prayers were offered to the Almighty; death was expected at any moment.

The prisoners looked from the windows of the western walls of the castle. How tense they felt! Half of them would be freed after up to five years' captivity. The other half would go into captivity – for how long? Soon the curtain of this drama must rise.

There they were! Five enemy tanks had entered the open fields in front of Colditz forest. They manoeuvred there for a while unchallenged. No shells were fired at them. No hidden troops fired bazookas. Neither our own nor the enemy's aircraft attacked. Shells fired from the tanks set fire to a few houses in Hohnbach – no counter-attack from there, but what was this? A small-calibre shell had hit the castle on the roof of the lodge on the stone bridge. Some of our soldiers, with Captain Vent, were waiting there for the Americans, but nobody was hurt so they moved into a room in the big tower. A second shell went through one of the windows of Wing Commander Bader's room, without causing casualties.*

At about noon, a battery of howitzers began firing at the castle and the town. The shells came from behind Hohnbach, so it looked as if the south-west side of the castle would be hit. One shell opened the whole front of an empty house which had been used by castle officials – just opposite the lodge at the stone bridge. Another shell hit Prawitt's quarters where the kitchen and a room was demolished. Nobody was hurt. A third shell exploded in the outer yard between the southern terrace and the official's house. Here Feldwebel Baer of the Guard's Company was wounded. He was taken to Doctor Giering in the Terrassenhaus nearby, but in vain. Shell splinters had torn open his bowels and he later died. He was the only one killed among the guards. The tanks later disappeared towards the Hohnbach valley, leaving the battlefield empty. Three German guns, sited somewhere in the Tiergarten, kept firing almost without interruption at a target we could not see, possibly an American battery.

So this spring Sunday ended, without any decision. During the battle we had tried to blow up the bridge over the Mulde, but as the charge was insufficient, only one side of the concrete roadway had been torn away, allowing passage for one-way traffic.

During the night of 15th–16th April, the shooting became more vehement: machine-gun fire with tracer bullets continued for some hours. It was concentrated between Lastau and Colditz where, among the rocky and hilly banks of the Mulde, the Germans had their centre of resistance in a kaolin pit. During this firing, the factory of Eismann & Stockmann was burned down.

The Americans had managed to cross the river by the railway bridge near Lastau and they started to turn the German flank. To avoid this, the Germans evacuated the kaolin pits and the nearby Tiergarten. Just before dawn on Monday 16th April the firing stopped and the last hours of Oflag IVC began.

* It is believed that Wing Commander Bader was knocked to the ground and Major Dollar, who was with him at the time had his spectacles broken. – *John Watton*

Early that morning, a heavy shell fired from a mortar exploded at the foot of the rocks of the castle. I was, theoretically, on duty and stayed in the inner courtyard. The British had made a Union Jack and the French a Tricolour which they at once hoisted from the windows of the Saalhouse overlooking the river from where the Americans were expected to arrive. Had their artillery observers seen the flags? As there was no safe spot in the castle against such heavy shelling, something had to be done, so I went through to the German courtyard where I met Prawitt surrounded by almost all his staff officers. I asked him whether there was any reason against our displaying both the Allied flags from the roof of the Saalhouse. Prawitt had no objection, so I arranged for the flags to be shown from the roof. Soon afterwards the heavy battery stopped firing.

Our German unit had retreated from the region of the Tiergarten to avoid being rounded up by the Americans who, having crossed the Mulde, began to occupy the town later in the morning without opposition. Small groups of GIs crossed the damaged bridge and infiltrated into the streets. During this time I had been with my family in the Kommandantur building. Most of the German officers were waiting in the German yard. Captain Vent was watching the town from a room in the castle tower. Colonel Tod ordered some of his officers to be ready to guard the castle entrances. Captain Eggers got ready a complete list of the names of all former prisoners of Oflag IVC.

Soon after 9 am an American patrol of three or four GIs entered one of the outer courtyards. No British were there to greet them as Colonel Tod had made them all stay in the inner courtyard. Some British officers, however, were in the Saalhouse, in Bader's room, and waved to the first Americans from the windows. Captain Eggers went to the US Sergeant, the leader of the patrol, and explained the situation. The Sergeant immediately brought Eggers to his officer who was quartered in a small house at Thumirnicht on the western bank of the Mulde. Captain Eggers reported to him and delivered the lists of prisoners' names. The American captain telephoned to his superiors and then sent Captain Eggers back to the castle with the order that all German officers should wait there until the Commanding Officer, Colonel Shaughnessey, or an officer of his staff, should come for their formal surrender. Instead of this, some other American soldiers arrived bringing us the order that all German officers should come forthwith to the local Commandant, the Captain at Thumirnicht. At this time, Captain Eggers had the bad luck to be in the cellar under the magazine building where he had stowed his luggage for captivity. When he came back into the yard he found everyone had gone, so he hurried out after his comrades, not realising at the moment that he was now a prisoner-of-war himself. Fortunately, Colonel Tod who had been looking over the German quarters in the castle, met him and called for Lieut. Walker to act as a guide and to escort Captain Eggers safely to the Americans.

I remained in the castle, as Brigadier Davis, Colonel Tod and Colonel Duke (USA) had ordered me to stay in my quarters. An officer was posted there as my guard and I was provided for in the best possible way, as were my wife and son. We could go for walks down to the park with the friendly company of our guard. Late in the afternoon I was ordered to come to our former officers' mess where I met the American, Colonel Shaughnessey. He appointed me liaison officer between the rest of the Germans and Colonel Tod at the request of the leading Allied officers.

Besides myself, Paymaster Heinze was the only member of our staff who had remained in the castle. He offered to provide food for the now liberated prisoners. This offer was accepted, but not just in a friendly manner. Heinze had often been destructive when the prisoners made special requests, but generously, the British declined to use this opportunity for petty revenge.

During this time I had lived undisturbed with my family in my own dwelling, and had seen little of the events around me. I well remember seeing two radio sets working at full power, but I never saw the famous Colditz glider.

I was asked to pack my baggage for my captivity, as the British wanted to take me with them to England. We travelled in trucks to the airfield at Koelleda in Thuringia, but here the American officer in charge of air transport refused to let me board a plane. Colonel Duke dictated a letter to one of the American officers, explaining my situation as a prisoner of the British army. Besides this, Colonel Duke stated that I had carried out my duties correctly and in accordance with International Law, but to no avail. The Americans took me to the prisoner-of-war concentration place at Naumburg/Saale where I met my Colditz comrades. With them I was taken to the next camp – Wellda in Thuringia. Together with Prawitt, Eggers and Ullrich I was kept back by the Americans as hostages for the *Prominente* until about 10th May when they reached the Americans safely. The four of us were then sent to Hersfeld on to Schwarzenborn and back again to Hersfeld, where I had the opportunity of seeing life from the other side of the barbed wire until I was returned to my home at Halle/Saale in June 1945.

Colonel Leo W. H. Shaughnessey

Leo W. H. Shaughnessey

On 15th–16th April 1945 he was commanding the Task Force of the 9th US Armoured Division that took Colditz.

Born in Woburn, Mass. in 1910. Attended Boston College and US Military Academy at West Point – graduated 1934 and commissioned second lieutenant, US Army. Various duty assignments in United States, at Infantry School, Fort Benning and Command and General Staff College at Fort Leavenworth. Overseas tours included Military Police duty in Panama, several years in Europe during and after World War II with 69th and 3rd Infantry Divisions; as military attaché in Saigon; with the Atomic Energy Commission in the Pacific. Retired from army 1962. Arizona State University: Masters Degree in Education (1964). Now lives in Phoenix and teaches mathematics. Married, with four children. Awards include Silver Star, Bronze Star Medal (with cluster), Army Commendation Medal, Combat Infantryman's Badge, Parachutist Badge.

XVII

How Colditz was Conquered

BY LEO W. H. SHAUGHNESSEY

A United States Army task force is credited with the liberation of
Colditz on 15th–16th April 1945. This task force consisted of elements of the 69th Infantry Division and the 9th Armoured Division. I had the honour of commanding that unit.

The 69th Infantry Division, commanded by General Emil F.
Reinhardt, entered combat in the Siegfreid Line in early February
1945, as part of the First Army. My battalion, the 3rd Battalion,
273rd Infantry, engaged in pill-box action in the vicinity of Uden-
breth, Germany. We had several engagements in that area and after
the Siegfried defences fell, we proceeded eastward toward the
Rhine. Soon after the 9th Armoured Division captured the bridge
at Remagen we crossed the Rhine by boat just south of that point
and we continued to move to the east in what was shaping up as the
pursuit phase of the war. We crossed the Fulda River north of
Kassel in early April.

Shortly after this the 3rd Battalion of the 273rd was attached to
CCR, 9th Armoured Division, commanded by Colonel Charlie
Wesner. We were organised into a task force by the augmentation
of some armoured infantry, artillery and engineers. Our task force
was completely mounted on wheels or tanks and we set out across
the north German plain.

There were several divisions operating abreast, each with five to
eight somewhat parallel columns clearing the countryside of pockets of resistance and uncovering groups of refugees and Allied prisoners of war. We by-passed some towns and occupied others as
night stopovers and re-supply areas. There was not much personal
reconnaissance on our part and we depended on intelligence reports
for information as to what to expect ahead.

My task force was on a line which would take us somewhere between Leipzig and Dresden. We met varied resistance but, in general, our pace was rather rapid. Resistance increased as we
approached the environs of Leipzig and on 13th April we were held
up all day at the small town of Altengroitzsch. In late afternoon we

got an air strike to knock out that strong point, but only after my Company L had lost a dozen men. We continued our advance on the 14th to a place called Wilderhain just west of the Mulde River.

We moved out on Sunday 15th April, and were halted in the early afternoon in the town of Hohnbach by orders from Colonel Wesner to concentrate on the city of Colditz. Our instructions were to take Colditz in order to liberate a large number of Allied prisoners-of-war. Further information indicated that there were some VIPs among the prisoners.

Reconnaissance showed that there was a small, moss-covered, concrete bridge over the Mulde River directly into the city and a railroad bridge downstream a few miles. The concrete bridge appeared to be lightly defended with indications that it was mined. We weighed the chances of using either or both of these bridges.

We put artillery in position to shell the city as a prelude to launching an attack in the late afternoon. I was near the O. P. on the west bank when the early rounds were being zeroed in on the most prominent aiming point across the river. This was one of the towers of a rather large and imposing castle. After several rounds hit the turrets we observed three Allied red, white and blue flags appear at the upper windows of one of the buildings. This thrilling sight was the only signal we needed to know that the castle was the prison where the prisoners-of-war were being held. We moved the fire to other areas of the city and continued the attack.

Resistance was brisk in the early stages and we suffered some casualties, particularly three platoon sergeants whom I had recommended for battlefield promotions. We cleared the west side of the Mulde River before midnight and resumed our efforts at first light.

Because of the departure during the night of what we were told was the SS garrison of the city, we had no difficulty moving into Colditz on the morning of the 16th. Obviously the centre of interest was the castle and its inhabitants, both Allied and German. However, the security of the area was of greater importance militarily and this was my prime concern. Advance elements of my troops moved to the castle while others moved through the city to the high ground to the east with no opposition. We set up our CP in the castle.

When I got to the castle I was amazed and delighted to find the situation so well organised, patently by the Allied prisoners. The German guards were in custody and it was no problem accepting their surrender. I noted that these guards were well past the usual age for active military duty. We placed them under necessary security in their barracks, pending their being sent back to one of our PoW enclosures. I found it interesting that the 'sighting in' barrage we had directed at the castle the preceding afternoon landed in the quarters of one of the most hated prison guards and that this individual was the only casualty of our initial attack on the castle.

The matter of sending the guards, now turned prisoners, back to confinement was a task for my higher headquarters, the 9th Armoured Division. These details were taken care of by Colonel Johnson, the G-1 of the division. He arrived on the scene shortly after the area was secured and announced the arrangements. The newly acquired prisoners left with dispatch except for three or four who were permitted to remain at the request of the liberated Allies. One of these was a Captain Püpcke who, Colonel Florimond Duke, the senior American, suggested would act as German Liaison Officer on my staff, certainly a most unusual situation.

The 9th Armoured Division Commander, General John L. Leonard, visited Colditz Castle on the 16th. He commended my men for their performance while attached to his division. Also on that first day we were visited by American and other Allied war correspondents and photographers. It was not possible for me to be of much assistance to these newspeople as I was not conversant with all the details of the prison and my major concern was the security of the town and preparation against possible, though unlikely, counter-attack.

On that first day I was privileged to be asked to participate in a French-conducted *Te Deum*. Personnel of all faiths joined in this opportunity to express thanks for their liberation and deliverance.

Following the departure of the German guards, the next big event was the evacuation of the Allies. Colonel Johnson and his staff handled this and on the morning of the 18th the convoys to freedom started. It was indeed a happy and meaningful occasion for all of us, especially the liberated, some of whom had been held captive since Dunkirk. Besides the PoWs in the castle, there were more in another Oflag on the other side of town. These were, presumably, of lesser importance than the castle inmates or perhaps they were not as notorious in the art of attempting to escape.

There were reports and evidence of a small Jewish concentration camp in the city. My only recourse in this instance was to request Division Headquarters to notify the Red Cross. The individuals who had been in charge, allegedly SS personnel, were no longer in the vicinity.

It was not possible for me to grasp much of the details of the lives and backgrounds of the liberated inmates of Colditz Castle. From what little I assimilated, I learned that the prison was a special one for highly-feared or much-respected captured personnel, most of whom had a record of escape from other PoW camps; it was a 'post-graduate' prison. I heard that Colonel Duke was there because of his participation in an attempted coup in Hungary. Another American, Colonel Schaefer, was under sentence of death for refusing to obey an order in another prison camp.

I was told that some VIPs, called 'Hostages' or '*Prominente*', had been at Colditz until a few days before our arrival when they were moved out to the East, towards Dresden. Some of these were political prisoners, reportedly being held as hostages for exchange at the time of Germany's impending, inevitable defeat.

Besides the two colonels I've mentioned, I did not find out the names of the other Americans at Colditz; I understand that there were only about a half-dozen US prisoners. The only British officers whose names I recall directly from my experience at the prison camp site are a Brigadier Davis and a Colonel Tod. There are also only two French prisoners whom I remember first-hand: they are General Daine and his adjutant, Lieutenant Jean-Louis Thuilot: I know this last-named officer particularly because he wrote me after his return home to thank me for my part in his liberation. I visited him in Caen, Normandy, and corresponded with him for several years after the war.

From reports I heard later of Colonel Schaefer, he never returned to full active duty as he was incapacitated by his ordeals as a prisoner-of-war.

It was with Colonel Duke that I maintained the only close contact. We had frequent exchange of messages and visits until he passed away in April 1969. During the ten years prior we lived only a few miles apart in the environs of Phoenix, Arizona. Each 15th April we commemorated "Colditz Day".

The passage of time makes it difficult for me to recall completely my feelings and reactions of those several days at Colditz in April 1945. In a way, the mission to take Colditz was a routine assignment, consistent with the activities of my unit in the several days prior to that beautiful mid-April Sunday. However, to overrun an encampment of almost two thousand prisoners held in that area because of their importance, talents, and skill in attempting escapes, was certainly not a routine event.

I was impressed by the organisation and discipline of the prisoners. It was as if my task force did not capture Colditz; they had already done so and, on our arrival, they turned the establishment over to us. They were organised to help us help them. My observation of their morale was under the circumstance of their being about to be free but I sensed an aura of stability and courage among them. Much of this attitude might reasonably be expected of military men but they exhibited an *esprit* which had not been broken by

some four or five years of captivity, much of which was undoubtedly oppressive. They conducted themselves in the town and they
participated in staff meetings with 9th Armoured Division personnel in a way which indicated that they were certainly not demoral-
ised in spite of their ordeals.

In general, they were loath to discuss their ideas and ways of
trying to escape as if this reticence were part of a prisoner-of-war
code. They did show me their famous glider with great delight and
they explained the almost incredible project of launching it across
the Mulde valley in the spring when the leaves on the trees would
hide the flight of the glider from ground view. It was most impressive; I was proud of them and the way they had obviously conducted themselves in extreme adversity.

The 'Battle' of Colditz was certainly not a major military operation. The phase of the war, the diminishing potential of the
German Army, and the impending link-up of the American and
Russian forces made the actual capture of the city a rather com-
monplace action. It is true that the initial attack did meet frenzied
last-ditch resistance. Also, a defended Colditz Castle would indeed
have been formidable to take by ground attack without a long siege.

The most significant factor in the liberation of Colditz prison was
the fact that the prisoners themselves, alert to the situation, had, in
reality, captured the prison from within and had full control of
everything necessary to deliver it to us. The events of the next few
days, particularly the return to freedom of several hundred out-
standing military men held captive by Nazi Germany for many
months, made the capture of Colditz a noteworthy humanitarian
triumph rather than a military episode.

Reinhold Eggers

Reinhold Eggers

Born 1890. Trained as a schoolmaster. World War I: served with Marine Infantry Regiment I; became lieutenant; won Iron Cross classes I and II and Hess Medal for Bravery. Slightly wounded by French bullet 1915. Studied at Halle University 1929–34; qualified to teach in secondary schools; Doctor of Philosophy 1934. Disqualified by NSDAP for anti-Hitler utterings. Primary school teacher until war. Camp Officer at Hohnstein 1940, then Camp Officer at Oflag IVC Colditz until February 1944 – thereafter Security Officer. PoW of the Americans April-August 1945. Released and returned to teaching, and lecturing at Halle University. Captured by Russians and imprisoned 1946–55 at Sachsenhausen concentration camp and Torgau prison. Retired as headmaster since 1956. Now lives at Bodman/Bodensee.

XVIII

The Other Side of the Fence

BY REINHOLD EGGERS

Allied Occupied Territory

The run had ended the night before. For five years I had been playing the lead in an all-star non-stop drama entitled *Escape Fever*.
From 1940 to 45, I had been on the Staff of the ace Allied escapers'
prison camp, labelled Oflag IVC. The backdrop was the castle of
Colditz, in Saxony, Germany.

The prisoners' little joke throughout those years – "This is
Allied-occupied territory" – was now an established fact. US Army
Colonel Shaughnessey's 273rd Regiment held the stage now, and
we the late principals were waiting for our new casting.

It was Monday, 16th April 1945. Anticipating a very different
part from the one just played for so long, I had collected a few
props for future use. Alas, they had disappeared! I had overlooked
Stage Direction No. 1 – "The PoW never takes his eyes off his personal belongings." They had been liberated, down to the last razor
blade, matchstick and candle-end. This part was going to take some
learning. Above all, I must learn the feel of the other end of the
stick. I was the PoW now.

Suddenly, as several of us waited under guard down by the river,
there came a shout in English, but with a strange accent – "Commandant and Security Officer, front and centre!" This was my cue.
My Commandant went out in front, but I took centre stage, with
my knowledge of English. So it was for the next four months, the
two of us playing not a stage show on the same old set day after
day, but as it were in a film, with constantly shifting scenes.

The first was set in a farmhouse at Ballendorf, a few miles to the
west of Colditz Forest, where the US regiment had its HQ. It was
all bustle and movement, in which local German civilians played a
crowd scene side by side with American GIs and no animosity on
either side as far as we could see. That's what we expected anyway
with front line troops. Back down the line, later, we came up
against the *Etappenhengste* or Lines of Communication troops, the
jackals that swarm on every battlefield after the lions have fought.

Overhead like vultures flew the American Air Force, but for the first time in years we had no fear of them.

Our first interrogation was not directed so much at ourselves but as to the fate of several very special PoWs, *Prominente* as we called them, who had been in our charge at Colditz almost to the end. An American colonel with what seemed to us a surprising informality, told us to take a seat at a table, help ourselves to the food laid on it, and answer his questions.

"Where are these men?" Between hunger and anxiety, I told what I knew, while real cocoa, made with milk, steamed under our noses. Bread of an almost unknown colour – white! Margarine of a suspicious delicacy – butter! Meat of an unwonted texture – ham! All lay untasted before our raving eyes.

"Safety first, *Herr Kommandant,*" I muttered, and went on – "Sir, the prisoners you ask for were taken by me upon German High Command orders to the prison camp at Königstein, the generals' camp, Oflag IVA, last Friday, the 13th."

"Nice day for the ride," interrupted the colonel superstitiously.

"There were two nephews by marriage of Sir Winston Churchill – Giles Romilly and Lieut. de Hamel," I reported. "Also Captain Lord Haig, son of the Field Marshal; the Earl of Hopetoun, son of Lord Linlithgow, ex-viceroy of India; and two relations of the British Royal Family, namely Lord Lascelles and Captain the Master of Elphinstone. Likewise the son of the American Ambassador in London, Lieut. Winant, and the Polish General Bor-Komorowski, who organised the Warsaw rising, with his staff. I delivered them all safe and sound, and returned to Colditz on Saturday."

"Go ahead and eat. And here's a smoke."

Relieved but puzzled by the Colonel's casual manner we disposed of the food with such haste as was seemly, bearing in mind Stage Direction No. 2: "Eat up – you may soon be elsewhere." And so began my four months in American captivity.

Half an hour later we were away to Bad Lausick, and the same questions all over again. This time I was word perfect, but there was no food to fall upon. We were indeed getting into the back areas. My commandant and I were somewhat protected by special passes signed by senior British and American officers, our late PoWs at Colditz, but our comrades, other German officers with whom we now piled into trucks for almost daily transports, were not so lucky. They were manhandled, beaten up, knocked down, assisted onward or faster with kicks and rifle butts, that's just how it was. "Give these baskets some of their own medicine!" "Clout the ——g Kraut." "Super-dupes what now?" The American Eagle sure heaped it on us.

Before my particular convoy left Bad Lausick a day later the local GIs gave us a frisking to end all friskings, or so they hoped "Come on you swine, part up! No one gets back of here with anything on him worth a cent." Forcing their way among us, they wrenched at our wrists, tapped our pockets, shook out our few belongings. They collected all possible souvenirs, rings, watches, razors, cuff-links, pens, money – all disappeared into the hoard of these rapacious camp-followers. "Get out of here, you! You've had your liberation for today. Take 'em away, Joe!" And off we went at breakneck speed as always.

What a contrast with the searches we had carried out at Colditz! When we confiscated private property, we always gave a receipt for it. And the last day that we were in charge of the castle, everything was returned to its owner, even three five-pound notes, also against receipt!

Our third stop was at Naumburg, well behind the front at that time, where they had a monster cage for German PoWs. At one brief halt on the way we picked up a German general, in civilian clothes. We knew him personally, for he had been in command of No. IV Army district, Dresden, retiring two years previously to live here on his farm. Now a Polish worker had denounced him, and the Americans pulled him in with the rest. The General came in our truck, and he turned out to be a gift from the Gods (Polish or otherwise). We stuck to him like leeches, my Commandant and I, until he was snatched from our sight. Stage direction No. 3: "Never miss a trick! See one, play one!" The General turned out to be a trump, for high rank, even of a prisoner, carries with it an aura of privilege.

At Naumburg the set was in the old ammunition dump. There was here a cast of thousands – hundreds upon hundreds of PoWs, not a single general! Before they let us inside the big yard we underwent another search. Or so it was called. Was this really a search? Search me if it was! They lined us up and we faced the front. A long rope was stretched out on the ground, and then the searchers began to go along the line, like customs officers in a dockside shed.

"After search, step over the rope," yelled one of the searchers, but in German. The searchers were our own people in US employ. No wonder we were all so thoroughly liberated this morning. Those GIs must have known what sort of search was coming next. That's why they took the lot, or our own men would have the stuff. Imagine us at Colditz having the British or French orderlies to do the searching! They could hardly have been less efficient than some of our NCOs I could mention. I pointed this out to our German Colonel – contraband at Colditz had been a sore point with him, but surely here his sense of humour might have kept his sense of one-time duty quiet. No – once a soldier, always a soldier, so I prompted him to act like a prisoner. In a moment he was hard at it, milling around like the best of them, spreading noise and confusion as to the manner born, like any seasoned prisoner, and so we got across the rope unobserved and without being asked what we had to declare. We hadn't between us an awful lot to lose, but having kept what we did have, our next worry was not to lose a night's rest. That, at any rate, we knew we should not find on the straw at our disposal on the barrack floors. It may be said that my Colonel's lack of humour gave his brain more room to manoeuvre. In a short while, he had thought of a master plan. First of all a quick reconnaissance. Crowded compound, crowded barracks. No room for us. No place for a general! Near the camp entrance, its door leading our way, was a house. Over the door there was a sign: "Commandant".

"I think," observed my former immediate superior, "that this officer will see eye to eye with one of his own standing." He became less reflective. "Eggers," he barked in his last week's voice.

"Colonel," I replied automatically.

"Get inside and tell this American officer there is a German general here with two of his staff. They require accommodation befitting their rank."

This struck me as rather high hat. General, yes, but were we his staff? But then, I thought, what the heck, who'll check? I'm a PoW now, never miss a trick, and here's one worth playing. I pushed into the front room of the villa. I threw the sergeant seated at the table a smart heel-click and a full salute. He beamed. We were, of course, well into the rear of the lines of communication. This guy had never had a captain salute him, German or otherwise. He beamed wider.

"Whaddya want?" he asked. This seemed to me a studied politeness, compared with what I had experienced from the lower orders in the US Army so far.

"Who runs this joint?" I replied, showing that I too was cultured enough to have learnt a foreign language and its vernacular.

"Why! the Commandant, of course. He'll be right back. Siddown. Smoke? You a German captain? What's it like up front?"

"The front is moving fast, but not fast enough for me," I said, "The further and faster you fellows go before you meet up with the Reds, the better. We don't want that lot inside Europe. Your President is playing with fire."

"I reckon Roosevelt knows what he's doing all right," replied the sergeant "What the heck would Russia want with Germany? The place is blown to hell! It's one great helluva mess. Nobody wants it. You couldn't keep a goat in some of your cities I've been through!"

"No goats," I said, "only ghosts." At this moment enter the Big Shot. Was this the commandant? A lieutenant, and bright pink at that. Uniform unstained, creases in the proper places, tight where it was right. He looked a piece of cake.

"Sir, I report the arrival of a German General officer, with two of his staff. He makes a request for accommodation suitable to his rank," said the sergeant.

"Name, please, and unit," said the Big Shot, after a second or two.

"General von S., late commanding No IV Army District, Dresden." A pause. Was this going to work? This lieutenant, too, had probably only very rare contact with shots as big as this, if any. I felt the prompter hiss, and the scene reached its climax.

"Wait outside, near the door, all three of you. I'll send a man outside to show you to your quarters," ordered the Lieutenant.

"Will you want our parole, Sir?"

"No, – or – er – yes. Or – no." Perhaps he was wondering if a lieutenant could take the parole of a General officer. "But if the General escapes," he added, "you two others will be shot at once."

This was surely where we came in? At Colditz the High Command had warned us that if one of our special PoWs got away, the Commandant and Security officer would answer with their heads. And now this man was putting our heads in exactly the same noose on account of one of our own officers, and the Allies already had another noose round our necks over the *Prominente* we had left at Königstein. We had learnt that if harm came to any of them, we were in for it automatically, although their transfer to Königstein was done under direct High Command orders.

Let all that be as it was. We were after comfort at that moment. Death could wait.

Within half an hour we were being shown into a house outside the wire.

"This floor is for you," said the GI: "I'll come back at five with some food. Help yourselves to what's here already." He went downstairs and locked the door. Security? There was none, except that laid on the head of the General's staff! I said no word of this to my Commandant, though, but had a quick look round the house. Lots of food packages about, tins of Nescafé, potatoes. At five o'clock came cocoa, cheese, white bread and real jam. Cigarettes were promised for supper. Until then we played the radio, had hot baths and washed our smalls. The General had nothing but what he stood up in.

"Herr General," I said, "Help yourself to whatever clothing you want."

"But that's stealing from the owner of the house."

"And where is he, do you think? This is American occupied territory, and all this is American owned property, the spoils of war. Our last orders were 'help yourselves to what's there already'. You must, as a PoW, obey the orders of the holding power!"

"But the original owners?" The General's conscience seemed to be irrepressible. I felt it needed crowning! I crowned it.

"When the peace is declared, Herr General, you will return to Naumburg and pay for what you have borrowed."

We fitted him out with underwear, towels, soap etc. and went to bed with comfort. That was the last really relaxed sleep I had for years and years and years and years. I was too tired to worry. I was too unexpectedly full of food even to think. The future could look after itself. I would find a place in it for myself, so I thought, and with this I slept. But the future was not sleeping. The future was just waking up to what it could do for me. . . .

Down from the Heights

Next afternoon, alas so soon! the shouting and yelling started at two o'clock.

"All outside the gate. Into the trucks!"

"Where for?"

"Bloody well wait and see! Get on up!"

They packed us in like herrings, and once more we roared off towards the West. A long convoy, with a lieutenant in charge, more or less. We stopped off at one point, well out in the open country, and the drivers and guards on each truck came back and robbed us of whatever they could find of value.

"Well, Goddam for a rotten miserable bunch of scarecrows! Christ, if I don't have your ——g cap for a souvenir." Hereby went my headgear. I am no egghead, but quite thin on top, so I wrapped my handkerchief round my head, and thanked heaven that the fellow hadn't gone for my boots.

In the evening we thundered into Heiligenstadt, and they quartered us in the school playground after another search, shorter, of course than the last. The loot got less each day.

Our own treasure, the General, was still with us, and we very much with him. Again we tried our trick on, and again it worked! Once more we got luxurious private accommodation, but this time our sleep was less easy to come by. On the stairs outside there was quite a bit of noise – delighted squeals and appreciative grunts. The US Army was in rut, and the Hitler maidens were shedding their status with a will, fraternisation or no fraternisation.

Before dawn we stumbled down the stairs and once more went

away, this time not so far as usual, but to stop in darkness before a great circle of floodlit wire on the open side of a hill.

"All out!" was the cry, and we fell or clambered down, stiff with cold.

On our way into the prisoners' cage I tried to find an ear for our General's plight and need for suitable accommodation. No luck at all. "Shurrup, you. Keep your mouth shut. Your bloody General can wait till the morning. Git in there!"

In the cage, the General took the only blanket we had between us, while my commandant and I stamped around trying to keep warm. At seven in the morning some of our own foul ersatz coffee came round. Those who had mugs helped their comrades who had lost theirs. We made out the name of the place Wellda/Thuringia on the railway station in the valley below. Then the loudspeakers started up, bawling all day for troops and officers of all ranks and every kind of unit, sorting out the mass of men there, from every conceivable unit of our Armed Forces, and the para-military units of the Hitler regime.

"Come out any of you – Hitler Youth, the Führer's most beloved children!" "All SS-swine to the gates!" "Gestapo bastards outside! Don't try to hide! We know you!" And suddenly, "Is there a General in there?" And so we lost our great asset and passport to comfort.

Towards evening my name came through and a GI took me over to a tent for yet another interrogation about what I began to think of as "these —— *Prominente*", and also about myself. They were getting down to grading us politically. My questioner was again a young fellow, from Vienna I thought. He went on and on, questioning apparently aimlessly. If he was feeling for some hidden Nazi ideology, he was wasting his time. By and by it was I who took over; I led him gently back to his home town, and we discussed Austria, and Vienna of the past, and future, if any, which depended who got there first – Russians or Americans. What did I think the Russians would do? I ventured to hope that they'd be no worse than the Americans. Oh, how bad were they? I took the plunge.

"You've liberated us, as you say. But liberation means only one thing now. It's a bad joke, and as you know, it means to steal. Or, if you like, to collect as spoils of war whatever can be moved. We've been plundered at every opportunity by our liberators in the name of Freedom and Democracy and the new life. It stinks. Why don't you officers do something about it? You will never live this down."

He'd been a refugee, in America only a few years. I had him there. "Well, confidentially," he said, "this had already worried me. I have taken it up in higher places. But you know what they say?

You did it yourselves, all over Europe. Sauce for the goose, sauce for the gander. And some of those concentration camps of yours — —?" He began to counter-attack, so I kept quiet. Yes, maybe we Germans were at the top of the list in brutality ratings. But we were not the only ones on the list. And I thought perhaps someone we all knew could be found to share our high place. But I said no more.

Back in the cage I made a report to my commandant. "This guy sounds a sucker. We'll work him some way," he observed, brutally. Obviously prisoner morality was fitting him like a glove. We both had been made fools by our charges in Colditz over and over again. Now it was our turn. Whenever we made them a concession they exploited it cynically. I thought of the tunnel under the chapel, the hospital escapes, the smuggling with the welfare parcels. Certainly, now it was our turn. Now it was we who would steal, lie and deceive. And supposing the news came that the *Prominente* had indeed been killed somewhere, somehow. What chance had we of making a case against being shot as hostages, which is what we had been told our fate would be? Would they give us a court-martial, had we a right of appeal? No. We were part and parcel of unconditional surrender. We had no rights whatsoever. No Protecting Power looked after the interests of German PoWs, as had been the case for the PoW we had held. The Swiss or the Swedes kept an eye on their interests. No one had any interest in Germans at that time, 1945, or for a few years thereafter. My Commandant was thinking. "Eggers, go and tell this damned Austrian interrogator of yours we want to sleep in his tent!"

For Heaven's sake! We of all people needed quiet and unobtrusiveness, and here was this damned Colonel of mine sticking his neck out and mine, when we had only just slipped out of one noose in the shape of our General. I hesitated. "Get on with it!" he cried. I went to the gate, feeling all kinds of a fool. The Lieutenant from Vienna was in a cordial mood. So I ventured, "How about me, the Colonel and our two comrades sleeping in this tent of yours when you are through with the day's work? We could be out before you come back in the morning. No harm done. After all, the tent's going to be here all night, and it is still inside the main perimeter. We can't escape."

Holy Moses! It worked. "I'll send for you in the afternoon. Look, there are two boxes with tinned food. They are at your disposal, help yourselves!" We stayed about two weeks at Wellda, exposed to all weathers by day, and sleeping most nights in the interrogation tent, provided the Lieutenant didn't forget to have us called out when he went off duty. The normal ration for us PoW was one-third that of the GI, so we four were in clover, except for water which was very scarce as they had to bring it up in tankers for 20,000 of us, and there were not many tankers available. My Commandant beamed when he saw that our appeal to American generosity worked. *"L'audace, toujours l'audace!* That's what Danton said, and did."

Our next move was to Hersfeld, down in the valley of the river Fulda. The US staff came with us, but we never profited from the tent. There was no room for us hoboes now. Tramps we all looked like now, and three days later, why did they move us at all for so short a time?

We were all on the move again, to Mollsdorf, near Gotha, but the US Sergeant in charge lost his way. When we arrived late in the afternoon, the camp with nice clean barracks was full so they sent us back, back to the open cages of Hersfeld. Long after midnight we clambered down from those damned trucks with no food or drink for a whole day. We were really down.

On 1st May, ten officers/were bawled out by name for transfer again. Only ten! Why so few? Why were we among the chosen people? Were we what we call in Germany *Todeskandidaten*? Candidates for death? Had the *Prominente* met a sticky end somewhere? Was this going to be our fate as well? Through peaceful villages and small towns we went up into mountainous country and stopped at a small training camp, Schwarzenborn. We were suspicious and depressed and asked at the Commandantur for special accommodation and showed our safe conduct document. We tried our old trick in a new form – in vain. Things looked bad for us, and even worse when we discovered that this was a place where Nazi officials were interned. We saw Düsterberg, a leader of the 'Stahlhelm' (Steel helmet), Prince August Wilhelm of Prussia, then a high leader in the SA. We were now graded as 'Gestapo officers', and handled accordingly. Could we protest? Who was there to protest to? As Gestapo types we were on the lowest level of all, but at least we slept under a roof on the bare barracks floor. The beds and the rest of the furniture had been thrown outside the rooms and lay rotting in the rain. But thank God for small mercies too.

The *Prominente* were always in our minds. I could have prayed for their wellbeing, for Hopetoun and Haig and Lascelles and Elphinstone.

"Don't worry," said my Colonel. "They're tough those Scots. And don't forget, the Devil looks after his own."

"Yes," I said, "those nephews of Churchill – Romilly and de Hamel – they'll be all right. The bulldog breed. Good stock always lasts, they say."

"You can't kill weeds," murmured the Colonel, quoting an old

German proverb. We could apply this to ourselves here, especially when we were escorted to our midday meal, to the kitchen barracks. We were near starvation and the guards knew it. "March there!" they ordered, and kicked us down from the road into the mud. In strict silence and exemplary military order we walked along. In the big eating hall the sentries were sitting on the tables and under their grim supervision we silently devoured some very good pea soup, but alas! Only one plateful. In our pockets we carried our evening meal: three potatoes. The last tin from the boxes of our generous interrogation officer was emptied here. From now on hunger, real hunger, tortured us till the day when the first bread came.

On 10th May we were called to the interrogation barracks and told that the *Prominente* had reached home in safety. Consequently we were no longer hostages but normal PoW. So back we went to Hersfeld, out in the open once more, relieved from a nightmare and with a blanket apiece which we had liberated from our gaolers. There were no flies on us now. There was nothing left for them to eat on us anyway. After barely two months of American captivity we were down to the scarecrow grade. Hersfeld camp in the meantime held up to 60,000 PoW. Discipline, of course, became stricter according to the growing number. The cry was, "*Schnell! Schnell!*" yelled menacingly along the cages when the trucks brought new masses of PoW. Once one man with one of his legs amputated flipped over the tailboard and lay a second on the ground.

"Get up, you bastard!" screamed one of the MPs.

"Hold on, he is an amputee!"

"Amputee be f——. Get up you filthy Hitlerite! *Schnell! Schnell!*" Those of us around began to whistle and to groan and soon the whole camp fell in. The MP carried on unaffected.

After a fortnight, just at Whitsuntide, we were at last moved to the other side of Hersfeld where was a comparatively decent camp in which three months ago French PoW were housed. We had to walk these few kilometres through the town. It was a very hot day. The people looked at the remainder of their Army, miserable figures that more stumbled than marched, under the escort of compassionate negroes who picked up those who couldn't stand the strain any longer. The new lodgings seemed very luxurious to us: a roof overhead! Water as much as you like! Plenty of wood (first taken from the barracks) to heat your soup! One drawback remained: we had to sleep on the bare floor. Little by little things improved: one day bread arrived, and from then on, one pound of white bread daily! At first everybody had to cook his own meal, but later a common kitchen was installed, and a Leipzig professor of botany became our cook, and an excellent job he did. We began to organise our own lives in the manner of all prison camps, so that lectures were going on, study groups were formed, and a thin cultural veneer spread over the raw basis of our uncertain present and non-existent future. But no mail inwards or out.

My Home Run.

Then, in June, things started to move. A trickle of releases passed out through the gate. In that way I got a message to my wife at Halle. In July all of us were regraded. We now became 'Arrested persons'. When we objected, they told us we'd be released sooner like that than as PoW. We were asked where we'd like to be dropped on release. I said at Naumburg.

4th July. My name came up out of the hat! Oh joy! Was this to be my Independence Day too? I drew forty marks, three days' rations and my papers. Hundreds of us crowded down to the truck park, just plain excited, with one set of worries behind us; the next not yet taken up. We waited and waited. Some started to eat a bit of their rations. No trucks. Back into the camp! Why? Someone spread the rumour "4th of July, American Independence Day"; they don't work that day. Well, hadn't they known that before? Next day the truth came through. The whole release operation was now held up. The Russians had moved their boundary westward, and much of central Germany had been handed over to them by the Americans and the English! Just handed over! Was this to be believed? The whole of Saxony, including Leipzig, the former Prussian Province of Saxony-Anhalt, with Magdeburg and Halle, the whole of Thuringia with Erfurt, Weimar, Eisenach – just handed over. Halle, my home town, was now in the Eastern Zone. Naumburg was no good to me now.

How did all this take place? I never found out. The Russians and their Western Allies had met on the Elbe. Colditz, on the Mulde, for some time was just at the demarcation line. Who had ordered this withdrawal, abandoning the heart of Europe to the 'Red Peril'? What in God's name were Truman and Churchill up to? Too busy with their atom bomb and Japan, perhaps, to see the powder train they were laying for themselves close to home? Refugees came through from the Russian Zone. I met and asked them, "Was it safe there for ex-Army officers? What was it like? Was it worth going back at all?"

In the end, of course, most of us decided, when the time came, to go back to our families whatever the risk. Several weeks later we were told that those who had wanted to go into the the Eastern Zone could choose new places to be dropped, places in one of the Western Zones. It then was left to them to make their way home as the Russians did not allow Allied convoys to enter their territory. There was no longer any transport to Naumburg, so I chose a small neighbouring village, Oderode. A friend had told me he could house me for some time on a farm there.

Papers, rations and money, all over again. (They really were generous, I admit.) And on 8th August I was free! Free to move at will, free to make my own decisions. Is man able to do this under his full responsibility? How far can he see in order to judge the consequences of his doings?

I went into the town of Hersfeld and found life was in more ways than expected back to normal. The Red Cross exchanged my ragged uniform for a civilian suit fit for a man seven feet high and three feet broad. I bought a rucksack for my belongings, including my precious blanket. I had a meal in a restaurant without needing food coupons to which I had been accustomed for the last six years. Astonishing!

But, at Oderode, my friend was absent. I decided to keep moving, but before that I called at the hospital to pick up any messages to be delivered to my home area. There I was approached by an officer whom I knew from the barracks. He was an amputee and used crutches. His wife had come over from Thuringia with permission of the Soviets to fetch her husband. I thought at first that if she could cross, then I could, but then I felt that three is a crowd. She was far gone in pregnancy, and he had only one leg and could hardly walk far. She could move only slowly. I was by now no athlete so there could be no creeping along on all fours. No dashing for cover bent double. We were all far too weak for anything but a steady tramp on even ground.

But "*L'audace, toujours, l'audace*", as Danton (or was it Napoleon?) used to say. So on 10th August we set out, aiming for Wallhausen-Vacha and Dorndorf, the first villages in the Eastern Zone, about twenty miles away. The railway brought us to Philippsthal, the last town in the American Zone, where three women who had come over the previous night gave us a tip: be careful when you go round Vacha. There is a Russian sentry high up in an apple tree. For the rest just follow your noses. We left Philippsthal and took to the woods. Somewhere near the ridge of the hill we had to be cautious because of American sentries patrolling the area. There they were! "Halt!" I went straight forward to them. They lowered their rifles and asked for our papers and where we were going. I told them. With an eye on the woman the Sergeant said, "We respect women. I shall help you. These woods we are in are safe. There are no Russians in them. Stay hidden till dark and then move down the other side of the hill. Don't run when the Russians see you. They will just mow you down. Stand and argue. And don't say you met our patrols close by." He offered us some cigarettes and showed us a way in the direction of Vacha. We thanked him and moved on deeper into the woods down a hill and hid in a deep hole some hundred yards from the edge of the trees. Both my companions had bravely stood the strain. She was well six months gone and he had been in captivity for four months; so had I. How any of us got as far I didn't know, but all of us were determined to get where we wanted.

I cautiously went to the edge of the wood to have a look around. There yonder was an apple tree, complete with a Russian guard in its branches. I noted a few landmarks, spurs, open ground, a ravine, bushes. Then I rejoined the others and lay down with them in our hiding place, until all of a sudden the Russians were upon us.

"*Was machen hier? Dokumente!* (What are you doing here? Show your papers!)" We brought out our papers. "*Nix gut. Frau kann passieren. Mann zurück!* (No good. The woman may pass, the men have to go back!)" But she would not leave her husband and tried to persuade the Russian lieutenant. In vain. He ordered the guard to search us. They didn't take anything, not even our precious American tinned food.

"Back to the Americans," we were ordered. Was the voice of fate speaking through him? Later I was inclined to believe so. But at this moment we had to obey, so we slowly went back up the hill and deeper into the woods which were not so safe as we had been led to believe. The Russians met us once more, but only fired their revolvers into trees and into thickets. We felt safer when we'd climbed the hill and rested to take stock of our position, as indeed we had hardly started to get home. I convinced the couple that we should stick to our plan, so we crept into a fir thicket and waited for the night. It soon became dark – not with the night, but with a colossal thunderstorm which soaked us through. We hailed the rain as something to keep the Russian patrols from moving out of whatever shelter they might have. As for us, we could not have got wetter had we had to swim a river.

About midnight, by my rusty, often concealed, unliberated old watch, we moved up and out of the woods. When we looked from their edge to the eastern horizon we could have shouted with joy for the Russians had handed us a trump! Vacha was floodlit, with searchlights all round it, and all we had to do was keep outside the limelight as we moved forward. In this scene, we were just 'noises off'. We pushed on, literally, through waist-high potato fields, sugar beet, meadows, puddles, drains – until the other two gave up.

"We're all in. Can't go on," they gasped. I could not leave them,

but plodded on looking for shelter, until I found some clay work-
ings, where they sank exhausted, on the wet soil for rest.

Half an hour later I was shivering with cold and had to get up. By
dawn we were up and away again with Vacha and the frontier soon
behind us. Ahead were the three tall smoke-stacks of the potash
works of Dorndorf. We came to a road, and decided to follow it, as
we knew our scarecrow appearance would cause no comment, for
we were leaving the frontier, not approaching it. At the first farm I
hobbled in with the others shuffling along behind me. I knocked on
the open door and an old woman emerged from the darkness of the
corridor.

"We have just crossed over. May we please sit by your fire a
while to dry our clothes. We need nothing else as we have our own
food," I begged.

"Who in the hell let you lot in here? Get out before I set the dog
on you," she screamed. What a welcome to the Eastern Zone! On
we went.

Next came a concrete works where we found shelter, fire, strong
coffee, hot soup, and rested on the beds where some months ago
French PoW had slept. The foreman warned us to stay there for a
while. "They're raiding Dorndorf, picking everyone on the streets
for screening, perhaps for deportation anyway. Forced labour for
the men – for the women." Later in the day the all clear was given
so we went into the village. In front of the town hall the Russian
trucks were lined up, packed with people, if you could call them
that. A mass of despairing, weeping, mute, terrified humanity, and
no one dared so much as look at them as he passed, for fear a sign
of recognition would bring him a share in the same fate. . . .

We got to the railway station at last. Trains had started running,
and I bought a ticket to Eisenach. We had a halt there and went to
the market place. From the walls of the town hall red posters told
us: "We welcome our Red Liberators!" Well, liberators were here
before; some months ago the same walls told the same bystanders:
"Never are we so near victory as now! Germany will never be
defeated!" What was wrong with these walls, or perhaps with the
world? Deep in reflections in this subject we came back to the station and succeeded in getting some hot soup from the Red Cross. I
took a ticket to Naumburg, the town where my odyssey began four
months ago. At Thuringia my friends left the train. At Naumburg I
spent the rest of the night on the floor of the station, which was
packed with refugees.

Sunday, 12th August, at noon, still looking like a scarecrow, I
arrived at Halle, my home town. Nobody in the tram recognised
me. The usual daily thunderstorm was going on when I went from

the terminus in the suburb to my home. The streets were empty. For protection I had wrapped my blanket around my shoulders. There was the lonely street where my house stood, apparently undamaged by the recent battles. The house was still standing as I left it on 4th April, with only some old damage from a bomb dropped nearby in my neighbour's garden. How many times had I done this stretch on foot during the last five years! And with what feelings! Hopeful, depressed, happy or worried. At this moment I could not think of anything, past or future. I could only feel the hellish present. A lorry, Russian, was waiting in front of my neighbour's house. Perhaps a raid too? Nobody was to be seen. I passed by quickly. I pressed the bell at my garden gate. No answer. I pressed a second time and longer. Behind the curtain a face appeared and, seeing me, disappeared at once. I must have caused a fearful impression with my blanket overhead. I pressed again and whistled my signature tune. I heard the cry of our housemaid, "The chief is here!" And then they came running out. "We are together again!" I said, "There, quiet now."

Another war was over, so we thought. Later we learned that it was going on grimly, demanding sacrifices and victims we had never believed possible. At any rate, at the moment the soldier enjoyed the moment of triumph; he was home again on the trailing wings of defeat. Five years of his life thrown away! Really? And one son lost as well. Had we anything more to lose? Unconditional surrender would soon show.

Meanwhile, to work again, teaching. The new masters of the country, the Communists, had nothing against me. They knew that I had been no Hitler man. They promoted me. But already, and how blind I was to it! another play was being rehearsed. Soon they were to find another part for me to play. . . .

On 3rd December 1946 a Soviet Military Tribunal sentenced me to ten years' forced labour because I had supported a Fascist regime through my services as an officer at Colditz. I passed these ten dreadful years in the old concentration camp of Sachsenhausen (December 1946 to January 1950) and then until 28th December 1955 in Torgau prison. On my order for release were the words: "The bearer of this order has been informed that he has to leave the territory of the DDR on the prescribed route in the shortest possible time."

XIX

Colleagues

BY REINHOLD EGGERS

(*Dr Eggers recaptures his impressions and memories of some of the German staff he worked with at Colditz.*)

Colonel Schmidt

I had been initiated into my work as a prison camp officer from August to November 1940 at Oflag IVB Hohnstein. When this camp was closed, I was transferred to Oflag IVC Colditz, where Colonel Schmidt was the Commandant. I already knew of his reputation as the strictest Commandant in the whole of District IV.

After my arrival at Colditz on a dreary day in 1940, I met the Adjutant, Captain Kunze, and then went to the Commandant's office.

"Lieut. Eggers reports – transferred from Oflag IVB to Oflag IVC," I announced in my best military manner. The Colonel, seated behind his desk, examined me for a moment and asked me to take a seat in front of him. After answering some questions about my service at IVB and the situation there, he decided I should join the camp officers' team, the head of which was Captain Priem. The Adjutant would help me to find a room and so on. Then I was dismissed.

I had the impression of a mighty head, perhaps not quite balanced on huge shoulders. The cold grey eyes showed no emotion. The hair, already thin and grey, revealed his whole forehead. His movements and words were brief. On the whole an imposing figure, confirming my idea of a Prussian colonel. When I saw him later in the mess, he impressed me even more. Over six feet tall, he was by far the biggest of our staff and of all my previous commandants. An atmosphere of an inaccessible superiority surrounded him; his high order of the Saxon "*Pour le mérite*" emphasised this. His subordinates addressed him in the third person. I had got used to this at IVB with Lieut.-General Niethammer and in World War I. Although Hitler had tried to change this old custom by ordering that higher ranks should be addressed in the second person, *Sie*, accompanied by their rank, here nobody bothered about this order. In Hitler's party and in the SA and SS the word *Herr* was forbidden. Superior officers were addressed as in the British army, by their rank or rank and name; Hitler personally by *Mein Führer*. No *Herren* any longer.

*Colonel Schmidt,
Commandant of Colditz*

His belonging to the old Prussian tradition was further stressed by his exterior appearance of austerity and simplicity. The dandy-caricature of German officers in magazines was reduced to absurdity by Colonel Schmidt whose uniform was well kept by his orderly, but he had surely worn it all through World War I! His everyday footwear was a normal soldier's lace-up boots with gaiters. Only on Sundays or when important visitors were expected, would he wear high boots and a uniform of the best quality.

Even after only a week's service I saw the outline of the Colonel's personality clearly. He was excessively punctual, very rarely entering his office later than 8 am. He often made a snap inspection through the camp: security, mail control, administration. After this he would sit down to have a look through his mail and newspapers. The entries in the log books of the main guard and of the guard near the main gate to the PoW yard were examined by the Colonel's vigilant eyes each morning. The NCOs on duty were summoned and severely reprimanded if everything was not in accordance with his exact orders. Nobody liked such scenes!

A walk round the castle, to check the guards or to examine the camp kitchen or sickroom was to be expected at any time. Often he inspected the drill of the guard company or the changing of the guards. He greeted the assembled soldiers with, "Good morning, *Landesschuetzen*", and he expected the old loud reply: "Good morning, *Herr Oberst!*"

Every morning at 11 am the whole staff had to meet in the Colonel's office, where he made known news from the mail, new orders and dealt with daily events and offences against orders. As an old experienced soldier he knew very well that authority which is not exercised each day, will soon fade away.

His austere way of executing his authority was uncomfortable but effective. When he once transgressed the limits which even old colonels are allowed, one of our best officers, Captain Lessel, over sixty, and serving only voluntarily, protested against his "*Feldwebel* manners", left Colditz and retired.

In 1941 the guard company was under the command of Lieut. Hirschbeck, a called-up schoolmaster from the Sudetengau. Somehow he continued to practise the ways of the Imperial Austrian Army which the German soldiers of World War I called "*Kamerad Schnuerschuh*", meaning that they took their duties more easily than we did. Their officers had big baggage trains, appeared often in parade uniforms when serving behind the lines. Discipline was more lax somehow. The spirit of the guard company displeased the Colonel – one member had even brought two ladies into the castle at night.

Now, on one fine Sunday afternoon, the Colonel, in his best uniform was sitting in the Waldschenke restaurant, near the Colditz Forest, having a glass of beer . . . and of course observing the soldiers who were also relaxing there. Then the door opened and in came Lieut. Hirschbeck. He wore leather shorts and a shirt, and was bare-headed. On his arm he carried a guitar. He was accompanied by some of his NCOs. They had all been strolling through the forest, enjoying the sunshine and singing *Wandervögellieder*. Seeing their Colonel the group halted and gave him the Hitler salute. Then they found a free table some distance away. Nothing like this had ever happened before in the Colonel's life. He acknowledged their Hitler salute with a slight bow of the head, but one could read in his face his utter disapproval of their behaviour. He later had a word with the Adjutant, Captain Kunze, an old

Wandervögel too, who smiled and assured the Colonel that there was nothing wrong and he had no grounds to rebuke the Guard Company Commander. But even so, the Colonel asked the Generalkommando to relieve this Company Commander and to send another one to Colditz.

The more intimate side of the Colonel's personality could be recognised off duty, when in the mess during meals he still exercised his authority. Although from time to time he invited important guests from the town to a party in the mess – Kreisleiter Naumann of the NSDAP, Ortsgruppemleter Headmaster Starke, the Mayor – he never accepted invitations as a private guest from any family in Colditz. On the other hand he was the only one of our commandants who had the means to invite his whole staff to a dinner once a year. He could afford to do this, because one of his daughters was married to the owner of the sugar factory of Klein Wanzleben, near Magdeburg. A big estate was attached to the factory and the sugar beet firm. I, with my small estate of one and a half acres at Reideburg, was the only officer who could afford to return this hospitality. In this way the Colonel relaxed the atmosphere of inaccessibility which surrounded him. This was so, too, in our Skat club. He liked cards, but his way of playing was boring for he usually lost, and he expected to lose. So we played for very low stakes. Even the worst player could not lose more than a few marks. Besides, all losses were paid into a common pool. From time to time we had a party and paid the bill with this money. The Colonel comforted himself by saying: "I am a big eater!" I never saw him drunk.

According to old soldiers' traditions the Colonel avoided political discussions. He undoubtedly had no more than a formal loyalty to the Hitler regime. His straightforward nature abhorred hypocrisy, so he concentrated on the fulfilment of his military obligations. He stated: "The NSDAP has given the German officer a status he did not even have in the reign of The Kaiser, so our loyalty is assured." I never saw him give the Hitler salute. He certainly, at that time, did not know details of crimes like Auschwitz, etc. With his authority he never violated international law. He rarely used to the full his power to punish his prisoners. When, near the end of his time in 1942, their behaviour verged on mutiny, he did not employ force to restore military authority in the camp. When once the Kreisleiter asked him to open fire on the shouting, howling mob in the castle, the Colonel answered: "Before I give orders like that, I shall make sure from a legal expert that such an order is lawful." He preferred the court martial as a weapon. Of course it was a painful defeat to him when the Polish Lieut. Siewert was acquitted for having refused to salute the Commandant after the command: "*Achtung!*"; after this acquittal the prisoners found they had more scope for opposing the Germans than before. His appeal to the Senior Officers of the different nations to keep things under control and to behave like soldiers remained without effect. Only the Dutch and the Poles were not guilty in his eyes, so eventually the OKW was compelled to put an end to the mutinous situation by partially dissolving the camp in 1943. But bloodshed was avoided.

Colonel Schmidt retired on 31st July 1942 when he was seventy years old. His troops said of him: "He was a great soldier, austere, harsh, but just." Officers, myself included, felt relieved of an uncongenial regime; but nobody could deny that it was effective; nobody could refuse the highest esteem for this personification of our old military virtues; devotion to his country and to his duties. An artillery officer in World War I, he was straightforward and kept to the traditions of the *Frontschweine*, taking no personal advantage from the life in the *Etappe* Colditz. He obeyed the same orders that he asked us to follow.

He moved from Dresden to Klein Wanzleben after the air-raid in 1945, and was arrested by the GPU. He was shortly released, only to be rearrested and interned in the GPU cellars and in the camps of Klein Wanzleben, Gross Wanzleben, Magdeburg, Mühlberg, Frankfurt/Oder and Reval.

The few men who came home from the Russian camps who had seen him there reported that he was never tried by the Russians but that he stuck firmly to his principles during those dreadful years. I found no-one who knew the exact details or even the date of his end – in a hospital in Riga in 1946 or '47.

Major Menz

Menz was our second-in-command* from 1939–41. He was still a *Rittmeister* (the rank of a captain with the calvary), when I first reported to him on my arrival at Colditz, Oflag IVC. I saw a man of formidable stature, a real *Kuerassierfigure* (cuirassier), over six feet tall, massive and imposing. Up to 1918 he had been a professional officer, a lancer. Between the wars, as a member of a rich banker's family, he lived on a big estate in the manner and style of a *grand seigneur*. On his estate he had been fond of hunting, so at Colditz he was the only officer who kept a dog.

He was soon promoted to major. We have a saying "Debts like a

---

* In small camps like Colditz the second-in-command was usually superfluous. He had no office, no clerks, no real function, except to stand in when the commandant was on leave – a task for about a month a year only – not enough to tax the energy of a normal man. – *Reinhold Eggers*

major", which was true of our second-in-command whose major's salary was insufficient to meet his mess bills. His mother was still alive, so the fortune of the family was not yet at his disposal. Major Menz was accustomed to drinking wine throughout the day and half the night. We did not try to keep pace with him as his service obligations were of a kind that did not require him to be completely sober. Yet I never met a man who was better able to keep his head whatever his state of drunkenness.

Christmas 1940 at Colditz with Major Menz as Second-in-Command

One of the top events to him was the visit of the Dresden Russian Orthodox 'Pope' and choir-members to our ancillary camp, the Schuetzenhaus, where White Russians were lodged. To honour them we held a party in the mess or in the Cross Hotel, as the 'Pope' liked the bottle too and could stand enormous quantities of schnaps.

I admired Major Menz for being able to hold his liquor so well, a quality I lacked, so I asked him how he did it. He told me: "Whenever I expect an evening like those we have with the 'Pope', I take a spoonful of olive oil before starting to drink. The oil-film protects my stomach from the alcohol." Unfortunately this recipe was of no use to me; I have always drunk extremely little and consequently only a small quantity of liquor has a perceptible effect on me. But besides olive oil you need regular training to reach our Major's perfection. He had been brought up to drink wines and spirits from his childhood. Of necessity I had been obliged to lead an abstemious life from my youth.

What degree of activity his second-in-command could deploy depended on the commandant. Colonel Schmidt did his commandant's job himself so throughly that Menz had an easy time, except during the month when *der Alte*, sometimes called the *Neandertaler*, was on leave for a cure. As Major Menz had neither office nor special duties, he strolled through the camp at his ease. He gave no directions to us, the camp officers. Like Priem, he was the best of comrades, but his massive body could consume twice as much alcohol as Priem without producing the slightest visible result.

I was responsible for giving our major an opportunity for an unusual activity. Colonel Schmidt had checked my *Wehrpass* (passport) and found out that there was no entry to show I had sworn my soldier's oath. I had done this at Leipzig in my original regiment in 1914 with the full ceremony, but before the clerks had noted this down in my passport I was transferred to an interpreter's course at Dresden, hence the gap in my passport. So Colonel Schmidt ordered his second-in-command to carry out the ceremony of swearing the oath with me. We both went into an empty room and Major Menz drew his mighty sword, the old sword of a Lancer from World War I, and pronounced the words of the oath which I repeated, putting my right hand on the sword. So I renewed the mass oath of Leipzig in an individual ceremony at Colditz. Had it therefore a particular validity? I have forgotten the text of the oath, except for two things: to keep my country and the Führer, Adolf Hitler from any danger. The remarkable thing was that both Menz and I were opposed to Hitler when we were civilians! He despised Hitler and his party. He told me that quarrels he had had on his estate with the functionaries of the NSDAP and with the local head of the SA. They had wanted to recruit him at least for the SA, which as a para-military organisation appealed to many old soldiers. Menz refused. Now, as soldiers, we were both bound to the Fatherland and to the current leaders of our poor country.

There were catastrophic consequences to all this for Major Menz. In 1941, the war in Russia brought millions of new PoWs who were not protected by the Geneva Convention, to which Stalin was not a signatory. Numerous new PoW camps were founded, mostly in Russia. Many new commandants were needed and Major Menz was appointed to be one of them. He left Colditz in August 1941 to become commandant of some miserable camp somewhere in the Baltic. He, an outspoken adversary of Hitler, found himself engaged in the work of annihilating millions of those unhappy human instruments of Stalin – just as more than one million German human instruments of Hitler were exterminated by Russian Commandants of German PoW camps.

Major Menz's end is unknown to me, but in my diary are some entries based on letters he wrote to Captain Lange. Here are brief extracts from a few of them:

27th September 1941. Major Menz wrote from Riga to say he is commandant of a prison camp of 9,000, the capacity of which was planned to be increased to 30,000, together with a hospital camp of 2,000. The 9,000 were camped in the open air without shelter, not even tents, so they dug holes with their bare hands in the soil for shelter, inside the barbed wire. Many died each day from starvation. In such conditions only one kind of regime works – revolver and whip.

14th October 1941. Major Menz writes that unbelievable conditions prevail in German-controlled PoW camps in Russia. He says he was obliged to have thirteen prisoners shot because they had resorted to cannibalism. For weeks the Russians remained without shelter, living in holes in the ground. About ten prisoners were shot each night when trying to escape. Their corpses were eaten by others if they could be smuggled away before the guards reached them. Up to twenty prisoners died from some cause or other each day.

5th December 1941. Menz again wrote to Captain Lange, from Polotzk, about 300 kilometres to the south-east of Riga, where he is commandant of a PoW camp of about 21,000 Russians. Here the daily death rate is about 70–80. This was only to be expected, having received no supplies, he was simply ordered to "Live off the country."

8th March 1942. Major Menz wrote that from his camp of about 21,000 PoW more than 15,000 have died from starvation and spotted fever. Among them were his security officer and a number of German soldiers. His own self-constructed log-house was burnt down and he only got away with his life. All this luggage was lost too – and he, *grand seigneur* that he was, had so much luggage to lose.

I do not know how this tragedy ended.

Lieut. Colonel von Kirchbach

As successor to Major Menz the Generalkommando sent us Colonel von Kirchbach; he was second-in-command at Colditz from August 1941 to February 1942. He came from a famous old Saxon officer's family with the best traditions and moral standards. He had lost an arm in World War I. With his level of intelligence, morals and manners, he quickly won sympathy from all sides and many of us hoped to have him as Colonel Schmidt's successor. It was he who was on duty when, on 17th December 1941, the three French officers, de Frondeville, Durant and Prot, escaped from the civilian dentist, Michael, in the town late in the afternoon. We had just been celebrating our Christmas party in the Waldschenke when the news of the escape reached us, but his countenance remained unmoved during this critical situation. How would old Colonel Schmidt have reacted? – but he was on leave.

11th December 1941 – the memorable day of our declaration of war against the USA. I heard the news on the radio in my room in the tower of the castle, when Adolf Hitler made his masterly speech between 3 pm and 5 pm. Colonel von Kirchbach was my guest in front of the *Volksempfänger* [people's radio]. He has been our chief for the past three weeks as Colonel Schmidt was on leave. Von Kirchbach was much impressed by the speech, but he avoided any comment; his situation is similar to mine for although, as soldiers and Germans, we look on the achievements of our people since 1933 and during the war with the utmost esteem, complete loyalty and devotion is impossible to us as a consequence of actions of the NSDAP generally against us personally.

Early in February Lieut. Colonel von Kirchbach, to the utmost regret of the whole staff, left Colditz and became commandant of the camp at Zeithain. He was a personality of the highest standards, as a soldier as well as a man. Would he have found a way out of the difficult situation in the 'Bad Boys' Camp'?

For a time Captain Priem became our second-in-command. Then from Vienna, the older Colonel Kalivius with his wife, 15 years younger, brought a more Austrian flavour into our otherwise Prussian tradition in Colditz. But when in February 1943 Lieut. Colonel Prawitt was appointed commandant Colonel Kalivius, a much older and more senior man, could not remain at Colditz.

Major Amthor
Major Amthor, second-in-command from May 1943 to February 1945, was some years older than Lieut. Colonel Prawitt and younger than the rest of the staff. He was a stout man of middle size. If he became excited his red face quickly deepened its colour to purple. The PoW soon found out that the Major's temper could easily be inflamed, a spectacle they frequently enjoyed, and called their victim "Turkey".

His temperament made him a more active second-in-command than the others we had. Being free from office work, he bustled round the whole castle; his vivid blue eyes and vigilant mind kept their owner always well informed about what was happening, the persons concerned and even the statistical details of the camp – much in contrast to the Commandant, Prawitt*. All this had made

---

* Prawitt, born in 1899 in East Prussia, was an infantry officer and became Commandant of Colditz from February 1943 to April 1945. He died in 1969, at Moelln, near Hamburg.

Amthor a successful merchant in private life but not a particularly convenient superior for the rest of the staff at Colditz. His sense of importance made him swollen up with arrogance and rudeness, so there were numerous quarrels and arguments with members of the staff and with the PoW. The Commandant willingly left him to the job which up to then had been the Commandant's business.

There was another important contrast between our two most senior officers of the camp: Prawitt was openly an adversary of the NSDAP, Amthor was a devoted follower of Hitler so, wisely, the Generalkommando had sent Amthor to complete the Commandant's personality by this second-in-command. Amthor showed his adherence to the party by wearing party decorations on his uniform, such as SA sports and rider medals, and he told us that there was no SA spirit in our little community. We found it ridiculous to salute our commandant with "*Heil* Hitler! *Herr Oberst!*" We, as ever, said "Good morning!" After the attempt on Hitler's life on 20th July 1944, Hermann Goering ordered that the Hitler salute should be introduced in the army without exception as a thanksgiving symbol for the Führer's rescue. Prawitt could not resist this order, so we all, even the PoW, had to use the Hitler salute. What a roar of laughter there was in the yard when Püpcke and I first used that notorious salute! But Amthor was happy.

So the SA spirit at last seemed to fill our minds but it only appeared so, for on Prawitt's orders Amthor tried to force the PoW to obey by the use of arms, even on small violations of orders like saluting, no camp officer was willing to comply. The attempt to sow hatred and to take reprisals for personal losses in air raids or on the battlefields, failed too. So in the end Amthor became resigned to the toleration of small vexations and Prawitt retired to his quiet office in the castle. Thus a compromise reigned throughout the last fifteen months.

There follow some extracts from my diary at the time:

14th to 28th July 1943. Today I again had a sharp argument with Major Amthor, who wants more severity, even brutality in dealing with the PoW. But what did he do when, in his presence, during an identity roll-call, the prisoners threw waterbombs? Nothing.

He had got a letter from his home in Cologne after a horrible air raid on the city just after his leave there. He lamented and tried to excite hatred in revenge for the Allied air raids. Did I complain about my second son's death as a pilot in North Africa? No, I did my duty silently, but types like Amthor are intolerable to me. I sharply paid back his insults and went to the Adjutant to announce that I did not wish to serve here any longer under a second-in-command like Major Amthor.

14th to 31st October 1943. Today Püpcke and I again had a serious dispute with Amthor. He said, to me "Your whole work here is shit! An

NCO could easily do what you do, for he at least would be more obe-
dient than you." Now Püpcke stood up to him for, when Amthor,

Lieut.-Colonel Prawitt   Major Amthor

almost bursting with arrogance like a blown-up frog, insisted that he
was our superior whom we must obey, Püpcke retorted: "I am a captain, fifty-two years old, and as such I am not as readily influenced as a
new recruit." Afterwards Püpcke and I both wondered what we could
do about such an impertinent colleague as Amthor.

14th to 18th November 1943. I told Amthor that I was going to apply for
a posting because of his insulting behaviour to me, so he could then
engage a corporal to do my work as, in a way, a corporal could do my
work better than I could. At this he apologised for his insults and said
that he had not intended to offend me, but had wanted to say that, with
my qualifications, I was too good for the work here. Since then he has
begun to be more friendly, shaking hands and so on.

Yesterday, during the 4 pm roll-call, he entered the yard. I commanded the prisoners:" *Achtung*! for the second-in-command!" Then I turned
to Major Amthor to report while the PoW were whistling. Colonel
Broomhall, the then Senior British Officer, commanded "Attention!"
and saluted. Amthor ordered an extra roll-call for 5 pm because of the
whistling. The SBO announced the order while I was counting prisoners
in the sickroom. The answer to Amthor's order was a roar of laughter
followed by howling and more whistling. Amthor, who had gone into
an office off the courtyard known as the Evidence Room, at once came
out into the yard, to be greeted with renewed roaring laughter.

At 5 pm Amthor returned for the extra roll-call. There was another gale of laughter, howling and whistling, so he ordered a further roll-call for 6 pm – but this time he wisely decided not to appear so all was quiet. *23rd January to 16th February 1945.* Major Amthor became chief of a new unit of volunteers entrusted with the task of destroying the Russian tanks which are approaching Dresden.

So Major Amthor (a member of the NSDAP) went off to enjoy the active service of which so many foolishly talked. He would have a chance to prove, like the old fighters, if he really wanted to risk his life for his convictions. In the meantime his family, who had lost their house in Cologne in an air-raid, found refuge in the castle, where they lived in a four-room apartment.

23rd February to 3rd March 1945. Major Amthor, the '*Panzerknacker*', is away again for training at Dresden where, in the pioneer barracks, spirits were high! He had said: "We – – lose the war? There is no question of it!" Such people must be very single-minded not to see what is going on. In August 1918 Hindenburg and Ludendorff went to the Kaiser and reported: "We report to your Majesty that according to our conviction we cannot win the war by military means." We then stood deep in France; we had peace with Russia and our home industry was intact, but today he who dares to say the same would be hung.

As for Amthor, he failed, but avoided captivity. He left the castle in February 1945 to fight the Russians but his élite commando could not prevent the conquest of Dresden. In 1971 he was still alive and a merchant in Bremen.

Captain Paul Priem

On 13th October 1942, we had our Skat evening, and Captain Paul Priem introduced us to our new second-in-command, Colonel Kalivius from Vienna. We all went to a wine restaurant and although both Kalivius and Priem were already in high spirits, they started drinking gooseberry wine. Priem's good humour grew rapidly as he talked much and wittily. When a few of us left at half-past midnight, we could imagine how it would end. Gooseberry wine is dreadful! And they drank rounds of it right up until four in the morning.

When I went into the mess for breakfast, only two and a half hours later, I found Rittmeister Kunath lying on a sofa in the games room, the carpet of which showed what he had eaten and drunk the evening before. He was flat out. Teichert, known as the 'Tiger', had fallen and lost much blood from a wound on his head. Paul Priem, with a considerable bit of luck, had staggered home with his hallucinatory monkey. When I saw Priem that morning, he stared at me as if he was out of this world, for during the night he had suffered from a long attack of asthma. Our doctor had to look after him. I understand Priem suffered from a slight heart condition.

Captain Paul Priem was our most memorable officer, both to the

Captain Priem (left) *with Captain Kunze*
outside the chapel at Colditz

British and to ourselves. He was born in the early nineties of the last century in the region of Bromberg-Schneidemühl, the district which is now Polish. It was then part of the German Reich of Kaiser William II, with a population of Germans and Poles.

Frontier districts between different races produce belligerent types on either side; thus Captain Priem joined a free corps to fight for his homeland in 1918 – to help keep the region under German rather than Polish control. Hitler easily won numerous and fanatical adherents from frontier districts, fulfilling for a limited time their hopes to win back provinces conquered in 1772, 1793 and 1795 by the Prussian kings. The Poles in 1919 won back their land only to have it reconquered by Hitler in 1939. Little wonder then that Paul Priem, a schoolmaster from Briesen in this lost country, was an adherent – not a fanatical, but a belligerent follower – of Hitler.

Priem was of medium height, with a good soldier's physique and gleaming blue eyes. He was lively and he reacted promptly to any surprise situation in which he found himself. He was above all a charming companion, especially at a good dinner party. When he had had a few drinks, his mind worked at double speed, producing an unbelievable number of fantastic ideas, *bons mots* and so on. There was no one in our whole staff who could match his ready wit. He was a born *maître de plaisir* and a much sought-after speaker at festivities. On the whole we found him a jolly good fellow, and so did the British, who described him as "the only German officer with a natural sense of humour." He was certainly a rarity, the best of comrades, noble and trustworthy.

His mercurial temperament, however, had its disadvantages when he dealt with prisoners. It was true he could be trusted to master every situation, but as an old headmaster he should have known that, for a new teacher, discipline is best established in the first few days of authority. Priem preferred the elegant way he managed the prison camp from 1939 to 1940; but when Colditz became a *Sonderlager* for hard cases, full of spirited, rioting officers and expert escapers, it became evident that his methods were leading to disaster. I have served in some camps on the staff, and as a guest in others, but nowhere have I found discipline on such a low level as it was in Colditz. Priem's laxity was partly the cause. Püpcke and I, made from a different clay, tried in vain to rectify matters, but our hopes of doing this had been dashed by Priem at the start.

As I wrote in the Preface the distinction between front-line and back-line troops, between *Frontschweine* and *Etappenschweine*, is far more marked in the German than in the British army. Can Captain Priem be honoured as a *Frontschwein*? Certainly. His audacious courage, quick action and reaction, honest principles, even his carousing, qualify him. Besides this, he did not abuse the hospitality of the rich citizens of Colditz to enjoy the pleasures of the *etappenschweine*.

Camp Officer at Colditz from 1939, Priem was dismissed from the army in January 1943 on medical grounds – he was subject to apoplectic fits. He died of a heart attack in August 1944.

Staff-Paymaster Heinze

Heinze was born in the late 1880s and was by dialect and temperament a true son of his native Saxony. A vigilant and clever organiser, he liked to pose in the role of a grim warrior. He always wore his long sword and spurs – although he had no horse. Instead of a coat he preferred a cloak dating from the time of the Kaiser, which explains his nickname, 'General Faltenwurf'.

As chief of the Colditz administration 1939–45 he liked to hunt escaping prisoners. As soon as the alarm sounded he would put on his steel helmet and arm himself with a rifle. "If I see the cur I will shoot him at once," he would say, and then go out and search the woods. Happily he never encountered an escaper.

He was a merchant by nature and training, and lived in Dresden, where his wife and daughter had a narrow escape from death and his house was partly destroyed in the air-raid of February 1945. As the end of the war drew near he threatened to shoot his wife, his daughter and then himself. "But before I do this," he said, "I shall enter the inner courtyard and kill as many of those curs as I can."

After the deaths of his two sons in the war Paymaster Heinze

Captain Lange   Staff-Paymaster Heinze

hated the British even more, and he once overreached himself. It was when three British prisoners were found in a drain. When they emerged, Heinze spat and said "*Schweine!*" This was at once reported to Colonel Tod, the senior British Officer, who wrote a letter of protest to Colonel Prawitt, the Commandant. Prawitt decided that the British had been insulted, so he asked Heinze to write a letter of apology. This he did, explaining he had not intended to insult the British but only wished to express his horror of the dirt and the stench in the drain.

When Colditz fell to the Americans, Staff-Paymaster Heinze offered his services to Colonel Tod and the Americans. Although they knew how ill-disposed Heinze had been to the British, Colonel Tod accepted his offer and was thus able to keep his officers supplied with food. After a day or two, Heinze was no longer needed and so rejoined his colleagues in a prison camp at Wellda in Thuringia, from where he was moved to a larger camp in France, and finally to captivity in Russia. His end is unknown to me.

Captain Lange

Hans Lange was born in Dresden about 1890, the son of an old officer's family. He served in World War I as a regular infantry officer, and was decorated with the Iron Cross of both classes, as well as Saxon orders. Between the wars he earned his living as a merchant. He joined the 'Steel-helmets' and with them became a member of Hitler's party. He was Security Officer at Oflag IVC Colditz from 1939 to October 1943. He was the father of six children. I do not know what became of him in the end.

Colonel Glaesche

Edgar Glaesche was born in 1889. Our second Commandant, he came to Colditz in August 1942. He was a man of medium height and with a slight squint in one eye – a less imposing person than his predecessor, Colonel Schmidt.

Although accustomed to instant obedience, as he had previously been a regimental commander on the Eastern front, Colonel Glaesche lacked the aggression needed to enforce his orders on the mob of prisoners we had in Colditz. Finding himself at a loss, he avoided contact with them, never inspected their quarters, observed their parades from a high window near a mounted machine gun, installed a new alarm system and improved the guard posts with a high wooden watch tower and with cat-walks for the sentries.

All these precautions only made matters worse. His reign as commandant brought escape attempts to a climax; the punishment cells could not house the crowds of prisoners who disobeyed his orders. He was helpless for the Geneva Convention prevented his imposing more effective punishments. So Colonel Glaesche had to go after only six months and we lost a man whom we all respected; whose instructions on cultured behaviour belonged to the little jokes we enjoyed so much like a certain General Wolff's opinion that a German officer should change his uniform three times a day, or a Colonel Gerloff's belief in the importance of always having one's plate only half filled, of wearing white collars one on top of the other to effect a quick change, or of leaving a room by walking out backwards. We missed Colonel Glaesche, who went back to the east to his new appointment – District Commander of Russian

prisoners in a group of camps in the Ukraine. Glaesche died at
Stuttgart-Degerloch in 1968.

Colonel Glaesche

Colonel Glaesche's fundamental conviction was that "German
officers are one of the main pillars of our culture. In their style of
life and behaviour they have to act accordingly." He not only
declared this openly but realised it. During his term of office at Colditz, festivities in the officers' mess were on the highest level. The
consumption of alcohol was the lowest we had ever known.

Captain Müller – 'The Assassin'
(*Captain Martin Müller, a member of the German staff at Colditz,
himself recounts how he came to be known as 'the Assassin'*)
I was born in December 1885, the son of a peasant. I went to school
in Zschopau in Saxony and then to the training college there. After
my military service as a volunteer for one year with the 104th
Infantry Regiment at Leipzig 1906–7, I continued my studies to
become a master at a secondary school. Besides pedagogical training my subjects were mathematics, physics, chemistry. Just before
the end of my studies World War I broke out and I rejoined my
former regiment and was wounded at Vitry le François during the

Marneschlacht in 1914, when a shell splinter went into my right knee. So the war ended for me. I completed my final examinations in 1915 and was awarded the degree of Doctor of Philosophy at Leipzig University. I became a schoolmaster at Zschopau, where I married, my wife dying in 1971. We had no children.

In 1941 I again became a soldier and was sent to Oflag IVC, Colditz. During my first months there I assisted in the postal department supervising the PoW mail under Captain Vent. In the autumn of 1941 I became a member of the central staff with Colonel Schmidt as Commandant and Captain Kunze as Adjutant. I was the Adjutant's deputy, and in addition I was responsible for the technical installations such as alarm apparatus, courts martial and punishments of any kind, precautions against air raids and fire. I also acted as the Commandant's assistant.

I particularly remember one Senior British Officer, Colonel Stayner, who conducted a few attacks against me, as for example when Lieut. Sinclair was wounded while impersonating Feldwebel Rothenberger. I was on duty at the time and I at once sent Sinclair to the hospital at Bad Lausick, during the night of 2nd–3rd September 1943.

I had also been on duty when on 20th June 1942 the French Lieut. Fahy had been wounded by a bullet fired from a soldier under my command. I had called out the main guard at about 9.30 in the evening as there was a tumult in the PoW yard. For reasons unknown to me the PoW were shouting and pouring water from the upper storeys to the lower ones. It was an enormous hubbub so I ordered the prisoners to be quiet and to stay inside. Laughter.

I called a group of our soldiers, ordered them to load their rifles and repeated my orders to the PoW. No result. So I gave the final warning, otherwise the soldiers shoot. Insults from above.

One of my soldiers fired and Lieut. Fahy was wounded when a bullet hit his neck. (I was later told that he had not been among the revolting mob.) He was tended by the camp doctors and treated in the Bad Lausick hospital. For this the French baptised me with the name *L'Assassin*. I am convinced that my way of acting was in accordance with my orders and with the Geneva Convention.

My duties included registering all judicial proceedings; interrogating accused or suspected PoW and supervising the communication of the accused with their defender, the lawyer Dr Naumann, who was paid 200 marks for each trial, about £16 at that time. He was appreciated by the PoW for his fair attitude to them and for his skill. The Court Martial court of the 404th division at Leipzig, too, was esteemed by the PoW to follow a strictly neutral line and to observe International Law. Flight-Lieut. Tunstall was accused in a number of trials, and of all the Bad Boys, I remember him best.

I was the senior officer of our staff, when in December 1944, in my sixtieth year, I applied to retire from the army. The General-kommando at Dresden granted me this in February 1945, but Colonel Prawitt delayed my return home until my successor arrived. However he never came, so a few days before the Americans conquered Colditz, Prawitt sent me home. I thus avoided captivity and hoped to continue teaching at Zschopau after the schools were re-opened, but the authorities dismissed me in late 1945 and left me without a pension or other income until 1950, when I became sixty-five, and could then claim a very modest old age pension of less than 200 marks per month. I lived by giving private lessons in mathematics, physics and chemistry.

In Colditz I think that, on the whole, I followed Captain Eggers' line in dealing with our Bad Boys. We acknowledged and some-times admired the skill, courage and imagination with which our PoW fulfilled their legitimate wish to escape from our custody. We despised the often childish and at any rate anti-Geneva Convention means some contingents of our PoW used to provoke us to use force and perhaps create martyrs. We strove to keep discipline by the legal means, to the limit and strictly. I regret that Lieut. Fahy was wounded in the course of my endeavours to restore order in a situation nearing mutiny. I was never able to hate any of the men in our custody, although they tried to infuriate us at times.

Lieut. Colonel Prawitt (1899–1969)

A regular Infantry Officer, appointed Commandant of Oflag IVC from 13th February 1943 onwards. (He claimed he had been pro-moted to full colonel in February 1943 in a telephone message from the Generalkommando.)

He was a martinet, and once publicly admonished the guard commander, Captain Thomann, for allowing one of his men to go on guard duty with his collar up to keep out the snow.

Colonel Prawitt often attended the parties given by rich families of Colditz, partaking to the full of the food and wine available. (When offered a cigar, for instance, he sometimes took more than one.) Although his outward appearance and bearing were generally those of a model German officer, he was in fact openly in opposition to Hitler, concealing his attitude only after the assassination plot of 20th July 1944.

XX

As I Saw It Then

BY REINHOLD EGGERS

(*Extracts from the Colditz diaries kept by Dr Eggers.*)

16th January 1941. At 3.30 am the Lieutenant of the Guard took two young ladies into his room in the castle. The Commandant, Colonel Schmidt, found out about this and punished him with ten days' room arrest. Later, the Guard Lieutenant had to leave.

27th February 1941. In the Castle, Captain Aurich raged against the British and Polish prisoners who had been complaining about trifles. It is absurd for such a neurotic and emotional person to have to deal with unruly prisoners. The British are delighted they have put Aurich in such a rage, and continue to oppose him with protests which he counteracts with legal trickery.

Today, during supper, the prison staff officers were debating how we should treat our prisoners of war. Some of us recalled how, during the occupation of Germany in 1918, French officers used the riding whip to encourage discipline. They recalled too, the treatment of some German prisoners in France in World War I. I said it was no use our following the example of a few hard cases from an old war. An unshakable, cool, correct treatment would be the best to follow in the long run.

1st to 5th March 1941. Recently the atmosphere among the German staff has been explosive. Captain Aurich and Captain Priem (a few weeks junior to Aurich) had been quarrelling. Eventually Priem said, "One of the two of us must go." Colonel Schmidt intervened by appointing Aurich the Commandant of the ancillary camp, the Schuetzenhaus, which made Priem and Aurich equals under the order of the second in command, Major Menz. Priem was now responsible for the castle and I was his assistant. Aurich's assistant was Lieut. Püpcke, from Halle.

30th April 1941. We had our monthly guest night. Our guests were usually officials of the town; the Burgomaster, leaders of the NSDAP, the headmaster and other notables. At half past one, I'd had enough as I'd emptied my bottle of red wine, so I took my leave and went to my quarters. Some of my fellow officers who liked the bottle continued the party until next morning.

At 8 am an orderly asked me to take the roll-call of the prisoners, as Captain Priem was not able to walk. He was later brought to Major Menz's room where he fell asleep and remained so until half past six in the evening. Then we went to Zschadrass, a mile or so away, where we had ordered a supper of roast duck. It really was a glorious supper.

15th May 1941. Lightning struck. All officers were ordered to appear at twelve noon in the Commandant's office, "*Ordonnanzanzug*," which meant full uniform with sash and revolver; so something serious was afoot. We also had to sign that we had read the order.

Colonel Schmidt had found out about our drinking bouts and gave us a severe lecture. He ordered that no drinks were to be sold in the Officers' Mess after midnight and that, in future, lights-out had to be at one am.

"We cannot go on like this," said the Commandant. "The prisoners are playing games with us. Two have just escaped, but none of my officers can tell me when, how, in what disguise or by which route they got out of the camp. How can I report such things to the OKW? You are not fulfilling your duty as you should. That is why I have restricted serving drinks in the Mess."

29th June 1941. It is Sunday and I am on duty as Orderly Officer. One of my duties is to deal promptly with telephone messages received in the Guard Room, in case Berlin or Dresden have urgent orders to give us. In the afternoon at about half past four, I was lying on my sofa enjoying the peace when all of a sudden an orderly came running up from the Guard Room to tell me the Commandant wished to speak to me on the telephone. I pulled on my boots and was away as quickly as I could, but when I reached the telephone, the Commandant said, "I gave orders to fetch you to the telephone. It has taken you thirteen minutes to get here. *The Orderly Officer has to stay in the vicinity of the telephone.* Please do so in future."

This is what we call a *zigarre*. In this way, the old Colonel controlled his staff.

Monday 30th June 1941. Colonel Schmidt invited us to be his guests in the Waldschenke. This was one of the rare opportunities when he was not a rough soldier and even displayed the charm of a *grand seigneur*. Frau Schmidt was my lady partner at the dinner. I enjoyed her interesting conversation, but what old-fashioned views she still has! She was careless enough to utter opinions about the 'browns' (Hitler adherents). When such topics come up in conversation I feel obliged to keep silent or to change the subject to something more harmless. Her two daughters were sitting opposite and from them I heard similar careless conversation. These are the people Goebbels calls the "*Plutokraten.*"

The menu was rich: soup; back of venison with a wonderful sauce, and mushrooms (very big portions); new potatoes, apple sauce with red whortleberries and ice cream. We ended the meal with real coffee and strawberry fancy cake. Although there were twelve of us in the party the Colonel did not ask us for ration coupons, which was much appreciated. But had Churchill seen us, he would have given up hope of defeating Germany by hunger.

4th October 1941. Tomorrow the Commandant will return, his energies refreshed, after five weeks recreation at Bad Reinerz in Silesia. We had a fine time during his absence. Now everyone is sighing, some even loudly, at the prospect of his return.

15th January 1942. The British prisoners have stolen eleven bulbs and some flex from the White Russians' Christmas tree in the Schuetzenhaus. I appealed to the Senior British Officer, Colonel German, as a gentleman, but to no avail.

Tomorrow, the Reichstatthalter of Saxony, Mutschmann (known by us as "King Mu"), with his attendants, will visit us in Colditz Castle. I am anxious to find out if the prisoners will whistle and howl when they see his much-hated uniform.

28th January 1942. About 220 Indian soldiers arrived at the Schuetzenhaus camp on the bank of the Mulde, up-river in the direction of Lastau. These men are members of different religions and castes – about 150 Moslems and the rest Hindus.* They are commanded by a sergeant and his squad of military police who wear red army badges and carry wooden batons about sixty centimetres long and about two centimetres thick. They use these sticks to beat the soldiers if instant obedience is not observed.

The caste system gives us much trouble. Some of the Indians

* In July 1942 they left Colditz for an Indian Camp. They had been sent to Colditz from the Annaberg Camp because they had refused to co-operate with the Germans who planned to found an Indian Legion.

refused to sit down on a privy, but stood on the seat of the water closet pedestal and so often missed their mark. Soon the closets were in an indescribably filthy state, but the Indians firmly refused to clean the place up, as such work had to be done by a lower caste, unhappily not represented here. What we did was to remove the planks from our old-fashioned closet in the park, so the Indians could climb up into the rafters and operate from there.

8th February 1942. One of our guards shot himself with Captain Vent's revolver. Vent is on leave and nobody knows the reason for the suicide.

We found that our guards were accepting coffee, chocolate and bribes of German money in return for tools, files and saws. Because of this, the Commandant, Colonel Schmidt, wants to replace our guard company.

4th January 1943. The prisoners, the British and French in particular, are doing all they can to get me out of the camp by making life unbearable for me. They have reason enough – I discovered the church tunnel and their attempts to get out from under the stage; I was their main antagonist in the saluting war; I discovered one of their radios. Today Colonel Stayner began a definite attack against me. I had recently brought Lieut. Sinclair back from Weinsberg and the Colonel complained that I had not treated Sinclair well during our train journey for when I ordered a meal in a station restaurant I did not invite him to dine with me. This beats everything! Such arrogance surpasses all my experience!

The difficulty was later smoothed over and explained away as a misunderstanding due to language difficulties.

1st March 1943. The prisoners are more insolent than ever as they can see that the fall of Germany is imminent. The French and British have mixed razor blade splinters with the kitchen swill, to kill the pigs who feed on it. The razor blades were concealed by sliding them into thick potato peelings. For this the prisoners were punished by banning the theatre, park walk and football. Then the British damaged the electric wiring and the Commandant held up its repair, so they have no light. On evening roll-call, the French cried "*Lumière!*", and threw burning newspapers from the windows into the courtyard. The British smoked on parade. I reported three of them to the Commandant.

20th April 1943. Hitler's birthday – I was decorated with the War Merit Medal, second class. At roll-call, when the French saw my new ribbon, they howled and jeered, shouting, "Aha! *Décoration pour prison!*"

The British laughed. The Dutch and the Poles behaved as soldiers are expected to do.

13th May 1943. A Swiss representative of the International Red Cross arrived at Colditz Castle. In the afternoon, the Commandant, Colonel Prawitt, invited him to look over the prisoners' quarters. Before starting their tour the Commandant stepped into the prisoners' yard to check that all was well, but found many officers sunbathing on blankets they had spread out on the sunny side of the yard. The Corporal who accompanied Prawitt shouted, "*Achtung!*" but nobody took the slightest bit of notice, so Prawitt sent the Corporal to fetch me from the office to order the prisoners, in their own languages, to leave the yard and return to their quarters. When this was done, Prawitt told me I could go back to the office while he stayed in the yard to make sure it remained fit for the Swiss representative to see. But the prisoners were angry because their sunbathing had been interrupted, and started to shout insults at the Commandant while he stood in the yard. He ordered, "Get back from the windows or we shall open fire on you!" There was continued shouting.

The Swiss and I who were in the office heard a volley of shots followed by several single shots. The Swiss Red Cross man seemed uneasy, but when the firing stopped we joined the Commandant to visit the quarters of the Poles and the Dutch, which seemed quiet. All went well, with the prisoners saluting and behaving properly, until we came to leave. But when we tried to get out of the Dutch quarters we found the outer door shut and its handle removed so we couldn't get out. I had to call from the windows for a guard with a French bayonet, which is cruciform in shape, to prise open the door. The British all shouted scornfully at us as we left the yard and then continued their sunbathing. Nobody had been hit by the rifle fire, but hate and scorn had been demonstrated.

As a result of this disturbance, Major General van Graevenitz pointed out to the senior British and French officers that the Commandant was justified in opening fire. "You forget that we are still at war. You are prisoners and not guests here for the cure."

14th September 1943. General van Schwedler, in command of District IV at Dresden, came to inspect us. He is about sixty years old, quiet and sympathetic. He inspected the guards around the castle, looked in at the kitchen and the inner courtyard. Colonel Prawitt, the Commandant, told him of all sorts of fairy-tale escape attempts, getting the facts all wrong. When the General, during a meal in the mess, asked how many German soldiers were serving in the camp, Prawitt promptly answered, "Five hundred": But Major Amthor, our second in command, a well-informed busybody, at once corrected his superior by giving the exact number of the guard company, which was 276. Later, when the General wanted to know how many civilian internees we had at Colditz, Prawitt told him there were three. He had counted Bader among them.

Prawitt is the most ignorant commandant I have ever had. His verbal reports amuse us, who know what is really happening, but a visiting General is much impressed by such stories because Prawitt reports them with such conviction. This is all part of the training of a professional officer, who is able to bluff his superiors in this way. But perhaps our adversaries are not bluffed so easily.

25th September 1944. Lieut. Sinclair was shot down in the park. He had staged a daring repetition of Mairesse Le Brun's audacious attempt of leaping over the barbed wire. The guards had ordered Sinclair to stop and fired warning shots, but he had taken no notice, so he was shot and killed. (When this happened, I was absent at Teplitz-Schoenau in Bohemia for a training meeting of security officers, and returned just in time for the military funeral. Captain Püpcke laid a wreath on the grave and commanded the firing of the last salvo for this unique soldier, honoured as 'The Red Fox'.)

16th April 1945. Colonel Prawitt and his whole staff, except for sixty-year-old Dr Müller, were marched off into American captivity. Prawitt had cleverly steered our Colditz staff through all the difficulties which are involved in an unconditional surrender.

It was possible for Prawitt to make good provision for the comfort for the whole German Colditz contingent together with their families who had found refuge in the castle – Frau Prawitt and baby son; Frau Amthor; Frau Püpcke and son; Frau Vent and two children; Frau Heinze and daughter.

Colonel Shaughnessey, the American Commander, gave us a meal that was far richer than we were used to. Prawitt was particularly happy to have a pack of American cigarettes.*

---

* Later on, Prawitt proved to be very clever as a prisoner. He was able to take advantage of every situation and to trick his American guards, who were not in the least concerned about him. In the autumn of 1945, he went to Leipzig without Russian permission, and met his wife in Colditz, secretly at night. The police tried to arrest him but he had gone, leaving the Soviet zone, and so avoided the fate I had as a Russian prisoner. He did in fact spend about five months in prison, without a trial, after being caught in 1946. He later settled at Moelln, near Hamburg, where his wife and son came to join him. He died in 1969 when he was nearly seventy years old.

Aftermath

BY REINHOLD EGGERS

To instruct such untrained officers as we were at Colditz, what to do and how to do it, the OKW published some regulations for Security Officers (I was not officially appointed Security Officer to Colditz until February 1944).

As one may expect, we were told that the main instruments of the Security Officer were men of confidence (i.e. traitors). As it was impossible to find any of these among the Colditz inmates, we had to find them elsewhere. But when Lieut. Grey* arrived, having offered himself for such services, he was spotted by the British on the third day. They told us that they knew all about him and were keeping him under a 24-hour watch. We had to take him outside the camp to save his life, so instead of any profit we had a lot of trouble instead. We were thankful when he joined the British Free Corps, leaving the Colditz Security Officer as blind as he was before.†

When the Russians questioned me on this matter in 1946, and I told them about our lack of traitors, they laughed and said, "A Security Officer without an agent is like a house-keeper without a broom! We'll send you to Siberia for ten years, and then the names of your Agents will come back to your memory."

My predecessor in the Security Office, Major Horn, was cruelly beaten by the Russians who wanted the names of his agents. This occurred in the GPU cellars of Finsterwalde. There was no result, as indeed we had no agents.

On the 3rd December 1946, Major Horn and I were sentenced to ten years hard labour for having supported a Fascist regime. We

---

* Not his real name, but the one I used in my *Colditz: The German Story.* – *Reinhold Eggers.*

† There was, however, one French traitor. He was soon discovered and escorted to the courtyard gates by the French prisoners who made a noise like a flock of sheep. The traitor gave his compatriots a mocking salute as he went through the gates to the German quarters.

There was one Polish traitor, too, who was ceremoniously stripped of his buttons and military insignia by the Poles, before he was handed back to the Germans. – *John Watton.*

were transported, in fetters, to the concentration camp of Sachsen-hausen near Berlin, where barrack number 51 became our home, together with 350 criminals like us and thousands of innocent lice, fleas and bugs.

Major Horn was convinced that the Americans would free us soon, but I said, "I don't think the Russians were joking when they said 'ten years'. I think we had better get used to the idea." Major Horn became extremely angry at the thought of this. In 1947 he fell ill and was taken to the Central Hospital where he died. About nine years later I wrote to his wife to tell her of his death about which she had not been informed. Nobody was informed of the deaths of more than 30,000 prisoners in this camp. Nobody ever bothered about them, except their next of kin.

Major Horn's stay at Colditz lasted only about four months. He was sent back to the army on the Western front where he was encir-cled with his men near Echternach. He refused to surrender and managed to break through with most of the troops. For this he was awarded the Ritterkreuz he longed for so much. He was a soldier and a patriot, although no Nazi. If anyone, he deserves the highest honour – a *Frontschwein*, a fighter to the last round.

1500 of us who survived the concentration camp at Sachsenhau-sen were brought to the prison at Torgau. Once when I looked out from my cell window there, I saw three men working in the yard, repairing the pavement. I could hardly believe my eyes when I saw that one of the men, clad in rags and down to the last of his strength, was my former arrogant highly cultured dandy, Captain Aurich, only to be addressed in the third person. But I had no opportunity to meet him until December 1950, when some of the most pitiful of us prisoners – I was one of them – skeletons weighing no more than fifty kilogrammes, were selected to be given extra rations and to be moved to larger quarters. There I found my former superior, Captain Aurich, who at once greeted me with the friendly German *Du*. He said, "I heard that you were here and have been wanting to see you, for I have an apology to make. There were times when I went a bit too far at Colditz. May I offer you a little food from my parcel?" This was very generous of him as he was ex-tremely hungry and had just received his first parcel, containing a small cake.

Many of our friends in this hell had forgotten their good upbring-ing. Their morals and manners had deteriorated into rough vio-lence. This was not so with Captain Aurich. Even the way he used his cutlery – a spoon made of tin – revealed the dignity of his upbringing; a glimmer of that behaviour which was traditional in well-to-do families like his, who were used to silver spoons. His conversation and contributions to the common entertainment were still on the level of a well educated man. The loss of his military prestige had laid bare the fine essence of his inner being, improving the total standard of the community in our big cell. We remained together there until after Christmas 1950, when our weight had risen to over fifty kilogrammes and we could then do without the better rations. After that I only saw him occasionally helping to repair the pavement, in one of the four big paved yards, year after year, in sunshine and in rain.

Roll-call in Colditz, Christmas 1942;
Polish PoWs in foreground
British in background

Home Runs 1939–45

A. Escapes under the responsibility of the staff of Oflag IVC, Colditz Castle

From the main camp in the castle:
1. Lieut. Le Ray. French. 11th April 1941
2. Lieut. Colin. French. 31st May 1941
3. Lieut. Mairesse Le Brun. French. 2nd July 1941
4. Lieut. Steinmetz. Dutch. 17th August 1941
5. Lieut. Lariva. Dutch. 17th August 1941
6. Major Giebel. Dutch. 21st September 1941
7. Lieut. Drijber. Dutch. 21st September 1941
8. Lieut. Durand. French. 17th December 1941
9. Lieut. de Frondeville. French. 17th December 1941
10. Lieut. Prot. French. 17th December 1941
11. Lieut. Neave. British. 5th January 1942
12. Lieut. Luteyn. Dutch. 5th January 1942
13. Lieut. Fowler. British. 9th September 1942
14. Capt. van Doorninck. Dutch. 9th September 1942
15. Capt. Reid. British. 15th October 1942
16. Major Littledale. British. 15th October 1942
17. Lieut.-Commander Stephens. British. 15th October 1942
18. Lieut. Wardle. British. 15th October 1942
19. Escaped, but missing: Lieut. Miller. British. 28th January 1944

From the Schuetzenhaus camp:
20. Lieut. Tatistcheff. French-Russian. 18th July 1941

B. Escapes of PoW belonging to Oflag IVC but who made home runs under the responsibility of military authorities other than the staff of Oflag IVC
1. Lieut. Kroner. Polish. From hospital. 20th August 1941
2. Lieut. Boucheron. French. From hospital. October 1941
3. Lieut. Odry. French. During transport from hospital to Colditz. 14th October 1941
4. Lieut. Navelet. French. During transport from hospital to Colditz. 14th October 1941
5. Lieut. Remy. Belgian. From hospital. 26th April 1942
6. Major Paddon. British. From court martial prison. 11th June 1942
7. Lieut. Bouillez. French. From hospital. 25th June 1942
8. Lieut. Darthenay. French. From hospital. 8th July 1943